SHIMON PERES

SHIMON PERES

A BIOGRAPHY

Matti Golan

*Translated from the Hebrew
by Ina Friedman*

St. Martin's Press
New York

To my son, Lee Shmuel

ISBN 0-312-71736-9

Library of Congress Cataloging in Publication Data

Golan, Matti.
    Shimon Peres, A Biography.

    Includes Index.
    1. Peres, Shimon, 1923-   . 2. Statesmen—Israel—
Biography. 3. Israel—Politics and Government. I. Title.
DS 126.6.P47064 1982   956.94'05'0924 [B]   82-7354
ISBN 0-312-71736-9

Contents

Illustrations

Acknowledgements

A man's life is made up of millions of details, the compilation of which involves a great organizational effort and, especially, the ability to pursue and uncover them. I could never have succeeded in this task without the aid of the many people who responded so willingly to my requests.

I wish to thank the staff of the IDF Archive, whose efficiency and dedication have created an institution that is a treasure for historians, and Malka Liff, the Director of Ben-Gurion House, whose patience and endless cups of coffee made the monotonous work of collation far more pleasant.

My gratitude also goes to the many people who agreed to grant me interviews: first and foremost President Yitzhak Navon; Knesset Members Gad Ya'akobi, Abba Eban, Chaim Bar-Lev, Yossi Sarid, Micha Harish, Aharon Harel, Dani Rosolio and Eliyahu Speizer; Shimon Peres's friends from his years at the Ben-Shemen Youth Village and Kibbutz Alumot: Elhanan Yishai, Avraham Greidenger and Mulla Cohen; his close aides in the Defence Ministry: Naftali Lavie and Brigadier Aryeh Baron; the Deputy Director of the Defence Ministry, Avraham Ben-Yosef; Labour Party activist Shraga Netzer; Peres's brother, Gershon; the journalist Mira Avreich; the historian and journalist Dr Michael Bar-Zohar, who, in addition to his remembrances and the material he placed at my disposal, was helpful through his biography of David Ben-Gurion; Peres's aides in the Labour Party: Boaz Applebaum, Yossi Bailen, Gideon Levi and Yisrael Peleg.

Finally, my gratitude and appreciation go to Shimon Peres, who did not make his co-operation conditional upon anything beyond the welfare and security of the State of Israel and who was far more concerned about the image of friends and adversaries than about his own.

1
A Romantic Education

It was a quiet Sabbath in the Polish town of Vishneva. Morning prayers had ended in the small synagogue, and the six-year-old Shimon placed his hand in the rough, wrinkled hand of his grandfather as the two walked out into the street. It was always with his grandfather that Shimon went to and returned home from synagogue. The other members of his family – his father, mother and brothers – were traditionalists who went to synagogue only on the high holidays. On Saturdays the Perskys usually slept late. Shimon alone would rise early to accompany his grandfather to prayers.

He loved and admired the old man, who embodied a combination of craftsmanship (handcrafting suede boots) with a thirst for Torah study and a deep love of poetry. Shimon's father was a timber merchant who spent long periods away from home on business; his mother was preoccupied with looking after the home. So the child's heart and mind were open to the influence of his grandfather, who passed on his two great loves: poetry and religion. The latter took pride of place during Shimon's early childhood:

> When I was a boy, I was an avid enthusiast of God. I was wholly convinced of his existence, feared his wrath, felt myself suspended between his broad, vanishing horizons. I tried to seek out his invisible visage and prayed for his well-being with inexhaustible fervour. I was zealous about observing the Sabbath as a day of rest.

The stooped man and small boy walked through the streets of Vishneva greeting passers-by, taking in the holy air of the Sabbath. But as soon as Shimon got home, the air of tranquillity was shattered. From a corner of the room, the sound of music emanated from a large, attractive radio. Great effort and no small amount of money had been invested in the purchase of this expensive instrument, which only people of means could afford. But now Shimon glared at the set with seething hatred. His entire being seemed to rebel against the desecration of the Sabbath. Without a word he strode up to the set and, pitting his strength against it, toppled it to the floor, where it smashed to smithereens.

Only when he heard it shatter did Shimon realize what he had done. He turned pale, but his expression remained obstinate. His father stared at him mutely; his mother brought a broom to sweep up the pieces.

In time Shimon's parents bought a new radio, but from then on it remained silent throughout the Sabbath.

The town in which Shimon Peres was born on 1 August 1923 boasted only 170 families, all of them Jewish. The schools were wholly Jewish-oriented – the language of instruction being Hebrew – and proved a breeding-ground for the Zionist revival. In effect, Vishneva was a Zionist town. All the residents were contemplating emigration to Palestine; the only obstacle was the dearth of immigration certificates issued by the British mandatary authorities.

Under his grandfather's tutelage, Shimon was also drawn to poetry – writing as well as reading it. 'I used to fill copybooks with poetry and became a collector of unusual notebooks – large and small, lined and blank, with thick covers and crinkled ones. I tried to hide this "weakness" from my parents and my brother, for I didn't think they would understand this curious penchant of mine.' He misjudged them, however, for his parents not only understood, they were proud of him. His father even sent some of Shimon's poems to Chaim Nachman Bialik, the reigning Poet Laureate of Hebrew. When an answer arrived from Bialik, the joy in the Persky household knew no bounds. Bialik encouraged the youngster from Vishneva to keep writing and even sent him a recently written poem.

Books were the other great love in his life – a devotion which bordered on obsession. When the other children were out playing, Shimon was reading; while his friends were busying themselves with boyish pranks, Shimon would make off with his personal heroes for wondrous, distant worlds. These loves cost him dearly, for he was guilty of the sin that children cannot forgive: that of being different. His schoolmates punished him for it by taunting and sometimes even beating him. But Shimon would not fight back; he wouldn't even try to defend himself. Physically the blows were not very painful, but they left a deep wound on his psyche. When his mother asked him why he didn't defend himself, he would reply in bewilderment and anguish: 'Why do they hit me? I haven't done anything!'

Eventually, Shimon's brother, Gershon, two years his junior, became his defender and avenger. In a fit of blind rage, he would take on anyone who tried to harm Shimon, sometimes striking the mark but mostly taking the blows. Their mother was more concerned by Gershon's outbursts than by Shimon's passivity, and when Shimon suffered a beating she tried to hide it from her younger son, though rarely with success.

It was at school that Shimon was cured of his piety and discovered Zionism in its stead. (His Hebrew teacher, Yehoshua Rabinowitz, is credited with playing a leading role in this process and, as matters turned out, decades later he would serve as the Minister of Finance in the Israeli Government whose Defence Minister was none other than his former pupil, Shimon.)

Of the various Zionist youth movements active in Vishneva, Shimon joined *Hashomer Hatzair*, the largest and most popular. Through his exposure to Zionist ideology, Shimon was taken with the idea of emigrating to Palestine; but because of the financial conditions attached to the immigration certificates, the Persky family was forced to split up. Yitzhak Persky emigrated to Palestine in 1931; his wife and two sons joined him two years later, when Shimon was ten years old. The next four years were a period of adjustment and search for a sense of identity. In the mornings Shimon studied at the Balfour School. Afterwards he 'wandered from one youth club to another trying to find a group that would meet my hidden expectations. Most of my friends joined the Scout movement. I was never a good dancer, and they spent a lot of time doing that in the Scouts.' When he completed primary school, the question of his future education had to be faced. His father, who was working as an agent for the sale of timber and produce, decided to send Shimon to a commercial school, and it was there that he met Mulla Cohen.

Mulla was the son of David Cohen, 'the father of *Hanoar Ha'oved*' ('Working Youth', the youth movement sponsored by the *Histadrut*, the General Federation of Labour). Together with other friends, Mulla organized a campaign to recruit his classmates into the ranks of *Hanoar Ha'oved*, and it was during this undertaking that he came upon Shimon. Thus began a childhood friendship which over the years

3

would turn into a bitter rivalry. Its climax came forty-three years later when Mulla Cohen led Yitzhak Rabin's struggle to depose Shimon Peres from the leadership of the Labour Party.

In *Hanoar Ha'oved* Shimon found the home he was seeking in his new country. 'I was excited by the kibbutzim, the agriculture, the blue shirts of the movement's uniform, the encounter with Yemenite youngsters and working youth. We would listen as David Cohen told legends in his inimitably hoarse voice, and I was enchanted by them. We would visit the tented camps pitched near the Moslem cemetery in north Tel Aviv, and I thought it was the greatest fun.' He also found Tel Aviv itself exciting:

> My parents bought me a bicycle to ride to school and, as I glided down Dizengoff, Bograshov and King George streets, I would check if the sycamore trees had grown any overnight. From time to time I would count the number of buildings to see whether any new ones had been added. I was very proud of the fact that Tel Aviv was considered a 'Little Paris' and deep inside I was convinced that a great injustice was being done to my city, for how could there be a more beautiful place than Tel Aviv? (Of course, I hadn't seen Paris yet!) Still, the open balconies, humming cafés, golden seashore, the crowded cultural centre and the Mograbi theatre with its open roof, the watermelons red as wine and the scent of *felafel* which you could watch cooking in boiling oil, splattering wildly – what could begin to compare with that?

Before long, Shimon began to be known for his rhetorical and organizational talents. The partnership of the athletic sabra, Mulla, and the sober-minded man of action, Shimon, was the core around which the life of their branch of *Hanoar Ha'oved* revolved. This did not go unnoticed by their leaders, who were convinced that Shimon's studies in commerce were a waste of his true, latent talents. In response to a request by one of these leaders and by David Cohen himself, the administration of the Ben-Shemen Youth Village decided to grant the two boys scholarships covering tuition and board at the village dormitory.

Shimon's parents had difficulty accepting this turn which their son's life had taken. His father believed he was destined for city life and hoped that Shimon would learn a lucrative profession. Neither was it easy for them to reconcile themselves to the youth village, situated as it was next to the Arab town of Lydda (Lod) and surrounded by Arab villages. Violent incidents between Arabs and Jews were almost daily occurrences in this area. But by now it was already too late to stop Shimon. He was under the spell of a way of life characterized by collective, creative living and felt that he had found the sphere in which he could make a deep and lasting mark.

As soon as Shimon arrived at the youth village, he knew that he had made the right choice. During the first year, he worked in the vegetable garden. 'I became a great admirer of cucumbers and, to this day, I think that the finest perfume is the scent of a fresh, young cucumber at just that critical moment when it is ready to be picked. Other than cucumbers, I still can taste that indescribable flavour of figs. We spent many hours hidden among the boughs of the fig tree gorging ourselves of this gastronomic masterpiece of nature.' Yet when it became time for him to choose a field of specialization, Shimon went in another direction. 'In the village I saw a cow close up for the first time in my life. She was so different from the cows on the chocolate wrappers – a hungry, weary, lowing and sometimes mud-covered creature.'

It was not the charms of the cow which attracted Shimon to the cowshed and certainly not any consideration of relative ease, because the work of a dairyman was considered one of the most difficult jobs. For one thing, it meant getting up at four o'clock in the morning; as yet the electric milking-machine was not even a glimmer in anyone's eye. But for all that, the status of the dairyman was far below that of the field hand, which was the most prestigious job in agriculture and the one in which Mulla Cohen had chosen to specialize. Perhaps that is why Shimon chose the dairy; unlike the strong, athletic Mulla, he felt a need to prove himself. At this time he was a chubby adolescent who hated sports and, in contrast to most of the other perennially tanned students in the village, always looked pale. He was known to be a talented writer and produced a stream of articles for the *Hanoar Ha'oved* newspaper, *Bama'aleh*. There was no doubt that he was gifted as a speaker and had superior administrative ability. But the Jewish community in Palestine was a labour-oriented society. A man's status was determined by his capacity for physical labour, and his other talents could supplement but not substitute for that ability. In this sphere, Shimon's desire to prove himself seemed to border on masochism. Everyone who knew him during those days remembers him as a devoted and diligent worker.

It was during this period that Shimon got used to making do with five and sometimes four hours' sleep a night – a habit which became second nature in his adult years. He used the daytime hours for

5

studies, reading, writing and youth-movement activities – least of all, we might add, for studies. 'I was best at literature and Bible and cut out of classes in chemistry and physics. I felt a sense of resistance that was almost a block against the exact sciences. I didn't believe we really controlled physics and chemistry. On the contrary, their control over us was stronger than we were willing to admit.'

What had not changed with Shimon's move to the youth village was his profound involvement in books.

Naturally I read Tolstoi, though I'm not sure that I understood him. I was too young to appreciate the maturity of his writing. And *War and Peace* seemed like such a distant, *goyish* world to me that a sense of estrangement diluted my enjoyment. The world of *Anna Karenina*, with its foppish princes and the adulterous matrons, a mixture of love with the pleasures of the flesh, seemed so alien to everything I knew that it revolted me. Perhaps shame also had something to do with it. But Tolstoi's writings seemed to be about another world, not a reflection of the one that seemed plausible to me.

Shimon himself wrote relentlessly – articles, stories, poems, even the personal confessions of others. 'We kept a collective diary of confessions in which everyone was supposed to divulge his innermost feelings. I wrote in it more than anyone else, and when I discovered someone who was delinquent, I wrote in his stead. Some of the youngsters claimed that I had a very profound influence on them, but I was reluctant to believe it.' In addition, he was always engaged in movement activities. The youngsters in the village were classified into four groups, according to youth movement, from *Hashomer Hatzair* on the left to *Hanoar Ha'oved* in the centre. This division along movement lines proved a constant source of ideological tension. Shimon played a central role in the endless debates that went on in the village, and it seemed almost natural that he was elected co-ordinator of the *Hanoar Ha'oved* group.

To prevent the ideological rivalries from getting out of hand, the director of the village, Dr Lehman, forbade the youth movements to set up clubs catering to the 'Children's Group', the younger level in the village (Shimon's level was called the 'Youth Group'). 'Little wonder, then, that we decided to establish a clandestine branch of our movement. Our meeting-place was the mule shed and, because of its secret nature, the cream of the younger children was drawn to our group.'

It was also during this period that the rivalry between Shimon and

Mulla Cohen began to develop – albeit covertly. At first their parting of ways was ideological: Mulla inclined towards the socialist faction of *Hanoar Ha'oved* while Shimon was a disciple of Gordonia, which did not follow the international-socialist outlook. Moreover, Shimon was an admirer of the head of *Hanoar Ha'oved*, Pinhas Lavon (who would later become Defence Minister and appoint Shimon Director-General of the Ministry).

As part of the whole new life-style he encountered in the youth village, Shimon also made new acquaintances in Ben-Shemen:

with Arabs, hostility and weapons. Together with my comrades, I was sworn into the *Haganah* in a candle-lit ceremony before a pistol and a copy of the Bible. We began training almost every night, and despite our relatively tender age, we were sent out on guard duty. That's when I began my military career, and I reached the rank of a position commander. (There were two people in a position: the commander and his deputy.) We would stand there wielding British rifles bigger than ourselves and peer out first at the beautiful moon, then into the darkness. Sometimes we were shot at and would return the fire. A night like that was considered an experience.

The director of the village tried to get us acquainted with the Arab villages around Ben-Shemen. We would go out hiking in the Judean Hills almost every Saturday, picking wild anemones and narcissus, and sometimes we would go over to an Arab village and be treated to *pitta* and *hummous* [flat bread and a paste of chick peas]. Our attitude towards the Arabs was mixed. They seemed so strange to us, so terrifying, and yet the creatures closest to nature.

Shimon's soaring imagination would later lead him to establish Israel's aeronautics industry, to build an atomic reactor and conceive of 'Operation Entebbe'. But at this time it led to his friendship with a young immigrant from Germany, who wore high leather boots and dressed in three-quarter trousers gathered at the knee with elastic bands.

He looked odd, almost ridiculous to us, but I taught him Hebrew and he taught me German. He brought along a book entitled *Klaferzahan Wundervoll* (*The Eleven Wonders of the Teeth-Chatter Family*), the story of a father (Klaferzahan) who raised eleven sons and formed them into a soccer team which beat all the others and became world champion. We wandered from country to country with the family, all over the world, and we were fascinated by the landscapes, people and fabulous tales. I promised myself then that I would not depart this world before visiting at least three places: the island of Zanzibar, with its giant date-palms and cured sharkskins; the

7

Kamchatka Peninsula extending from Russia into the Bering Sea, where people go wrapped in furs during the endless, freezing winters; and the Falkland Islands off the Straits of Magellan, where the inhabitants raise excellent sheep and sail around in private speedboats. (To my regret, only part of this dream has come true: I have been to Zanzibar and I wasn't in the least disappointed.)

One of the most important events in Shimon's life occurred when he received word that Berl Katznelson had read his pieces, enjoyed them and was inviting him to a meeting in his home. Shimon spent about three hours with the revered ideologue of the labour movement, talking about books, people and ideas.

> I was thrilled by the experience of meeting the man, by his patience, even more by his insatiable curiosity, and by the very fact that he was willing to spend an entire evening with a youngster who was known to him only from a few columns in an adolescent newspaper. From then on I visited his house almost every Sunday. I would sit in his room as if under a spell, taking in every word, following every movement of his handsome face and the quick changes in the expression of his eyes, which also took part in the conversation, like a voice in harmony. Whoever was privileged enough to have met Berl was graced with an unforgettable experience.

Despite all these activities, however, Shimon also found the time and the inner need to be a youngster. Although pranks were not typical of him, neither were they entirely alien to his personality. Once, on an outing in Tel Aviv with his friends while the city was subject to a blackout (it was during the Second World War), Shimon had the idea of impersonating blackout wardens. The youngsters wrapped white handkerchiefs around their sleeves and began reminding delinquent Tel Avivians to turn off the lights in their apartments, and dressing down people caught smoking in the street. They carried on like this until they met a genuine warden, who scattered them in all directions.

Neither was Shimon apathetic to girls, but his first romance in Ben-Shemen, with a girl named Ada, did not meet with his friends' approval. The problem was that she wasn't considered 'our kind of girl', because she was a recent arrival in the country. To the other boys, Shimon's flirtation with her bordered on treason; but his second romance was above reproach, from every possible point of view.

> I fell in love easily and I've been in love all my life. My love was total, full, nurtured by a rich imagination. The girl I loved at any one time – and I never loved more than one girl at a time – seemed perfect to me. And the

inevitable conclusion was that I was unworthy of her, so that I was inhibited about revealing my love and would suffer with it secretly. Only once – and with great difficulty – did I overcome this inhibition and that was for my great and unending love, the girl who became my companion for life.

Sonya, the daughter of Gelman, the carpentry teacher, was a thin girl with long plaits and a ready smile. Modesty was her most prominent trait – even by the stringent standards of those days – and she has remained a modest woman over the years. Their courtship went according to the norms of the times: Sonya would accompany Shimon on the nights when he had guard duty, and in the remote post, by the flickering light of a candle, he would read her poems and selections from *Das Kapital*. Because he also loved music, Shimon encouraged her to join him in learning to play the mandolin, even though he later confessed that 'I don't have any real musical talent. My tone is off and my grasp is not disciplined.' The greatest musical achievement of the courtship was mastering a duet of the national anthem, *Hatikvah*.

In August 1941 Shimon's settlement group left Ben-Shemen for a period of collective apprenticeship on Kibbutz Geva, where he continued to work as a dairyman and co-ordinated the group's affairs. During the stint on Geva, however, Shimon's public activities began to exceed the narrow confines of his settlement group and extended across the northern valleys of Israel. Formally speaking, *Hanoar Ha'oved* groups existed in all the kibbutzim organized in two of the country's three kibbutz movements – *Hever Hakevutzot* and the more leftist *Hakibbutz Hameuchad* – but they were dormant. In a single year, Shimon succeeded in revitalizing them by travelling from branch to branch and organizing activities and day seminars.

'Deep inside I am convinced that I am hopelessly shy,' he said recently, 'but I must accept the fact that many others perceive me as a man who tends to push ahead.' This is what the members of Kibbutz Geva thought, and Shimon was a creature they had trouble digesting. They complained to his friends that never before had they come up against a situation in which a youngster from the training group tried to manipulate them into doing what *he* wanted. They also took a dim view of his public activities because from time to time these required that he be released from work. The work schedule was drawn up in the communal dining-hall, and when the representative of Shimon's group requested that Shimon be exempted for a day or so, a public debate would often break out. It centred on charges that Shimon was 'goofing off' and didn't take his work seriously.

Yet Shimon's absences from work were only a partial, perhaps even a marginal, reason for the antagonism he generated among the members of Kibbutz Geva. Essentially, he was required to make a great physical and emotional effort during this period, for he would work at night and tend to the affairs of *Hanoar Ha'oved* during the day. He only left the cowshed when he left the kibbutz on movement business.

What irked the kibbutzniks far more were the unconventional ideas and objectionable mentality which Shimon brought with him. On the ideological level, he unabashedly aired the view that, in addition to agriculture, the kibbutzniks should engage in modern industry, science and technology. In a conservative society like Geva, where people believed that the kibbutz should be an intimate society engaged only in agriculture, these thoughts were tantamount to blasphemy, and their proponent was treated almost like a heretic.

(Many years later, Peres was to enjoy a sweet 'revenge'. As Minister of Transport and Communications, one of the ideas he tried to introduce was the activation of public telephones by magnetic cards instead of tokens. He had heard that cards of this sort were used in the Metro in Paris, so he approached the French and asked whether it would be possible to do the same with public telephones. When he received a positive reply, he asked who produced the cards and was told that they were not manufactured in France. The address of the factory, to his great surprise, was Kibbutz Geva, Israel. On a subsequent visit to the kibbutz, he found that the cowshed in which he had once worked had been converted to a factory for electronic instruments and magnetic cards. The dairymen with whom he had worked in his youth and who had been so reviled by his ideas now ran the modern, sophisticated machinery.)

From the point of view of his mentality, Shimon represented an approach that was likewise considered outrageous. The moral code of kibbutz society held that it was not seemly to desire a public position, far less to strive openly towards an appointment. Shimon refused to bow down to this attitude. He loved public work, wanted leadership positions to and didn't hesitate to say so. 'Ambition is not a dirty word,' he would argue. 'I admire people who are ambitious and don't try to hide it.'

It was during this period that the personal rivalry between Shimon and Mulla Cohen reached a peak. The *Palmach* (conceived as the 'shock-troops' of the *Haganah*) was being organized just then, and Mulla decided to leave the training group at Geva and join up, though this wasn't the only reason for his departure. In a heart-to-heart talk he told Shimon frankly and without resentment: 'You've got what you want. People follow you. I'll have to find my niche elsewhere.'

In September 1942 the training period on Geva came to an end and Shimon's group joined Kibbutz Alumot, overlooking the Sea of Galilee. Since the buildings to house the youngsters were not yet ready, the group took up temporary quarters on a hill near the settlement. In addition to their tents, they inhabited the ruins of a house which had once belonged to an English family, redividing it into rooms by hanging blankets between the dilapidated walls. Kibbutz Alumot was poor not only in housing but in land, so the members of Shimon's group were sent to work on nearby Kibbutz Ashdot Ya'akov. They would rise at four in the morning, walk to work and not return until late at night – again on foot. It was a great day indeed when an old truck was placed at their disposal.

Shimon worked alternately as a shepherd and a field hand, but he did not give up his public work. He started a weekly newspaper and wrote a regular column entitled 'A Woman's Diary'. A number of literary critics who read the column commented: 'Finally the authentic voice of a woman!'

By this time Shimon had already made a name for himself in *Hanoar Ha'oved* and beyond. He even caught the eye of Levi Eshkol, head of the Jewish Agency's Settlement Department. One day, during a debilitating heat-wave – a *khamsin* – Eshkol turned up at the kibbutz and asked to meet the secretariat. Near the abandoned house was a fairly deep well preserved from antiquity, when it presumably served as a cistern for storing rain-water. It was no longer used for that or any other purpose, but it was the coolest place in the area. So the members of the secretariat took their guest clambering down into the depths of the well, where Eshkol revealed the purpose of his visit: to ask that Shimon be assigned to work in the *Hanoar Ha'oved* secretariat in Tel Aviv. The idea was not greeted with much enthusiasm, but the members of the secretariat decided that it would be impolitic to turn Eshkol down – not so much because of his position in the Jewish Agency, but because as a member of Kibbutz Deganya he was a neighbour, and courtesy dictated that you couldn't refuse a neighbour.

In the *Hanoar Ha'oved* secretariat, Shimon was the only representative of *Mapai*'s kibbutz movement, *Hever Hakevutzot*. The rest of the eleven members belonged to *Si'ah Bet* (the B Faction), which traced back to the rival *Hakibbutz Hameuchad* movement. Some of them were members of Kibbutz Na'an, the first to be established by graduates of *Hanoar Ha'oved*. As such, they were surrounded by an aura of 'trailblazers', and anyone who did not belong to this élite group had to prove himself. Appointed chairman of the Organization Department, Shimon spent days and nights working to prove that he could hold his own among them. During this period he was hardly ever in Tel Aviv. He made his way systematically across the country's settlement map, establishing new branches and organizing new settlement groups.

One day Shimon had to get from Tel Aviv to Haifa (no mean feat at the time). Someone mentioned that David Ben-Gurion was travelling in the same direction and got him a ride north. Shimon was very excited about the prospect of meeting the venerable Zionist leader; he hoped to be able to talk and listen to him. To his great disappointment, however,

> almost the entire journey passed without him uttering so much as a syllable. Only as we were approaching Haifa did he turn to me and, out of the blue, say: 'You know, Trotski was no statesman.' To this day I have no idea what brought Lev Trotski into Ben-Gurion's mind at just that moment. But being eager to continue the conversation, I asked, 'Why not?' Now he began to warm up a bit and said: 'What kind of policy is that, no peace and no war? It's a Jewish gimmick. Either peace, and then you reconcile yourself to the heavy price it may cost, or war, and you take the terrible risk it entails. Lenin understood that.'

Shimon left the car in Haifa. 'At the time I never imagined that one day I would see Ben-Gurion decide both for war and on steps towards peace.' And he certainly couldn't have imagined that this man, more than any other, would forge his own fate and future.

A short time after this trip, the two men entered into a co-operative venture, albeit on a modest scale. One of Shimon's pet projects was the hiking society he had founded together with Shemaryahu Gutman. Its members were the first to discover the Snake Path leading up the slope of Masada.

This path was found as a result of considering the question of how the Jews under siege on Masada received supplies. Since it was known that the Romans made their camp west of Masada, the only possibility was that supplies came in from the east. The eastern slope of the mountain is very steep, yet after scouring it Shimon's group discovered sections of a path which, because of its tortuous nature, was christened the 'Snake Path'. To find out how these sections connected, Shimon climbed up the side of Masada one day. When he was half-way up the slope, he suddenly lost his footing and began to slide. He grabbed a rock at the last minute, but it came loose, so he dug into the arid ground with his finger-nails to prevent himself from plunging into the abyss below. The members of his group on top of the mountain saw the drama unfolding below them and formed a human ladder. They reached Shimon just as he was at the end of his endurance. The next day he returned to the goal he had set for himself and, together with his companions, uncovered the full course of the Snake Path.

During this trip the bond of friendship grew stronger between Shimon and Shemaryahu Gutman, who was soon to instigate another longer and far bolder journey. Shimon would begin the story of that trek with the words: 'A tale of fourteen youngsters who longed to dip their toes in the waters of the Red Sea. . . .' Only it didn't start exactly like that. One day Shimon told David Ben-Gurion that he and his friends would like to cross the Negev on foot to reach the Red Sea at the place then called Umm Rashrash (later the site of the port city of Eilat). Ben-Gurion was enthusiastic; even then, he envisioned the development of the Negev and the establishment of Eilat. Since this desert area was uncharted, he asked Shimon to have his group draw a map of their journey. Gutman and Shimon put together a group of fourteen people – seven from *Hanoar Ha'oved* and seven from the *Palmach*. A zoologist and a surveyor joined them. The funding of £300 was provided by Ben-Gurion and the commander of the *Palmach* on a fifty-fifty basis.

The group travelled by truck as far as Asluj, where they hired fourteen camels and loaded their supplies and equipment on seven of them. Some of the hikers rode on the remaining seven; the rest started out on foot and took turns with the riders. The entire adventure was quite illegal, because the mandatary administration forbade Jews to travel in the Negev. They were also forbidden to carry the arms which they had brought along in large canteens.

They spent twenty-two days making their way south, marvelling at the splendours of the desert, the antiquities at Avdat and the beauty of Wadi Ramon, but they never realized their dream of a dip in the Red Sea. When they were about twenty kilometres from Umm Rashrash, the hikers suddenly heard the hum of automobile engines. Once the dust settled, they found themselves surrounded by British and Arab policemen. Without so much as a word, they were loaded into command cars and driven to the police station at Umm Rashrash, where they spent the night. The next day they were transferred to the jail in Beersheba to await trial.

The commander of the jail was an Arab named Abu-Saba. On the second night there, Shimon persuaded him to let him out until morning. He took a taxi to Tel Aviv, made straight for Ben-Gurion's house and told him of the arrest. Ben-Gurion immediately ordered the legal adviser of the *Histadrut* to go to Beersheba and defend the members of the group at their trial. Shimon kept his word and returned to prison early next morning. Since he had given the impression of being responsible for the group, he received the toughest sentence: a month's imprisonment. The others were sentenced to two weeks behind bars.

When the affair was over, Shimon presented Ben-Gurion with an album of pictures and maps. After studying them, the leader of the state-in-the-making commented: 'This is something of great value. If we're lucky, we'll capture Umm Rashrash without a war. But if war is necessary, this will be very helpful.'

This was not the only yield of the desert journey. Along the way Gutman discovered a nest of the eagles called *peres* in the Bible. The geologist of the group, Dr Mendelson, turned to Shimon and said, 'Persky, why don't you change your family name to Peres?' Shimon took to the idea and shortly afterwards made the name change legal.

The barren desert left an indelible impression on Shimon Peres. He never stopped talking about its size and the great potential it held for people prepared to contend with it. He was convinced that the area would have to be part of the future Jewish state, and during the War of Independence, when the capture of the Negev was being planned, Ben-Gurion included Shimon in the consultations – to a large degree because of his participation in that excursion.

The mysteries of the Negev were not the only thing that Shimon had an urge to unravel; his seemingly insatiable curiosity, always in conflict with shyness, pressed him into other directions. For instance, he yearned to know what lay behind the doors marked 'Nightclub'. The most popular of these watering-holes was on Dizengoff Street, in the heart of fashionable Tel Aviv, and Shimon begged his friend Avraham Greidenger to come with him.

'But we haven't any money!' Greidenger protested.

'Don't worry. It'll be okay,' Shimon assured him.

Somewhat hesitantly, the two entered the nightcub and hastily made for a remote table. Soon afterwards the show began – a magician, singer and dancer – temporarily saving them from having to face the question of ordering. But finally the moment they feared was upon them: a waiter was making his way towards their table, eyeing their outfits gingerly – for they were hardly appropriate in these surroundings.

'What would you like to order, gentlemen?' he asked somewhat dubiously.

Shimon studied the menu at length and finally blurted out, 'Two sodas, please.'

His greatest pleasure during this period was reserved for his taste-buds: ice cream. Mountains of it. Once when he was in Whitman's, the most popular ice-cream parlour in Tel Aviv, he challenged Greidenger to a contest: whoever could eat ten portions of ice cream would be paid for by the other. Shimon shovelled the creamy treat in until the waiter refused to bring him any more for fear that he would expire on the spot. But Shimon convinced him that no one ever died of an overdose of ice cream, and he finished off ten helpings without any trouble. Greidenger paid the bill.

The new housing on Kibbutz Alumot was completed and the members of Shimon's settlement group left their camp to move to their new home. Shimon was enchanted by the spot 'on a mountain slope in the Lower Galilee overlooking the exquisite scenery of the Sea of Galilee and the Jordan Valley. Every shaft of sunlight streaks the Jordan's waters a different shade as it snakes its way through the valley, changing from a come-hither green to a gaudy silver.'

Another of Shimon's romances developed in a completely different direction. One of the kibbutzniks, Micha Talmon, noticed that Shimon had his eye on a young woman named Rachel, and he decided to play a trick on him. The kibbutz had a large communal mailbox divided in two: one side for outgoing, the other for incoming mail. Micha composed a love-letter addressed to Shimon and signed Rachel's name. Then he placed it in the incoming mailbox and waited until he saw Shimon arrive, pick up the letter and return a while later, placing what Micha assumed was his reply in the outgoing box. After Shimon left, Micha removed the letter and, as he expected, it was addressed to Rachel. Thus began an exchange of love-letters between Shimon and Rachel-Micha. For a time, reading Shimon's letters aloud around the campfire was a favourite pastime of the young men and women in Micha's crowd of friends. Eventually, one of the kibbutz-niks told Shimon what was going on. His reaction was vehement, for he felt humiliated, his most private and vulnerable feelings violated. Leaving for Tel Aviv the next morning, he did not return to Alumot for a month.

These trials came to an end when Shimon and Sonya Gelman decided to get married. Their decision created a serious dress problem, however. The members of Alumot had only standard-issue khaki shorts, which sufficed for everyday needs. There was one pair of long flannel trousers in the kibbutz, and this singular treasure was saved for just such occasions, when it was lent to the groom without consideration for his height or girth. To make matters worse, Shimon was told that he had better not show up at his wedding without a black dinner-jacket. The members of the kibbutz had only khaki battle-dress. His resourcefulness did not fail him. Shimon took his battle-dress and, with the aid of a special cream, coloured it black. When the great moment came, he appeared at the ceremony wearing grey trousers which barely reached his ankles and battledress whose black coating was beginning to peel. That evening, 1 May 1945 (the Jewish festival of *Lag Ba-Omer*), beside the swimming-pool at Ben-Shemen, Shimon and Sonya entered into not only a pact of marriage but an alliance of love and true friendship.

Shimon's devotion to Sonya became something of a byword on the kibbutz. One of her jobs was night duty in the children's houses, which were quite far apart. Sonya was afraid to cover the distance alone at night, so Shimon would join her in one of the children's houses – where he slept on a mat on the floor – and every half-hour Sonya would wake him so that he could make the rounds with her. The other women on the kibbutz were green with envy. 'A husband like that', they confessed, 'is a rarity these days.'

In addition to becoming a husband, it was also in Alumot that Shimon made his first strategic decision – and it did not bode well for a brilliant career in this field. A young Italian named Valvolio Vitale arrived at the kibbutz and introduced himself as a professional surveyor. Before coming to Alumot, he had been in Deganya, where despite the fact that he was handicapped – his right arm was shorter than his left – he earned a reputation for being very 'handy' with the women, including the married ones. This behaviour so irritated the members of Deganya that they asked Alumot to take him in. Not that he kept his hands to himself there. In fact, he earned the nickname

'*Leibediker Volf*' ('The Merry Wolf'). To add even more colour to his flamboyant ways he told everyone that he was descended from the false messiah, Shabbetai Zvi.

One day Shimon, then secretary of the kibbutz, was approached by a youngster named Yeshayahu (one of a group of immigrants newly arrived from Poland), who told him frantically that Vitale was a spy. Yeshayahu had come to this conclusion after purportedly hearing the surveyor speaking into a radio in Italian. When he questioned Vitale about what he was doing, the Italian pulled a gun and threatened to kill Yeshayahu if he revealed his secret. The story sounded fantastic to Shimon – especially as Yeshayahu had a reputation for exaggerating – but he approached Vitale anyway. Vitale's reaction was convincingly calm as he made light of the incident. 'So that's what he's going round saying about me, is it? Don't worry. I'll take care of him!'

Vitale continued to plant notes in secret hiding-places and speak into a radio, while the Pole became increasingly distraught – to the delight of Shimon and his friends. But on the day the War of Independence broke out, Vitale disappeared. It turned out that he had crossed the border into Jordan, whence he had been sent as a spy. The lesson Shimon learned from the incident was not to disregard any warning or item of information, however dubious.

Shimon was forced to make a decision of another kind when he was treasurer of the kibbutz. One day, after checking the money in the cashbox, he found that one pound was missing – an enormous sum in those days, in view of the kibbutz's financial condition. He immediately undertook an intensive investigation, discovered the thief and, without hesitation, ordered him to leave the kibbutz within twenty-four hours. The man was Avri Zeidenberg (Elad), who a few years later would become far better known by the codename 'The Third Man' – one of the principal characters of the Lavon Affair which so rocked the *Mapai* Party, Shimon's life and the lives of many others.

'Surprising as it may seem, shyness and nerve are two sides of the same coin. I'm afraid that I had more than my fair share of audacity and I had a way of challenging many conventions.' Shimon needed every ounce of that nerve in 1944, when *Mapai* was threatened by a split in the ranks. The Party's leftist faction, *Si'ah Bet* (B Faction), which was built around members of *Hakibbutz Hameuchad*, was threatening to secede from the Party. It was taken for granted that *Hanoar Ha'oved* was identified with *Si'ah Bet*. Thus *Mapai* was faced with the grave prospect of being left without a youth movement and consequently without a reserve of fresh forces. It was Shimon's hour to prove that not only was he in no way inferior to the élite of Na'an and *Hakibbutz Hameuchad*, he was actually far superior to them. So he set out to challenge the 'commonplace' that *Hanoar Ha'oved* and *Hakibbutz Hameuchad* were one and the same.

He did so quietly so as not to rouse the members of *Hakibbutz Hameuchad* from their smug complacency. In anticipation of the movement convention that was to take place in 1944, he stayed in Tel Aviv as little as possible and spent most of his time in the field, where he made the rounds of the branches, visiting each a number of times, speaking with the members, debating, organizing. After the festive opening of the *Hanoar Ha'oved* convention, the first item of business on the agenda was the election of the conference presidency. Since it was unseemly to speak openly of factions within the movement, the vying camps were named after those who led them, in this case 'Shimon's Camp' vs. 'Benyamin's Camp' (Benyamin Halili, a member of Na'an). But it was obvious that Shimon stood for *Mapai* and Benaymin for *Si'ah Bet*.

When the vote was called and the delegates' hands were raised, the people from *Hakibbutz Hameuchad* were aghast: the majority of Shimon's candidates were elected to the secretariat and *Hakibbutz Hameuchad* remained without a single representative on the secretariat of 'its' movement. And so it went in the voting for all the other movement bodies. A storm of protest ensued and there was even talk of a spit in *Hanoar Ha'oved*. To avoid that possibility, Shimon gave in to the urgings of Berl Katznelson and David Cohen and agreed to forfeit the majority which the conference had granted him. It was decided that the institutions would be composed on the basis of parity, but in essence *Hanoar Ha'oved* became *Mapai*'s movement.

For years to come, *Ahdut Ha'avodah* (the Party which grew out of *Hakibbutz Hameuchad* after its subsequent split with *Mapai*) would not forgive Shimon for its ignominious defeat. 'He's inhuman, a machine driven by the power of unconscionable ambition. His triumph at the *Hanoar Ha'oved* convention was merely the fruits of other people's menial labour,' said his critics. Shimon Peres would hear these accusations throughout his career. At first they hurt him deeply; later on he learned to live with them while keeping his sights on the objectives he set for himself.

After the victory at the *Hanoar Ha'oved* convention, Levi Eshkol brought Shimon into the *Mapai* headquarters to work on the elections to the Twenty-second Zionist Congress, scheduled to convene in Basel in 1946. Shimon himself was elected as a *Mapai* delegate to the congress in light of Ben-Gurion's unequivocal directive that not only tried and true activists should be sent to the congress, but also young comrades who represented the movement. At the age of twenty-three, Shimon Peres was one of these young people; the other, eight years his senior at thirty-one, was Moshe Dayan.

Shimon Peres and Moshe Dayan found themselves in the same camp as Ben-Gurion – and in some ways even outstripped him in zeal. They proposed that the immigrant camps established by the British in Cyprus be burned down as a way of forcing the mandatary authorities to bring the interned Jews to Palestine. The suggestion so scandalized Avraham Hartzfeld, secretary of the Agricultural Centre, that he burst into tears. It did not get a very serious hearing, but formulating and tabling it was the first contact between Peres and Dayan – a connection that would grow far closer over the years.

When he returned from Basel, Shimon was invited to join the Jewish Agency's newly founded school for diplomats, but after consideration he turned the offer down. But he had no trouble at all in deciding to accept Levi Eshkol's invitation to go to work in the 'Red House', as the *Haganah*'s headquarters were known.

His first position in May 1947 was Director of Manpower, subordinate to the headquarters' chief, Yosef Yizraeli. Shimon never returned to Alumot as an active member of the kibbutz, though he was careful to maintain his formal membership and tried to spend his vacations there. From time to time he would bring along important guests, including the Kings of Burundi and Nepal and a variety of French generals. But this desultory attachment began to irk many members of the kibbutz. In 1957, when Shimon Peres was Director-General of the Defence Ministry, the kibbutz general meeting decided that he must either return to live in Alumot or his membership would be revoked. Avraham Greidenger went to Tel Aviv to tell Shimon of the decision. It hurt him deeply. 'Why are they doing it to me?' he asked his old friend. 'How can I leave the Defence Ministry?'

Shimon did not return to live on Kibbutz Alumot and his membership was revoked, but his attachment to the kibbutz continued. Gradually the kibbutzniks even grew proud of their ex-comrade and, in 1966 after a stormy debate, the members decided to build an apartment for him where he could spend his vacations. But this project was never completed, for by 1968 the kibbutz was in a hopeless state: only thirty families remained and no reinforcements were coming in. That year Kibbutz Alumot was abandoned by its last remaining members.

2
The Architect of Defence

In May 1947 Peres came to the 'Red House' on the Tel Aviv shore, where the *Haganah*'s headquarters were housed. His job was to be responsible for mobilization and manpower and, a few days after he began working, he was invited to a brief meeting with Ben-Gurion. In an attempt to motivate the young activist, Ben-Gurion said, 'We must prepare for war. We don't have much time and we have to mobilize as large a force as possible.'

On 15 May 1948 Ben-Gurion proclaimed the establishment of a Jewish state, and the next day a ceremony was held at the *Haganah*'s headquarters to swear loyalty to the new state. The 'Red House' had now become the headquarters of the Israel Defence Forces, and its Chief of General Staff, Lieutenant-General Ya'akov Dori, called Peres in for a talk. 'I know what you're engaged in here,' he said. 'Take the rank of lieutenant-colonel.'

'I am a member of Kibbutz Alumot and have no interest in ranks,' Peres protested.

'So what do you want?' Dori asked.

'To be a soldier,' he replied.

Together with eleven other members of the staff, Peres went up on the roof of the 'Red House' and swore loyalty to the IDF and the state. Of the dozen or so men there, he was the only private.

The title Chief of Manpower Branch did not really express the scope of Private Peres's actual responsibility. In addition to manpower, he handled all matters related to arms acquisition, manufacture and administration. This last often involved him in the minutiae of army affairs.

During that period Teddy Kollek was head of the arms-purchasing mission in the United States and on a visit home he told Levi Eshkol that he would not remain at that post, unless someone at headquarters in Tel Aviv was appointed to be responsible for arms acquisition in the United States. Eshkol summoned Peres and asked him in Hebrew generously peppered with Yiddish: 'What are you doing now?'

'Manpower,' Peres replied.

'Do you know English?'

'No,' Peres confessed.

'Have you ever been to America?'

'No.'

'You're just the man I'm looking for!'

'What are you doing?' Kollek exploded after Peres left the room. 'You're taking a completely inexperienced man!'

'Don't worry,' Eshkol soothed him confidently. 'He'll do better than anyone else.'

A short time later, a number of mishaps occurred in the navy, and Chief of Staff Dori asked Peres to assume the position of chief of naval affairs at the General Staff headquarters – in addition to all his other jobs. Now Peres's work day was divided among three offices: in Haifa, where he presided as chief of the naval headquarters; in Tel Aviv, at the headquarters of the Naval and Air Branch; and in Ramat Gan, where the Manpower Branch was located.

During the War of Independence, Peres twice asked to be transferred to a field unit. Each time his request was turned down by Ben-Gurion and Shaul Avigur, his closest aide at that time. On the other hand, Ben-Gurion did comply with a request which Peres made of him immediately after the war. Peres was then twenty-six. Despite the responsible positions he had filled and the great trust placed in him by the leaders of the young state, he felt frustrated by the fact that he lacked a formal education. So he approached Ben-Gurion and asked to be granted a study leave. Ben-Gurion was amenable to the idea, but immediately linked it to a new job. He agreed to allow Peres to study in the United States on condition that he take over the Israeli arms-purchasing mission from Teddy Kollek.

Peres left for the United States in January 1950 and, immediately upon arriving, he registered for an evening course in English at the New School for Social Research in Greenwich Village. It was undoubtedly a move dictated by necessity, as was proven during his first class. The instructor chose to open the course with a lecture on 'The Role of Psychology in the English Language'. Naturally she made frequent use of the word 'psychology', which Peres did not understand. Upon returning to his apartment, he looked the word up in a dictionary under the letter 's', then under the letter 'c', but no such word existed. Puzzled, he came out and asked his instructor the next evening, only to discover that the word begins with a silent 'p'. By the end of the three-months' course, however, he proved to be an outstanding student. His transcript was a very boring document, as the only thing on it was the letter 'A'.

Almost as soon as he reached the United States, Peres discovered that political independence had not brought Israel up from under-ground – at least not in the realm of arms acquisition. It was useless to even talk about purchasing directly from the US administration because of the embargo Washington had imposed on the shipment of arms to the Middle East. Consequently, all his efforts centred on the huge market of army surplus from the Second World War. For the most part this mass of discarded materials consisted of scrap-iron or outmoded equipment which no state would dream of purchasing under normal circumstances. But the State of Israel was not only in unusual circumstances, she was poor in funds and weapons of any kind. For all that, the American administration placed severe restric-tions on even this pathetic collection of what had once been weaponry, and Peres, like his predecessors, needed every ounce of his imagination to circumvent the rules. The yield he provided was not insubstantial – considering the circumstances. We can read about some of it in Ben-Gurion's diary (for Wednesday, 13 September 1950):

> Shimon Peres arrived. He's working for the Defence Ministry and studying in the evenings. Up to now $1.7 million has been spent in the United States on arms. $1.1 million on the air force (80 planes, spare parts). $.41 million on the navy (a frigate, 12 landing-craft, 3 launches, spare parts). $.09 million on the infantry: explosives, .22 bullets, shells, etc.
>
> Canada is acting friendly. [Foreign Minister] Lester Pearson is helping out. Young McNaughton [the son of Canada's Chief of Staff during the Second World War] is our agent. The Canadians have sold us 5,000 armour-piercing shells, 200 used machine-guns ($80 each instead of $1,300); repairs will cost $20 apiece. A licence has been obtained to buy Mosquitos.

Things sound far simpler in Ben-Gurion's rendition than they actually were. The problem for Peres was not merely cultivating the proper relations with a foreign government, but also obtaining the funds to enable him to turn those ties to good advantage. The saga of purchasing artillery in Canada was characteristic of the difficulties he faced and his way of overcoming them. At this time the IDF had a grand total of four pieces of field artillery. Israel's chief arms agent was a Polish aristocrat called Stefan Czernski, who lived in France (in a marble-lined palace, we might add, built by Napoleon). Czernski claimed that he could get twenty-five recoilless cannon, which Israel was very eager to have. But when the Director-General of the Defence Ministry, Pinhas Sapir, wrote about this to Peres, he replied that he had established his own connections and believed he could obtain the guns direct. 'Excellent,' Sapir cabled, 'but we have no money.'

So Peres began to look for ways to drum up the necessary funds. He was told that there was one Jewish family in Canada that could probably help – the Bronfmans, Samuel Bronfman being the founder and President of the Seagrams Corporation. Peres also found out that the best way to get to Sam Bronfman was through Dr Nahum Goldmann, the President of the World Jewish Congress. But since the matter under consideration was classified, Peres decided to eschew Goldmann's aid and go directly to Bronfman's office. When he reached the gate of the Seagrams plant, he found it manned by guards who wouldn't let him pass. Identifying himself, he asked them to inform Mr Bronfman that he was waiting outside the gate; a few moments later Sam Bronfman came out and led the young Israeli to his office.

As Peres told the Canadian liquor magnate about the artillery, the number of pieces involved and the price, Bronfman wrinkled his brow. 'They're asking far too much,' he pronounced. Then he picked up the phone to the Canadian Minister of Commerce and Industry and requested a meeting. The next day the two men were on their way to Ottawa in Bronfman's car. It was the height of winter and the roads were covered with snow, while the temperatures dipped well below zero. Bronfman had an aversion to heating in his car, so they were wrapped in woollen blankets and for extra warmth were quaffing generous amounts of whisky – Seagrams, of course.

As soon as he entered the Canadian Minister's office, Bronfman began bargaining. To Peres's astonishment, it didn't take much to get the Minister down by half a million dollars. Peres was in seventh heaven, but his high was tempered somewhat when on their way back to Seagrams Bronfman asked him: 'Where will you get the remaining million and a half from?'

'From you,' he replied impulsively.

Bronfman peered at him for a long moment and finally broke into a smile. 'Actually you're right,' he said. 'Tomorrow night I'll invite a few people over and we'll drum up the money.'

As they left the car Bronfman noticed that Peres was wearing light-coloured socks. 'You can't come to my house in the evening wearing socks like *that*,' he pronounced, and ordered his driver to take Peres to a clothing shop where he could buy some dark ones.

At the appointed hour, the moneyed élite of the Montreal Jewish community gathered at Bronfman's home. By the end of the evening, Peres had at his disposal the remaining $1.5 million. When he reported his *coup* to Sapir, the man was flabbergasted. Thirty cannon that would not cost the State of Israel a cent! Sapir refused to believe it until he saw the guns with his own eyes. And a few weeks later, he did – all thirty of them.

This was Peres's first contact with the Bronfman family, a tie that was to carry over into the next generation. After the artillery deal was closed, Peres gave Sam Bronfman a gift of a silver-bound Bible; the book took pride of place on his desk until his dying day.

The 'Mosquitos' mentioned in Ben-Gurion's diary were small, swift bombers made of wood. One of the routes they took to Israel was over the North Pole, and during one flight a plane was lost over Newfoundland. After Peres got Ben-Gurion to intervene for this purpose, El Al agreed to lend its one and only plane – a Constellation – to carry out a search. The condition was that Peres personally join in the search to prevent any temptation to recklessness by pilots eager to find their lost colleague.

The base of the search was Goose Bay, Newfoundland, and every day the plane took off for a long sortie through the blinding snow. Disquiet and frustration mounted with each passing day of the futile search. The members of the search team spent their evenings together, and on one of those nights, Peres began to voice thoughts which struck his listeners as fantasies. The day would come, he said, when Israel would no longer be dependent on hand-me-downs from other countries; she would establish her own industry to manufacture sophisticated, reliable aircraft. The pilots regarded him with pity. True, the bitter cold had begun to affect them too, but not quite so dramatically.

No trace of the plane was ever found. The search team returned to New York and scattered, but Peres continued to be dogged by the thoughts he had expressed during that freezing night of growing despair. Soon he began to examine ways to bring it to fruition and, as sometimes happens, he found the solution right under his nose.

The planes which Israel had bought in the United States were not assembled and ready to fly at the time of purchase. The first stage in this process was to gather parts; the second was to put them together. And this latter stage, too, was executed in the United States, at a small plant in Burbank, California. Its owner was a young American Jew named Al Schwimmer, whom Peres described as 'a man of forceful opinions and rich imagination, probably the best technological leader I ever met'. When Schwimmer and Peres met, a rapport was established immediately. The American youngster and the kibbutznik from Israel were both eager for action; the more daring and challenging the mission, the more it fired their imagination. During one of Ben-Gurion's visits to the United States, Peres persuaded him to visit Schwimmer's plant. When the Prime Minister saw its pitiful collection of machinery, his mouth fell open in amazement: 'What? You can repair planes with these few machines? For heaven's sake, come to Israel!' That was precisely what Peres expected to hear.

A week later Schwimmer and Peres began to plan the establishment of a plant to assemble and overhaul aircraft in Israel. On one of their joint visits to the country, Peres took Schwimmer to Alumot for a weekend and introduced him to one of his close friends, Elhanan Yishai. It was summer then, and the three sat on the patio of Yishai's small apartment, nursing cold drinks. Out of the blue, Peres said to Yishai, 'You know, this American says he can make a jet.'

'What kind of jet? How is he going to manufacture a jet?' Yishai murmured doubtfully.

'Yes, I can make a jet,' Schwimmer confirmed.

'Listen,' Peres went on, 'you don't know him. If he says he can manufacture a jet, he'll manufacture a jet.'

Sceptical as he was, this vision kindled Yishai's imagination. 'You know what?' he proposed. 'Let's go for a dip in the lake. That way we'll remember his promise to build a jet.' And the three men stood up, marched down to the shore of the Sea of Galilee, stripped and jumped into the tranquil lake. The chilly water cooled their bodies, but not their enthusiasm. They would build a jet – and much more than that.

At that moment, Peres could not have known that the notion of an aircraft industry would play a decisive role in determining his future. When, after his stint in America, he returned to Israel at the end of

1951, it wouldn't have taken much to bring his brief military career to an end. Various people had differing ideas about his future. One of the leading figures in *Mapai*, Zalman Aranne, asked Ben-Gurion to direct Peres into a political career by appointing him chairman of the Party's Tel Aviv branch. According to Ben-Gurion's diary, the then-Director of the Defence Ministry, Ze'ev Schind, 'offered to make [Peres] Deputy Director with the title of "assistant". Peres doesn't agree to the title "assistant".'

In fact, Ben-Gurion had difficulty in deciding. On 21 January 1951, he wrote in his diary: 'I told Peres that I still want to clarify where he'll work, in the Defence Ministry or in my office. Or perhaps he'll be charged with managing manpower and youth, particularly for the army's needs. After consultations I'll make my final decision.' While Ben-Gurion was trying to make up his mind, he was visited by Al Schwimmer, Leo Gardiner and Dani Agron, who were in charge of establishing the Institute for the Reconditioning of Planes (known by the Hebrew name *Bedek*). They told the Premier and Defence Minister that 'they had purchased part of a maintenance base, transported it to New York and would bring it here. They were able to start working. What they needed was someone in government who would be a father to this enterprise, because it was necessary to co-ordinate mainten-ance, flights and so forth. They suggested Peres.'

Perhaps it was this suggestion which tilted the balance. At any rate, Ben-Gurion reached his final decision about Peres immediately after that meeting. On 1 February he wrote to Kibbutz Alumot:

> I have appointed Comrade Shimon Peres Deputy Director of the Defence Ministry, and I would like you to allow him to assume this post. In turning to you with this request, I know it is a difficult thing to ask. The membership of your kibbutz is not large, and Shimon has been away for quite a while. And were it not a vital and central position in the service of the state's defence, I wouldn't dream of imposing this heavy obligation upon you. . . . Without a vanguard, nothing will be accomplished in the realm of security. So consider the Defence Ministry part of your kibbutz – I would not object to a setting like that for it – and consider Shimon's work in the field of security one of the jobs on the kibbutz.

Peres was twenty-eight then. The first time he was invited to a meeting of Ben-Gurion's immediate defence staff, Chief of Staff Yigael Yadin could not contain himself. 'How can you appoint such a young man to such a focal position in the defence network?' he asked Ben-Gurion in front of Peres. Ben-Gurion replied with an adage that reflected his actions throughout his life. 'To be young is no drawback,' he said, adding, 'as for inexperienced, we'll see about that.'

Peres found a Defence Ministry organized to fit the needs of the state-in-the-making, a structure inappropriate to the demands of a sovereign national concern. Director-General Schind was a talented and affable man, but he also served as the Director-General of the Transport Ministry and therefore lacked the time necessary to change things in any fundamental way. Peres took this task upon himself with alacrity and in a short time had the Ministry restructured. No one was in the least surprised, therefore, when nine months later Ben-Gurion announced in a letter dated 5 October 1952 that 'Shimon Peres has been appointed acting Director-General of the Defence Ministry'. Within a few months *Bedek* had been founded, set in operation and was filling all the maintenance needs of civilian and military aeronautics in Israel.

Shortly afterwards, in November 1952, there was a seismic changing of the guard in the senior ranks of the army, as well. The Chief of Staff, Lieutenant-General Yigael Yadin, decided to retire and was succeeded by Mordechai Makleff. The latter's outlook on the relationship between the IDF and the Ministry of Defence differed fundamentally from Yadin's. Makleff saw the IDF as a body that should handle the full range of subjects related to security, from manpower down to the details of arms acquisition and manufacture. Peres thought otherwise. He believed that the IDF and its General Staff should deal exclusively with military matters; all the rest should be left to the jurisdiction of the Defence Ministry. Each side was pulling in a different direction, but evidently Peres's pull was stronger and more effective, for it prompted an uncharacteristic outburst from Makleff. 'I ate all the shit,' the Chief of Staff grumbled. 'I sacked thousands of civilians – and now suddenly I see the Ministry of Defence starting to surround and circumvent the army from every direction, taking all kinds of initiatives upon itself.'

As matters turned out, Makleff never managed to reach an understanding with the head of the General Staff's Operations Branch, Major-General Moshe Dayan, either. In a meeting with Ben-Gurion, he demanded that Dayan be replaced by another young comer, Yitzhak Rabin. He also complained about Peres making 'changes at the expense of the General Staff'. All these complaints brought Ben-Gurion to the conclusion that Makleff 'is suffering from an inferiority complex and therefore suspects people of trying to infringe upon his jurisdiction'.

For all that, Ben-Gurion refused to accept Makleff's resignation, which was submitted to him in May 1953 – though he also rejected the Chief of Staff's relentless demands to oust Dayan, Peres, Major-General Chaim Laskov and other high-ranking officers. But the frequent squabbles led Ben-Gurion to believe that something was probably wrong with the structure of the defence establishment, the army and the reciprocal ties between them. To study this matter in greater depth, he took an extended leave as Minister of Defence and, on Peres's recommendation, appointed Pinhas Lavon as his replacement.

Ben-Gurion took advantage of the leave to make tours and study the defence network in depth. He visited army camps, climbed down into trenches, studied the various branches of the Defence Ministry – and the conclusions he reached vindicated Peres's way of thinking. The most important of his verdicts was that the Defence Minister needed two assistants: the Chief of Staff, to be responsible for the armed forces; and the Director-General of the Defence Ministry, to deal with all the branches designed to serve the IDF but not strictly defined as combat-related. Since it was clear to Ben-Gurion that the framework he decided upon did not suit the tastes of all those who operated within it, when Makleff submitted his resignation a second time, on 11 October, he accepted it.

But Makleff was not the only one to go. Ben-Gurion himself was suffering from severe fatigue due to the strains of political life. On 2 November he notified the President of his decision to resign the premiership and retire to the modest wooden house that had been built for him at Sdeh Boker, a new kibbutz in the heart of the Negev desert.

Before his departure on 7 December, however, Ben-Gurion instituted a number of measures to ensure that the two institutions he considered most vital to the security of the state would be headed by people in whom he placed his unreserved trust. The first appointment was prompted by Pinhas Lavon, who noticed that the title 'Acting Director-General' appeared next to Peres's name in the Defence Ministry's correspondence. Lavon mentioned this to Ben-Gurion, who immediately summoned Peres. 'Why didn't you tell me that you're still listed as the Acting Director?' he asked. 'It doesn't bother me,' Peres explained. But that was only part of the reason for his silence. From the start of his relationship with Ben-Gurion, Peres had set an iron-clad rule for himself: never ask the Old Man for anything personal. Ben-Gurion often made a point of remembering that. At the end of December 1953, the secretary of the Cabinet announced that 'on the recommendation of Acting Defence Minister Pinhas Lavon, Shimon Peres was formally appointed Director-General of the Defence Ministry on 27 December 1953'.

Far more problematic was the second appointment, namely, a Chief of Staff to replace Makleff. Peres was strongly in favour of Moshe Dayan and recommended him highly to Ben-Gurion. But many *Mapai* leaders, including Moshe Sharett, Zalman Aranne and Golda Meir, were against the appointment. They called Dayan a 'partisan' and complained that he was disorganized, undisciplined and reckless. Even Ben-Gurion had misgivings about Dayan's character. But Peres assured him: 'You can trust him 100 per cent. He'll turn the IDF into a fighting force.'

In the end Ben-Gurion decided in Dayan's favour and appointed him Chief of Staff. Some time later, however, Peres was sitting in Ben-Gurion's office in the Defence Ministry in Ramat Gan when a panic-stricken officer burst into the room and fairly shrieked: 'The Chief of Staff is standing on his balcony and shooting all over the place!' Ben-Gurion flashed a reproachful look at Peres. 'See what your Moshe is doing.' Peres sprinted over to the two-storey building which housed Dayan's office and, sure enough, Dayan was standing on the balcony with a rifle in hand. 'What's wrong with you?' he shouted. 'What do you think you're doing?'

Dayan merely smiled. 'You've been invited to dinner at my place tonight?'

'Yes.'

'Do you know why?'

'No,' Peres admitted.

'It's my fortieth birthday today. I decided to invite forty guests and serve them the forty pigeons which I'm hunting right now.'

Even after three decades Peres tells this story without being able to conceal his admiration for Dayan's unfailing panache. Perhaps this is why he loved and followed Dayan throughout the years, because he himself was too inhibited or self-conscious to behave in such a way.

The man Ben-Gurion appointed to succeed him as Defence Minister was one of the brightest rising stars in the *Mapai* firmament. Pinhas Lavon had about him the aura of a leader. He was forty-nine and handsome, with silver hair which added a frame of dignity to his suntanned visage. His mind was acute, his speeches a work of art. But his striking appearance and dazzling wit camouflaged a number of traits perceived only by those who knew him well. In his personal relations, Lavon conducted himself with more than a dash of arrogance and a generous measure of conceit. The most telling observation about Lavon probably came from Labour ideologue Berl Katznelson in a comment to Zalman Aranne: 'A brilliant mind but a troubled soul.'

Peres and Dayan were pleased by Ben-Gurion's choice, primarily because they identified with Lavon's activist approach to foreign affairs and defence and considered it a necessary counterbalance to the moderate position of Moshe Sharett (who succeeded Ben-Gurion as Prime Minister). Before long, though – far sooner than anyone expected – the first strains began to show in the relations between the Minister of Defence and his Director-General and the Chief of Staff. As early as February 1954, some two months after Ben-Gurion's retirement, when Dayan and Peres visited the Old Man at Sdeh Boker, both were bristling with complaints about Lavon – Dayan about his unbridled activism, which was leading him into rash decisions and actions; Peres about his cuts in the defence budget, especially the clauses covering arms acquisition and manufacture.

One case in point, the question of purchasing the French AMX tank, climaxed with Dayan submitting his resignation as Chief of Staff on 16 June, and it was only due to Ben-Gurion's intervention that Lavon invited Dayan for a conciliation meeting. The interesting point about this talk appears in a sentence in Dayan's diaries: 'Lavon is shifting the entire misunderstanding on to Shimon's shoulders.' And Nehemiah Argov, Ben-Gurion's military secretary, wrote: 'The Old Man said that Lavon appears to have something against Shimon.'

This motif would reappear again and again throughout Peres's public and political career. It was difficult to strike against Dayan – a military man, a national hero, an all but legendary figure. And no one would dare take aim at Ben-Gurion. So anyone wishing to get back at one of these two men would inevitably do so by attacking Peres. Peres was aware of this syndrome and accepted it, either because he could do nothing about it or because he understood that it was the price he had to pay for Ben-Gurion's trust in him, which sparked off widespread envy.

Ben-Gurion's and Dayan's attitude towards the criticism of Peres – which would grow in direct proportion to his political advancement – were not identical. Ben-Gurion understood that Peres served as the target of barbs essentially meant for himself, and it never ceased to infuriate him. He often came to Peres's defence in letters to editors, from the Knesset rostrum or in Party debates. But the result was usually the opposite of what Ben-Gurion wanted: the more he defended Peres, the stronger the attacks on him grew. Ben-Gurion's enemies, both within his own Party and in the opposition, understood that the assaults on Peres touched a very sensitive nerve in him, and they never stopped aiming for it.

Dayan's attitude, stemming from his overall feelings about Peres, was as different as could be. He accepted as perfectly natural the fact that Peres served as a buffer for him whenever possible, but he did not see this as obliging him to adopt a reciprocal position. Rarely did he come out in Peres's defence or have a good word to say for him. And when he did mention Peres, orally or in writing, he did so grudgingly and only when the chronological order of events strictly demanded it.

During this period, Israel was not the only state in which major changes in leadership took place. In the spring of 1954, the power struggle within the military junta that had assumed power in Egypt after deposing King Farouk finally reached a climax. General Mohammed Naguib was ousted as Prime Minister of Egypt and replaced by a charismatic young colonel called Gamal Abdul Nasser.

One of the new Egyptian leader's first acts was to demand that Britain evacuate the Suez Canal zone so that he could nationalize the Canal. The United States seemed inclined to support this demand. Israel was justifiably alarmed, for she perceived the British military force stationed in the Canal zone as the bridle on Egypt's aggressive intentions. The spectre of Nasser going through with his plans kept many an Israeli awake at night, and a number of people active in defence and political circles felt that something drastic had to be done if the worst were to be averted. The most radical thinking in this direction was represented by Defence Minister Pinhas Lavon.

So it was that a plan of action began to take shape in the IDF's Intelligence Branch. Based on the premise that the British MPs opposed to the evacuation of the Canal zone should have their case strengthened by evidence that the new Egyptian regime could not be relied upon, it called for the execution of a series of sabotage operations in Egypt to create the impression of political anarchy. The clandestine campaign began on 14 July 1954, with the planting of firebombs, which were quickly extinguished and caused only light damage. But a week later agents of the Israeli Intelligence unit embarked upon similar missions in two cinemas in Cairo, two others in Alexandria and a warehouse in Cairo. During this second operation the agent sent to the Rio Theatre in Alexandria suffered a mishap. The firebomb in his pocket ignited and he was promptly arrested by the Egyptian police.

On 25 July items appeared in the Arab press and radio about the round-up of an Israeli espionage network responsible for committing acts of arson throughout Egypt. This was the first Prime Minister Sharett and Chief of Staff Dayan heard of the affair. In a subsequent clarification, the initiative was traced to Defence Minister Pinhas Lavon, who had not felt obliged to consult with or report to anyone about it. This revelation sent shock waves from Jerusalam clear down to Sdeh Boker, where Ben-Gurion wrote in his diary: 'He [Moshe Dayan] spoke of Pinhas Lavon's astounding order – given during [Dayan's] absence – for an action in Egypt which failed (and they should have known it would fail). Criminal irresponsibility!'

The trial of the captured Israeli agents opened in Cairo on 11 December 1954, while in Israel a committee of inquiry was secretly appointed to find out exactly who gave the order for the ill-conceived operation. The committee was composed of two members: Ya'akov Dori, an ex-Chief of Staff, and Supreme Court Justice Yitzhak Olshan. Its investigation brought to light instances of strained relations, intrigues and even the forging of documents in the senior ranks of the defence establishment. The Israeli Government found itself sucked into an invidious trap. On the one hand, day after day shocking facts about the affair were coming out. On the other, the official line remained that Egypt had perpetrated a base libel against Israel.

On 27 January 1955, the trial of the Israeli agents came to a close in Cairo. Two of the accused were sentenced to death; six to long prison terms; and two local Jews were acquitted. Four days later the death sentences were carried out. Before that, one of the two doomed prisoners, the Intelligence officer Max Bennett, committed suicide in prison.

Meanwhile, details of the Dori-Olshan inquiry also began to leak out to the press, but in an erratic and censored fashion. Lavon was sure that Dayan and Peres – particularly Peres – were scheming against him and leaking the incriminating information to the media. He told Prime Minister Sharett that if the inquiry commission cleared him, he would dismiss Peres together with other people in the senior echelon of the Defence Ministry. Sharett investigated the leak, declared the charges unfounded and so informed Peres in writing. On 13 January 1955, the Dori-Olshan Commission wound up its inquiry without arriving at a clear-cut conclusion: 'We can only say that we have not been convinced beyond a reasonable doubt that the Chief of Intelligence did not receive orders from the Defence Minister. However, neither are we sure that the Defence Minister actually issued the orders ascribed to him.'

This ambivalent judgment again set off tremors within the top ranks of *Mapai* and prompted a series of consultations about Lavon's future. When Lavon got wind of these doings, he promptly submitted his resignation, but tacked on the threat to reveal his motives to the people. The spectre of such a public laundering of *Mapai* linen alarmed the Party leaders even more than the prospect of Lavon remaining as Defence Minister. So a stampede now began in the opposite direction, with Sharett urging Lavon to retract his resignation. Lavon insisted upon a number of conditions, including the dismissal of Intelligence Chief Benjamin Jibli and the Director-General of the Defence Ministry, Shimon Peres. Speaking on Sharett's behalf, someone suggested to Peres that he take a six-month leave; but he flatly refused because he believed that a move of that kind would be equivalent to an admission of guilt. Jibli also turned down Sharett's request to transfer to another position. Then Sharett changed course again by informing Lavon that he was opposed to dismissing Peres because he found him completely innocent. Lavon was left with no choice: on 2 February he resigned irrevocably.

The official explanation for Lavon's departure was a series of disagreements over the structure of the Defence Ministry and the IDF, but in fact the resignation had been forced upon him because of the Egyptian affair, which remained suppressed from the public. Lavon was chosen by *Mapai* as Secretary-General of the *Histadrut* and it seemed as if the affair had been laid to rest. But this conclusion was little more than wishful thinking. In time it would rear its ugly head again and set off another political earthquake – this time strong enough to rock the entire Israeli public and bring about a dramatic change in the map of Israel's political leadership.

The dominant feeling was that none of this would have happened if Ben-Gurion had been at the helm of state, and a spate of delegations began to stream towards Sdeh Boker. On 17 February the public was informed that Ben-Gurion had agreed to return to government as Minister of Defence, while Sharett would continue as Prime Minister. Those who predicted that this *mélange* was doomed were very right. The friction was particularly sharp over the issue of the reprisal raids launched in response to infiltration by squads of *fedayeen* coming from Egypt. Ben-Gurion championed a policy of military pressure on the countries which allowed the *fedayeen* to operate from their territory; Sharett advocated moderation and restraint.

When general elections were held in Israel in the middle of July, *Mapai* retained its distinction as the country's largest Party, though it lost five seats. At the other end of the spectrum, the *Herut* Party, headed by Menachem Begin, picked up a number of seats. These results were viewed as an expression of the public's disappointment in the moderate line pursued by the Sharett Government. The voices calling on Ben-Gurion to resume the premiership grew consistently louder.

On 2 November 1955, the Knesset gave its vote of confidence to the new Government formed by David Ben-Gurion. As in the past, he kept the position of Defence Minister as well. Throughout this period tension had been running high along the Israeli-Egyptian border, as squads of infiltrators crossed the frontier almost nightly to sow death and destruction throughout the Israeli border settlements. Israel responded with retaliatory actions, and the conflagration soon spread to the Jordanian and Lebanese borders as well. But the worst blow of all fell on Israel in September 1955. After months of negotiations, Czechoslovakia and Egypt signed an arms agreement of unprecedented proportions. The deal called for Egypt to receive 200 MiG-15 and Ilyushin-28 jet fighter-bombers, 230 tanks, 200 armoured personnel carriers, 100 self-propelled guns and about 500 pieces of other mobile artillery, plus marine craft, torpedoes, 2 destroyers and 6 submarines.

The Czech arms deal shifted the balance of forces in the Middle East to Israel's severe detriment. The Western countries were no less conscious of this ominous situation than was Israel. Cairo was swamped with protests and demands to cancel the deal, but to no avail. Israel knocked at the chancelleries of all the Western capitals, but except for lip-service was unrewarded. Most disappointing of all was the attitude of the United States, towards which the major Israeli effort was directed. Secretary of State John Foster Dulles reiterated his promise that in light of the Czech deal Washington would reconsider her position on supplying arms to Israel. In the end, however, his reassessment concluded with a message conceding only that the United States would not object if other Western states sold arms to Israel. The frustration notwithstanding, a pro-American orientation continued to prevail in the Prime Minister's Office and Foreign Ministry in Jerusalem. Peres was almost alone in urging that greater efforts be made in the direction of France.

'Every Frenchman killed in North Africa, like every Egyptian killed in the Gaza Strip, takes us one step further towards strengthening the ties between France and Israel.' Peres sounded these words during a closed session on 19 June 1955, before the Czech arms deal was signed. Though not pleasant to the ear, this statement was an accurate reflection of the situation.

At this time France exhibited deep-felt support and admiration for Israel and her struggle. This was especially true in defence and military quarters. But Peres understood that a solid link between the two countries could not be based upon sentiment alone. A concrete interest must also come into play, and this interest was inherent in France's struggle to maintain her rule over Algeria. The Arab world, and Egypt most of all, backed the insurgents in Algeria. Israel was an enemy of the Arab world and, following the rule that 'my enemy's enemy is my friend', Peres saw this situation as brimming with potential.

The first tie with France had been established at the end of 1953. Until then Israel had purchased meagre quantities of weapons from France through the agent Stefan Czernski, who received – in addition to his 15 per cent commission – separate funds to 'oil the machinery'. When Peres was appointed Director-General of the Defence Ministry, he met Czernski and demanded to know who the recipients of the money were; otherwise he would stop paying it out. Czernski claimed that they were 'associates of Paul Renaud', the French Deputy Premier. Then Peres said that he wished to meet Renaud. 'No problem,' Czernsi told him and promised to arrange it.

A few weeks passed but no meeting was scheduled. Then Peres arrived in Paris, phoned Renaud and asked for a meeting. A day later he was received by the Deputy Premier and spelled out Israel's problems, difficulties and needs. When he asked for artillery, Renaud promptly replied: 'I'm your friend. I'll take care of it.'

After this meeting, Peres phoned Czernski and asked, 'What about Renaud?' 'He'll see you next week,' the agent promised. This convinced Peres that the claim about bribing Renaud's aides was a fabrication, and he severed Israel's association with Czernski. From then on the Israeli Government purchased arms from France without intermediaries, though the quantities remained small and the types of arms limited. In order to bolster the French connection, Peres needed a much freer hand than Defence Minister Lavon was willing to give him. That problem was solved when Ben-Gurion resumed the post of Defence Minister.

On 2 May 1955, Ben-Gurion wrote in his diary:

> Shimon Peres is going to England and France tomorrow on an arms mission. He believes it's a good time to buy from France because of the pique over Bandung [the Bandung Conference of Afro-Asian States] and the murder of the Syrian Chief of Staff. He suggests that Moshe Dayan write about it to General Koenig, who promised to treat Israel like the French army. I agreed, on condition that the Prime Minister [Sharett] approves.

With Dayan's letter in hand, Peres left to meet the French Defence Minister, Pierre Koenig, whose admiration for Israel, and particularly the IDF, was boundless. After Peres told him of Israel's needs, the French General asked him for a memorandum giving a list of arms and the reason for each item. 'When do you want the memo?' Peres asked.

'On Sunday at ten,' Koenig told him.

'You work on Sundays?'

'It's a day, isn't it?'

On that Sunday Peres happened to be in the Israeli Embassy in Paris when, promptly at ten o'clock a telephone call came from General Koenig's office. 'Where's the memo?' an aide asked.

'We sent it an hour ago,' Peres replied.

'Well, it hasn't arrived,' Koenig's chief aide complained.

Peres immediately made for the French Defence Ministry, where he found the messenger, memo in hand, standing at the gate. The guards had refused to allow him in because Sunday wasn't a workday.

General Koenig did not disappoint Peres and signed an agreement to sell Israel light tanks and field artillery. But the items which Israel had her eye on most of all were combat planes, and Peres found Koenig's ear attentive to this request as well. He agreed to sell twenty-four Mystère-2 jets. The quantity was small compared to the need, but Israel could not afford to be too fussy on this score; no other country was prepared to sell her so much as a spare part for a plane.

Despite the genial atmosphere Peres found in Paris, the French did have reservations about an overt and broad-based relationship with

Israel. Egypt and Syria were still considered French allies against the Baghdad Pact, and Paris feared that the supplying of Israel with large quantities of arms would kindle the wrath of these two Arab states.

At the other end of the Mediterranean, circles within the Israeli Foreign Ministry were no less concerned that to balance out her sales to Israel, France would have to offer similar deals to Egypt and Syria – perhaps in even greater quantities. Thus in the midst of his negotiations in Paris, Peres received an admonitory cable from Dayan on 10 May: 'If one is to judge by the blue cables, it seems that the Foreign Ministry is having second thoughts about our present arms-acquisition efforts in France, since it is not consonant with their efforts to prevent the sale of French weapons to Egypt. Is it necessary to hold a clarification that will ensure the Foreign Ministry's support for your present purchasing mission?' Peres replied in the affirmative and, following Ben-Gurion's intervention, the Ministry's objections were withdrawn. But not for long. From this point on, the effort to purchase arms in France was bound up with a relentless struggle between the Defence Ministry and the Foreign Ministry in Israel.

In September it turned out that the jubilation over the Mystère-2 deal was premature. Senior officers in the French air force made it known to their Israeli colleagues that the plane was riddled with defects. They recommended cancelling the deal and ordering Mystère-4 planes, which were then in the final stages of production.

The signing of the Czech arms deal promoted the subject of combat planes to the highest order of importance. Prime Minister Sharett himself made for Paris to meet his French counterpart. In essence, however, his trip was superfluous, for two days before Sharett reached the French capital, Peres had met the heads of the French Defence Ministry and had come to an agreement whereby Israel would receive twenty-four Mystère-4 planes. This undoubtedly was the reason why Sharett's meeting lasted only about ten minutes, during which the French Premier confirmed the agreement already reached. Still, that commitment was attended by the condition that the United States give its consent, since France had manufactured the planes for NATO by American request.

The United States hedged on the question and never really approved the deal. Meanwhile, however, a political earthquake shook France and threatened to scuttle the arrangement altogether. Edgar Faure's Government fell, and elections for the new National Assembly were set for the beginning of January 1956. Surveying the political scene in France, Peres came to two conclusions. First, there was little chance that the plane deal would come to fruition through conventional channels. Second, a final commitment on the planes must be obtained from the French before a new government was formed, for the policies and leanings of a future government could not be surmised in advance.

He therefore travelled to Paris to meet General Pierre Billotte, who had replaced Pierre Koenig as Defence Minister. The primary subject of their talk was the Mystère-4s, which were still held up pending a go-ahead from the United States. Peres came to the talk armed with the knowledge that the commander of the French air force would emphatically refuse to release Mystère-2s from his hangars. This allowed him to state that Israel was prepared to purchase the Mystère-2, while silently praying for the answer he expected. And he got it. 'Billotte jumped up and declared, "The Mystère-2 is out of the question. You must take the 4. I spoke to Faure about it and it's all right. But I must ask extraordinary secrecy of you, because of the Americans and the British. If you can see to it that France is assailed in the press, please do so. It will help matters." '

Peres had the feeling that the only problem with Billotte's statement was that it was too good to be true. 'When do we sign?' he asked. The Deputy Defence Minister, Croisier, produced a diary and they set a meeting for 5 p.m. the next day. 'We showed up at Croisier's office at the appointed hour in blue suits and a festive mood all ready to sign. Smiling, Croisier asked: "How is the weather in Israel?" We talked about the weather for five minutes and meanwhile there's no hint of any signing ceremony. Finally, I said we've come to sign. "Ah," he said. "Really. To sign. But there are two difficulties here – with the Americans and with our Foreign Ministry." ' It was necessary to make another round of visits to French officials and generals, but two days later the signing did take place for 155 pieces of field artillery and Sherman tanks – everything but planes.

Meanwhile, time was running out for the Faure Government. In December Peres went to France again and this time he found Billotte fuming. A few days before, Israel had executed a large reprisal action against Syria. Billotte contended that such operations jeopardized French interests in Syria and demanded that there be co-ordination between the two countries in the future. The report Peres submitted on 28 December 1955 concluded that: 'The incident in Syria helped somewhat because we finally have something to offer the French.'

Peres also added fuel to the flames of the traditional antagonism between the French and the British by telling Billotte that London had just wrapped up a deal to sell Israel fighter planes. 'You see what the British are doing? On the one hand they forbid you to sell us planes while they themselves sell to us without consulting you.' No French patriot needed to hear more than that. Billotte promised Peres that the matter would be dealt with forthwith. But difficulties arose again – and this time Billotte was nowhere in sight. Like the rest of his colleagues, he was preoccupied with the election campaign. So Peres went to his constituency, about 350 kilometres from Paris, and ran the General to earth in a sound-truck roaming the streets of Dijon.

Peres suggested that they circumvent the American obstacle by sending the planes to Israel dismantled. Billotte replied that Prime Minister Faure preferred to wait for approval, since he had reason to believe that it would be granted. But he did agree to issue an immediate order 'that an agreement be signed forthwith on the sale of twelve Mystère-4 planes. If the Americans permit it, they will be sent to Israel immediately. If the Dassault plant is able to manufacture twelve planes without the Americans' knowledge, they will be supplied by July 1956.' Billotte added in his own handwriting, at Peres's request, a clause ordering that 'a reasonable number' of components be transferred to Israel 'following a gentleman's agreement that we will be able to assemble an additional number of planes, above and beyond the twelve, in Israel'.

The results of the election led to a thorough-going change in the upper reaches of the French regime. The task of forming a government fell to the leader of the Socialist Party, Guy Mollet, and as his Minister of Defence he appointed Maurice Bourgès-Maunoury (who had been the Minister of the Interior in Edgar Faure's Government).

Peres was prepared for these changes, for during his pre-election visits to France he initiated a number of introductory meetings with personalities likely to assume key positions. When he joined Guy Mollet for lunch in November, he had reason to be anxious about the meeting and the man. Israel had had bitter experiences with the socialist parties that came to power in Western Europe, so when Mollet expressed his friendship for Israel, Peres rejoined by expressing his misgivings: 'Ernest Bevin was also a supporter of Israel, but he turned into an enemy when he came to power.'

'I won't be a Bevin,' Mollet replied decidedly.

Peres's acquaintance with Bourgès-Maunoury had been established when the latter was still Minister of the Interior. In a meeting with Bourgès, set up by his trusted chief aide, Abel Thomas, the Minister expressed deep friendship for Israel. In short, he said that France and Israel faced similar problems: 'We should work together and we can.' Peres could not have known it at the time, but this relationship would prove to be crucial in determining Israel's future both in terms of security and in her relations with France.

After Guy Mollet was sworn in as Premier, Peres approached him with a letter from Ben-Gurion. Breaking into a smile, Mollet reiterated, 'Now you'll see that I am not a Bevin.' He proved it immediately by ordering that all the commitments of the previous Government be honoured. On 11 April Ben-Gurion visited a military airfield in northern Israel. A ripple of excitement ran through the crowd as, over the horizon, one after the other, French Mystère-4s could be seen coming in to land on Israeli soil.

But there were some who felt a shudder of concern as well. Finance Minister Levi Eshkol complained about the high price Israel had to pay for its purchases. Ben-Gurion answered him on 12 March 1956: 'I hope that Shimon demands more for this purpose. For the meanwhile, you are asked to enable him, without delay, to sign whatever contracts can be written up immediately.' Far more disgruntled was Moshe Sharett, who had resumed the post of Foreign Minister when Ben-Gurion resumed the premiership. Sharett's resentment of Peres's independent enterprise in France had begun much earlier. At his instigation, the Director-General of the Foreign Ministry, Walter Eytan, sent Peres a letter on 31 May 1955, which read in part: 'This time, as on previous occasions, you left for France on an important mission without giving the Foreign Ministry prior notice and without allowing the Embassy the proper time to do the groundwork in Paris.' At the close of his letter, Eytan expressed the hope 'that in future the matter will be rectified'.

'As a rule I have consulted with the Foreign Ministry,' Peres wrote in reply, 'but this last time I was unable to hold a consultation because of the urgency of my trip.' It was a flimsy excuse which Peres made little effort to bolster. He also refrained from stating that he shared Eytan's hopes regarding the future.

In April 1956 the confrontation escalated to a head-on clash. At the beginning of that month, the United States turned down Israel's requests to purchase military equipment. It was also the start of a period in which tensions along Israel's borders were mounting and colossal amounts of arms were flowing into Egypt from the Soviet bloc. Meanwhile, all Israel's urgings – almost pleas – landed up on the desk of Secretary of State John Foster Dulles, whom Peres described as 'an odd combination of priest and prosecutor. Sometimes he resorted to the arguments of a lawyer, sometimes to mysticism. He began by stating that the Jews murdered Muhammad and wound up by proclaiming that the Russians are beginning to revise their way of life because America has succeeded. Dulles has a Jewish complex. He was defeated, for the one and only time in his life, in an election district with a high percentage of Jews.' Peres concluded: 'Dulles hasn't given and won't give us anything.'

The United States' reply to Israel's arms request infuriated Ben-Gurion, who promptly convened a consultation with Dayan, Sharett, Peres and the Director-General of the Prime Minister's Office, Dr Ya'akov Herzog. Sharett believed that it was still possible to win Dulles over, but Ben-Gurion was unequivocal. 'We must stop all mediation with the United States immediately,' he pronounced. In the course of the discussion, Dayan congratulated Peres on the success of the Mystère deal with France while criticizing the Foreign Ministry's acquisition methods. His remark evidently cut Sharett to the quick, for after the meeting the Foreign Minister sent a letter to Ben-Gurion (dated 3 April): 'My admiration for the energies and accomplishments of Shimon Peres notwithstanding, the fact remains that my conversation with Faure at the end of October [1954] broke the deadlock on the question of arms acquisition in France and rescued us from difficult straits.' On the following day, Ben-Gurion wrote back:

I don't see the problem or the importance of who achieved more or first. I view all the Ministries and all members of the Government as envoys in the same cause; and in the case of arms acquisition, the only question is that of effectiveness – not prestige or the right of precedence. I am no less pleased about the success of the [Israeli Minister in the Paris Embassy] than about Shimon's achievements, because the important thing is succeeding. I am not at all interested in an account of who should get *more* credit.

The Chief of Staff's way of thinking is, as I see it, generally logical: we should first approach the owners – the factory or the army (if the latter owns the weapons). Naturally the Minister should be informed of that. If [the owners] turn to the Foreign Ministry, the Minister should be allowed to act; but if Shimon, too, can meet with Pineau or another Foreign Minister or a Director-General, I don't see anything contradictory in that – as long as the approach is *effective*. This temperamental score-keeping is somewhat mystifying to me.

However, I believe that a man who deals with one job may succeed better than a man who deals with many tasks, and that is how I account for Shimon's success (when he succeeds).

In this letter, Ben-Gurion effectively granted Peres *carte blanche* to pursue his maverick mode of operation. He understood that Peres's approach was dictated by necessity, for a similar, in fact almost identical, state of affairs prevailed in France, where fundamental differences on the subject of aid to Israel divided the Quai d'Orsay and the Defence Ministry. At their very first meeting, for example, Bourgès had made it clear to Peres that he preferred to bypass the diplomats and make direct contact.

Peres commented on this situation in a lecture before senior employees of the Defence Ministry on 30 April 1956:

> The disagreements between the French Foreign Ministry and Defence Ministry are not just between two separate administrative units, but between networks that reflect two outlooks. The Foreign Ministry views France as a focal power in the Middle East, a power which can mediate between Russia and the United States. The Defence Ministry sees in Israel 1.6 million people, and it sees 1.6 million Frenchmen in Algeria. It views Israel as a second front against Nasser, contrasted to the primary front they have in Algeria. Israel's problem is which orientation to choose. We must take advantage of any factor in any country in order to get results.

Peres's analysis had much to recommend it. But Algeria was not the only subject of French concern just then: France also had an abiding interest in Syria. When Peres visited Paris in mid-March 1956 he was repeatedly asked: Can you assure us that you don't have any designs on Syrian territory? And what are you prepared to do in the event of an Iraqi invasion of Syria? 'I asked: What do you want us to do? But they backed down, said they were just asking. That's what we call "socialist fog". Many sentences end with a question mark; only a few end with a period.'

There was no dearth of sentences ending with an exclamation point, especially those proffered in reply to Israel's arms requests. Peres found Prime Minister Guy Mollet 'far less stodgy in real life than his pictures in the papers suggest. Occasionally his eyes glint with an intelligent smile that seems more like a Gallic wink. Throughout the meeting he gave me the feeling of comfort that goes with informality. When I said that Nasser should not be allowed to remain in a belligerent mood for so long, he grinned and said: "So, what are you waiting for!" '

It was a good lead into the subject of Peres's mission. What interested Israel most, Peres told his host, was the replacement of her large, outmoded collection of planes by new Mystères. On 23 April Peres was able to cable Ben-Gurion from Paris: 'This evening, at a festive party, we signed on another twelve Mystères. The planes will be supplied in May. The existence of the contract must be kept highly secret, at the request of the local Defence Ministry. Six Ouragans were also approved for us.' The next day, he cabled again: 'The contract has been signed. Am leaving Paris tomorrow.' Ben-Gurion could not resist cabling back (on 24 April): 'Congratulations!'

Acquiring arms from France now became the subject that took up most of Peres's time. He would talk to the head of the military mission in Paris, Yosef Nachmias, several times a day, and anyone listening in to these conversations would undoubtedly have thought that the two had lost their minds. For example, on 1 May 1956:

Peres: 'Did Carmen Miranda get married or not?'
Nachmias: 'Who?'
Peres: 'Carmen.'
Nachmias: 'She's gone.'
Peres: 'Hasn't found a husband yet?'
Nachmias: 'I still don't know whether the wedding's on or not.'
Peres: 'OK.'

It was not always clear who the two succeeded in confusing more, the enemy or each other.

Towards the latter half of 1956, it began to dawn on Peres that the potential he was capitalizing on in France might only be the tip of the iceberg. The sentiments he heard from Guy Mollet and Bourgès-Maunoury left little doubt in his mind that he could get much more out of France – perhaps far beyond what even his own rich imagination could conceive. In a discussion with Ben-Gurion, he therefore asked that the quantities under consideration be revised. 'Instead of 72 Mystères, let's start talking in terms of 150. Instead of 60 tanks, let's ask for 200.'

He also sensed that Nasser could serve as the catalyst for bringing these requests to fruition. The Egyptian ruler was inching towards an increasingly radical position, and the aid he was providing to the

44

Algerian rebels was on the rise. Behind closed doors, voices in the French Government began to call for military action against Egypt. In May 1956 Peres floated a trial balloon with Ben-Gurion by suggesting that Israel enter into a tacit military pact with France against Nasser. With the Old Man's blessing, he went to Paris for a meeting with Bourgès-Maunoury, to whom he proposed a package deal: Israel would be prepared to participate in planning a joint operation against Egypt in return for a massive infusion of French arms. The idea appealed to the French Defence Minister, and the two decided to convene a secret conference in France within days.

Back in Israel, however, Moshe Sharett did not take to the idea at all, and his opposition proved to be the proverbial last straw. Ben-Gurion came to the conclusion that he could not go on working with a man who disagreed with him on almost all the major issues of the day. On 19 June, therefore, when Sharett submitted his resignation as Foreign Minister, Ben-Gurion accepted it – officially with regret but privately with a sense of relief – and appointed Labour Minister Golda Meir to the vacant post.

Three days later, on 22 June, Chief of Staff Moshe Dayan, Chief of Intelligence Yehoshafat Harkavi and Peres boarded a French Nord plane at a small airfield outside Tel Aviv. Some twelve hours later they landed near Paris and were conducted to a nearby town, where they were put up in an ancient castle surrounded by a lush garden and a wall, to assure complete secrecy. That same afternoon discussions began with the French delegation, headed by Louis Mangin, the Director of the French Defence Minister's bureau, and including Generals Challe and Levaud and representatives of French Intelligence. The exchange of views and assessments produced an understanding about the need to topple President Nasser, and, without committing Israel, Dayan expressed her readiness, in principle, to co-operate with France towards that end.

After a brief respite, the two delegations met again to discuss the subject of arms. This time it was Peres who presented Israel's requests: 200 tanks, 72 Mystère jets, 40,000 75mm shells, 1,000 anti-tank missiles – all told, a deal worth $70 million. After he finished reading out the list, the Israelis held their breath. They quite expected the French to stomp out of the room in high dudgeon or, at the very least, fall off their chairs. Instead, Mangin asked softly: 'Are you prepared to sign?' Now it was the Israelis who almost fell off their chairs. Peres, the first to recover from the shock, immediately produced his pen and signed – as Yosef Nachmias whispered furiously at him in Hebrew: 'Are you mad? You don't have any authority!'

'The Paris talks were a special experience for me,' Dayan recorded in his diary. 'They filled me with hope, confidence and pride. We'll get arms – a lot of arms, good arms, and soon. Within a year we'll have a new air force and armoured corps, offensive and defensive weapons. We'll be relieved of the stress caused by the alliance between Egypt and the Soviet Union.'

When the delegation returned to Israel, Ben-Gurion approved the deal it had made. 'It's a somewhat risky venture,' he conceded, 'but what can you do? That's what our very existence is.'

While France became Israel's principal arms supplier, she wasn't the only one. Mutual friendship and interests notwithstanding, Israel did not feel obliged to put all her eggs in one basket. In Britain Peres obtained six night-combat planes and a number of cannon for torpedo-boats. On the other hand, a staff member in the Israeli Embassy in London reported (on 4 May) that 'recently the Vickers Corporation had received an order for twenty Centurion tanks from a large company in Nicaragua. [It] did not accede to the request due to the suspicion that the tanks were destined for Israel and the [Nicaraguan] company was merely serving as an agent.'

On 26 April Peres cabled Ben-Gurion from The Hague: 'We have signed an agreement wth the Dutch army for 155, 25 and 20 pound shells. Part of the payment is in cash and part is in kind in the form of products manufactured by the Israeli military industry.'

This combination of buying and selling became an important aspect of the arms-procurement effort. The export of arms from Israel consisted of the output of the local miliary industry and sales from stocks that Israel no longer needed. The most obvious market for these products was the developing countries. Burma was a typical example. On 7 August 1954, Ben-Gurion wrote in his diary: 'Shimon Peres came to see me. The Burmese have bought thirty armed Spitfires from us for $1 million and 50,000 rifles manufactured by the military industry for $700,000 dollars. They're sending seven cadets here to train with the air force.'

The event that everyone dreaded, but certainly expected, finally occurred on 26 July 1956. To roars of jubilation as he showered ridicule on the West, President Nasser announced his nationalization of the Suez Canal. All the Western capitals responded in anger. France and Britain instituted contacts over a joint military action to thwart the Egyptian ruler, who had become a sworn enemy of the Western world. They hoped that the United States would lend a hand in the operation, but Washington was quick to pour cold water on the idea. The Americans were resolved not to co-operate and vigorously opposed military measures of any sort.

The seeds of the Sinai Campaign can be traced to a cable which Peres sent Ben-Gurion from Paris on 27 July. It stated that he had been summoned urgently to see Louis Mangin, the Director of the French Defence Minister's bureau and Bourgès-Maunoury's adviser on special affairs. General Paul Ely, the Chief of Staff of the French armed forces, was also present, as was General Challe, his deputy for air force affairs. 'Without any preamble, they informed me that an urgent consultation is to be held in London tomorrow between [British Prime Minster Anthony] Eden and [French Foreign Minister Christian] Pineau regarding the steps to be taken in the wake of Nasser's announcement about the Canal.' What did the French want from Israel? 'By tomorrow the French Foreign Minister must acquaint himself with the latest Egyptian order of battle and its disposition. He wants these details from us before his departure.' Nothing more – at this stage. Most interesting of all, however, is the closing paragraph of the cable: 'They remarked with a smile that Israel will surely be prepared to play her role if asked to.'

On 1 August Peres wrote to Nehemiah Argov that 'although we continue to pursue the subject of acquisitions, funds and spare parts, it is impossible to hold a discussion in the [French] Ministry [of Defence] without getting into the subject referred to as Suez. The English and the French have decided in principle on a joint military operation to conquer the Canal.' But, Peres went on, 'the English have made it a condition that Israel not be included in the operation at this stage – not even to be told about it. According to [Abel Thomas, the Director-General of the French Ministry of Defence], the British contended that bringing Israel in on [an operation] will rally the Arabs around Nasser and turn it into an Israeli-Arab war.' Nevertheless, 'the question of our involvement in planning and consultations came up – and, if necessary, in more than that, e.g., "escalating the tension on the southern border" or "holding down Egyptian forces in Gaza". He has passed this information on to us because of his personal trust, on condition that no one in France except the two of us will hear of it, and in the hope that treatment [of this issue] in Israel will be marked by the same degree of discretion and caution.'

At the end of the cable, Peres made reference to a personal dilemma. 'To Nehemiah. Highly Confidential. Am personally distressed about the situation in which I find myself. Bourgès has asked me whether I will stay a few more days, since he wants to give me full details. Please advise whether there is any value to this information and whether the Old Man [Ben-Gurion] has any instructions about what, if anything, the French should be told.'

Before he received instructions, however, Peres was invited to another meeting with Bourgès. 'How much time do you reckon it would take your army to cross the Sinai peninsula and reach Suez?' the French Minister asked outright. Peres replied that the accepted assessment in Israel was between five and seven days. Bourgès shook his head sceptically. In France, he said, it is usual to accord an operation like that about three weeks. He went on to ask whether Israel was planning to act one day on her southern border and, if so, when? Peres answered that 'our Suez is Eilat. We will never reconcile ourselves to a blockade, and that would be the reason for an Israeli action – if ever there is one.'

Then another French participant in the meeting laid all his cards on the table: 'If France goes to war against Egypt, will Israel be prepared to go with us?' 'Yes!' Peres replied immediately. As they were walking out of the meeting, Yosef Nachmias mumbled to Peres, only half in jest: 'You should be hanged for such a commitment! Who gave you the authority to make it?'

'If I had said no,' Peres explained, 'that would be the end of the tie with France. On the other hand, it is clear that such an operation requires the approval of the Israeli Government. We can always change our minds.'

That link with France, which Peres wanted to preserve at any price, was no longer limited to arms sales alone. In meetings with the top echelon of the French Defence Ministry, he now put forward another request: for a small, 1,000 kilowatt atomic reactor. By the standards of the day, such a request bordered on insolence, and that is precisely how it was viewed in both Israel and France. Israeli Finance Minister Levi Eshkol dubbed the idea 'madness' – in and of itself and because of the enormous outlay involved – and all the senior officals who knew about it shared that opinion. The only one taken with the idea was Ben-Gurion, and essentially that was all that mattered.

48

The initial reaction in France was similar. The French mulled it over, mumbled ambivalencies to gain time and found it very difficult to make up their minds. Peres came to the conclusion that they would find it easier to overcome their qualms if Israel could offer something equal or similar in return – active military co-operation, for example.

From then on, the subject of the small atomic reactor was part and parcel of the process that led inexorably to the Sinai Campaign; it may even have served as an agent in that process. In any event, it is a fact that the Sinai Campaign was decided upon together with the fate of the reactor. At the beginning of September 1956, Peres met Bourgès in Paris and was told that the British were beginning to have second thoughts about Suez. They were talking in terms of a military operation taking place within two months, during which time the diplomatic efforts would continue. Then there was the American view, which posited a long-term subversive operation to topple Nasser, while the French preference on timing was to go ahead immediately. Bourgès explained that he was interested in moving immediately because the French Government itself might not last much longer. But in the existing circumstances, he admitted that it did not seem realistic.

From Israel's point of view, the British timetable seemed best, for the IDF had still not fully assimilated the wealth of French arms that had come its way. Yet Peres grasped that the new circumstances provided Israel with the quid pro quo she could offer the French: substituting for Britain in a military venture at a time convenient for France. He cabled Ben-Gurion his recommendation and on 21 September received the answer he was hoping for: 'As to the three options on timing, the partnership [with the French] is most to our liking. If they act at their convenience, we will back them to the best of our ability.'

The first sentence of this cable gives us an insight into the flip side of the deal: 'Congratulations! I am very proud of the agreement on the other matter.' 'The other matter' was the small atomic reactor, and the agreement to build it in Israel was signed on 21 September. Immediately afterwards, Peres left for the United States, but when he reached New York he was greeted by a cable from Yosef Nachmias stating that Bourgès wanted to see him urgently. So Peres returned to France, arriving in Paris the following morning and going straight from the airport (with Nachmias) to the Defence

Ministry in Rue Saint-Dominique – only to find it closed because it was Sunday.

The Defence Ministry was deserted. However, we managed to rustle up a duty officer and he was able to locate and get a telephone call through to Abel Thomas, Director-General of Bourgès-Maunoury's Ministry. Thomas told us where we would find his chief: at a weekend hunting-lodge near a small village several hours' drive from Paris. We telephoned the lodge and were promptly invited for lunch. Three hours later we arrived at the village, some 160 kilometres north of Paris, only to discover that the village we wanted bore the same name, but was 200 kilomètres *south* of Paris. There was nothing for it but to drive all the way back and then on. Only with the help of the local prefect of police did we find the village, the lodge and our host, arriving eight hours late. Bourgès-Maunoury and his friends had begun to worry about us, and when we appeared he greeted us with: 'No need to apologize. First, I am delighted to see you safe. Second, if you had been half an hour late, that would have been unpunctual. But eight hours! There must be a good reason for that.'

On 25 September Peres returned to Israel, where Ben-Gurion and Dayan were awaiting him at the airport. Ben-Gurion subsequently wrote in his diary about Peres's report to them:

What he told us may be fateful. In a meeting with the [Defence] Minister, Bourgès-Maunoury told him that after the London conference the [French] Government decided that it cannot accept that plan and is prepared to act against Nasser – with the knowledge and consent of the English. They [the French] want a three-man delegation, including at least one Minister, to come next week and hold discussions with Guy Mollet, Pineau and Bourgès-Maunoury on working together as equals.

Ben-Gurion brought a number of Ministers in on the secret, and to those who expressed reservations he said: 'This is the birth of the first serious alliance between us and a Western Power. We can't not accept it.'

The delegation invited by the French Government left for Paris at the end of September 1956. Headed by Foreign Minister Golda Meir, it included Transport Minister Moshe Carmel, Dayan and Peres. Under a cloak of absolute secrecy, they stayed at the Pavillion Henri IV, the royal palace in the Parisian suburb of St Germain. The talks began on 30 September in Louis Mangin's Montparnasse home – and on the left foot. For the head of the French delegation was supposed to be Guy Mollet, known for his wholehearted support for Franco-Israeli co-operation. But when the Israelis arrived, they were told that due to a sudden political crisis, Mollet would not be able to take part in the conference. This announcement got Golda's back up, and Peres made straight for Mollet's office to tell him that his absence had negative implications for the Israelis. Mollet expressed his understanding and regret; none the less he would not be able to take part in the talks.

His place was taken by Foreign Minister Christian Pineau, the other members of the delegation being Bourgès-Maunoury, Abel Thomas and General Challe. But it was Pineau who set the tone – and a very minor one it was. No longer was the subject under discussion a joint action. Pineau proposed that the battle against Egypt be initiated by Israel, whereupon France would come to her aid. There was a good chance, the French ventured, that such a plan would be acceptable to the British, who would then be good enough to join in.

The Israelis had the distinct feeling that France was loath to enter into a military venture without the British. But equally plain to them was Ben-Gurion's injunction that Israel must not be the party to initiate hostilities, for by now Egypt was not Israel's only security concern. Her front with Jordan was heating up as well, and Ben-Gurion's principal fear was that if Jordan were drawn into a confrontation, the British would come to the aid of their Near Eastern ally. And that was something he wished to avoid at all costs – including an alliance with France.

Thus as far as the military action went, the two sides essentially came away from the conference empty-handed. The only conclusion was that both countries would maintain current and frequent consultations. No doubt the absence of Guy Mollet had a decisive impact on the vapid outcome of the talks, but the members of the Israeli delegation nevertheless shared the feeling that in his enthusiasm for the French connection, Peres had exaggerated the prospects of reaching an accommodation and had surrendered to a state of unfounded optimism.

The one achievement of the St Germain conference was the appreciable supplement of arms which France agreed to supply to Israel. Peres was particularly pleased by the fact that Bourgès-Maunoury agreed to supply American-made tanks – and without payment at that! The understanding was that Israel would receive the tanks on terms closely akin to 'lend-lease', that is, the tanks would be lent to Israel and only in the event of a national emergency would they be returned to France. The sole guarantee that Bourgès asked for, and received, was a personal letter from Peres.

Throughout September the tension along Israel's borders mounted. Squads of *fedayeen* continued to infiltrate from Jordan and Egypt, spreading havoc in their wake, and Israel continued to respond with reprisal actions. Matters reached the point where Jordan, fearing all-out Israeli attack, asked Iraq to send a full division into Jordanian territory.

In a report addressed to the senior officials of his Ministry (dated 15 October), Peres mentioned the possibility of a pre-emptive war against Jordan. 'I don't know whether we'll be able to wait until the Iraqi thing burgeons and reaches us before we fight,' he said, while speaking of a joint operation against Egypt almost in the past tense. 'I am convinced that the French sincerely wanted, and still want, to fight Nasser. [But] I am very suspicious of British machinations.' Nevertheless, more from intuition than pragmatic logic, he added: 'Deep in my heart I also believe that the present course of the [Israeli] Government should be to cast the spotlight on Iraq's entry into Jordan – and not necessarily because this is Israel's main problem.'

These were difficult days for Peres. He feared that the French seedling he had been cultivating with such patience and devotion would wither before it had a chance to blossom. So he went to Paris to explain that 'when all is said and done, England and France are prepared to fight without Israel. And they certainly are not prepared to fight for her. Israel, for her part, is not prepared to fight for England and France and, if necessary, she will fight without them.' The French were sympathetic towards this position, but sympathy alone does not make for an alliance. What does forge a pact is a common enemy, a joint military operation – and these seemed to be fading into the distance.

Then a number of events occurred in close succession and altered the picture dramatically. Diplomatic efforts in the U.N. Security Council ran aground when the Soviet Union vetoed the Anglo-French resolution to internationalize the Suez Canal. On 20 October the French stopped an Egyptian ship carrying arms to the Algerian rebels and France decided to recall her Ambassador from Cairo. Then the elections to the Jordanian Parliament climaxed with a victory for the pro-Egyptian slate. Meanwhile, the Russians were tied down in

Poland, where a power struggle was going on between Wladyslaw Gomulka and his Stalinist rivals, and in Hungary, which was on the brink of revolt against the Communist regime. And in addition to it all, winter was at the gates.

All these events sparked off a new interest in France and Britain, leading to a series of meetings in London and Paris. The plan which emerged from these consultations was based on the premise that Israel would be the one to initiate the war, conquer the Sinai peninsula and draw to a halt at the Suez Canal. At this point the French and British would intervene and demand that both sides pull back from the Canal zone. If the Egyptians refused – as they surely would – French and British forces would enter the zone on the pretext of ensuring that the Canal remain in operation. The Anglo-French talks also concluded with a decision to hold a Franco-Israeli summit (to which Britain would send a representative) for the purpose of co-ordinating moves.

This was the first time that the British had approved – and in writing, at that – an operation that included Israel, and the French considered it a major achievement. 'It's the maximum you can get out of the British,' Bourgès told Yosef Nachmias. 'If Israel rejects the proposal, the last opportunity to topple Nasser will have been lost.'

Ben-Gurion learned of the Anglo-French agreement on 17 October, when Peres brought him a cable from Nachmias, and in a consultation with Golda Meir, Levi Eshkol, Dayan and Peres he summarily rejected the plan. 'He is vehemently against any set-up in which Israel will be depicted before the world – and even more so before the tribunal of history – as an aggressive nation,' Peres recorded in his diary. But no less strong was Ben-Gurion's mistrust of Britain's motives. In fact, he regarded the plan as 'the height of British hypocrisy, with the desire to damage Israel being even stronger than the enmity towards the Egyptian dictator'.

Ben-Gurion told Peres to inform Paris of his position while taking care to underscore that if, in these circumstances, Guy Mollet's invitation still stood, he would come to Paris. Not because he thought it was possible to arrive at a mutually acceptable formula for a joint operation (in effect, he had already laid that idea to rest), but because he regarded the British proposal as an attempt to scuttle the Franco-Israeli alliance, and he desperately wanted to foil it.

On the night of Thursday, 18 October, Nachmias sent Peres Guy Mollet's reply: 'Again invites Ben-Gurion, though he knows of his opposition to the British plan.' The date suggested for a meeting was

Sunday, 21 October. On the spot Ben-Gurion ordered Peres to cable back that he accepted the invitation.

To get Ben-Gurion to the meeting, the French sent de Gaulle's personal plane to Israel. In addition to the crew, the plane was also carrying Louis Mangin and General Challe. Peres and Dayan, who met them at the airport, understood that they had been sent to soften up Ben-Gurion's adamant opposition to the British plan, but their efforts were to little avail. On its return to France, the plane carried – in addition to the French – Ben-Gurion, his military aide Nehemiah Argov, Peres, Dayan and Dayan's adjutant, Mordechai Bar-On. After an exhausting seventeen-hour flight, they landed in Paris and were virtually smuggled out of the airport through a side gate. To keep Ben-Gurion's identity secret, his famous bushy white mane was tucked into a low-brimmed hat. Moshe Dayan wore dark glasses to conceal his eye-patch.

The French convoy brought the Israelis to an attractive villa surrounded by a well-tended garden in the Parisian suburb of Sèvres. Ben-Gurion was put up there together with Argov. The other Israelis stayed at the Reynolds Hotel in Paris. The talks began the following morning and went on for three days filled with drama, tension and surprises. On the second day the Sèvres Conference appeared to be doomed. The turnabout came on the third and final day, when the British Government decided to approve Israel's compromise proposal. The agreement finally hammered out called for the operation to start on Monday, 29 October, with an Israeli force parachuting into the area of the Mitla Pass, near the Suez Canal. On the following day Egypt and Israel would be asked to accept a ceasefire and withdraw their forces ten miles back from the Canal within twelve hours. If one of the countries refused to comply (and there was no question that Egypt would balk), French and British forces would enter the arena on 31 October.

In the end, therefore, Ben-Gurion yielded on the stand that Israel would not be the party to initiate hostilities, but not because of anything his prospective allies said or did. In essence he surrendered to the will of Dayan and Peres, who considered the point marginal compared with the opportunity to dispose of Nasser and strengthen the alliance with France. Thus at 7 p.m. on Wednesday, 24 October 1956, the representatives of Britain, France and Israel signed the Sèvres Protocols. The formalities completed, Bourgès-Maunoury strode towards Peres, who was standing in a corner, and the two men who had conceived the operation, lobbied for it and never despaired of it, even at the bleakest of moments, shook hands emotionally.

At the appointed hour on 29 October 1956, Israeli troops parachuted into Sinai, near the Mitla Pass. Likewise as planned, though with a slight delay, on the following day the French and British issued their call for a ceasefire and the withdrawal of forces from the Canal zone. Israel immediately agreed. Egypt refused.

This was the last thing to go according to plan. The British, who were scheduled to start bombing the Canal zone, reported a delay of twelve hours. As a result, the French also postponed their timetable for going into action. After a nerve-racking wait, the bombing finally began. Throughout this time the IDF continued to advance. Then the Security Council was convened in emergency session and issued a call for a ceasefire. Finally, the United States began pressuring Israel to pull back to her own borders. And all the while, the IDF kept up its race against time with the aim of conquering the Sinai peninsula before the ceasefire came into effect.

The original plan called for France and Britain to invade the Canal zone on 6 November, and all France's efforts to coax the British into bringing this move forward were futile. Since the British wouldn't budge, the French asked Israel to have her forces capture the Canal, in a radical departure from the agreed plan. But when the British commander of the joint expeditionary force got wind of this prospective change, he ranted, 'I won't have a single Israeli soldier going beyond the ten-mile limit!'

On 5 November, when Israel had completed the conquest of the Sinai peninsula, the French and British began their invasion of the Canal zone. After taking the city of Port Said, they advanced southwards along the Canal. But then the Soviet Union intervened. On the previous day, the Russians had successfully quelled the Hungarian revolt, and now they were free to turn their attention to the war in the Middle East. Soviet Premier Nikolai Bulganin sent letters to France, Britain and Israel that smacked of a threat to use nuclear-armed missiles against them unless they ceased firing immediately. Visions of a third world war sent a wave of panic sweeping through the world's capitals. The first to break ranks – which hardly surprised the Israelis – was the British Prime Minister Anthony Eden, who informed Paris that he was going to order his forces to cease firing. The French immediately followed suit.

By then these steps made little difference to Israel. On the day the British and French announced the cessation of hostilities, the Israeli flag was raised at Sharm e-Sheikh, near the tip of the Sinai peninsula. A wave of elation and pride swept through the State of Israel. Her military achievement was impressive, almost incredible. Without any real help from her partners, Israel had managed in eight days to capture the entire Sinai peninsula from an adversary armed to the teeth with Soviet weaponry.

In summing up the Suez Campaign before senior officials in his Ministry (9 November), Peres said:

> If what they write in the papers is true, namely, that there were three partners in this war [all three countries still denied any collusion among them], then only one of them has fully achieved its objective – and that is Israel. The other partners came out of it smarting. The French wanted to destroy Nasser, but because of British dithering they did not succeed. The British wanted to liberate the Suez [Canal] and instead they are being ousted from it for the second time. Israel wanted to put an end to the threat of an Egyptian attack and succeeded.

This description was accurate so far as the French and the British went, but it was excessively optimistic with regard to Israel. Her original aim had been to destroy the Egyptian army and *fedayeen* bases in Sinai, and that was fully achieved. But afterwards, when the magnitude of the Israeli victory became clear, there was an impulse to annex the Sinai peninsula to the State of Israel – and this aim was not achieved. As soon as the fighting ended, the major Powers and the UN began to exert strong pressure, including outright threats, on Israel to withdraw completely from the Sinai. The withdrawal was executed in full about three months after the campaign, in return for which the Union of Maritime Nations guaranteed free passage to all nations, Israel included, through the Straits of Tiran. As would later become clear, this guarantee was hardly worth the paper on which it was written.

Though she had been chastised by the Security Council, Israel's military victory in the Sinai Campaign actually opened a new era for her in foreign relations. No longer was she a young and weak state, a tiny country whose future seemed dubious and whose very existence constituted a burden on the community of nations. Now the world stood back in wonder at the sight of a small, poorly endowed country which, in eight difficult years of statehood, had become a military power on a global scale.

The corollary of this realization was not universally symmetrical, and actually the countries of the Middle East were the first to draw operative conclusions from the IDF's show of strength. After a series of extended and highly secret contacts, Ben-Gurion signed what later came to be known as the 'Peripheral Alliance', a pact between Israel and the states on the periphery of the region: Turkey, Ethiopia and Iran. This was the first lattice to open for Israel onto the Moslem world, and it would be impossible to exaggerate its importance. New outlets emerged for Israeli weapons – markets eager for whatever Israel could supply. The oil which Iran could and did supply to Israel was worth its weight in gold, and gradually the relations extended into the spheres of politics and security.

In contrast, the attitude of the largest of the Western Powers did not change at all, as the Eisenhower-Dulles team continued to impose a complete embargo on shipments of weapons to Israel. Peres, like many others in Israel, took a disliking to the American president:

> I had the pleasure of watching Eisenhower on television for forty-five minutes during his press conference. What came across was a man with healthy teeth, beautiful eyes and a warm smile who hadn't the vaguest notion what he was talking about. And what he did know, he couldn't express properly. There was no connection between one sentence and the next. The only question he could answer well was 'How are you?'

His admiration for John Foster Dulles was not much greater, though Peres appreciated his talents. 'He knows how to express himself well and has a phenomenal memory and inordinate capacity for work.' Peres provided a very lively description of a talk he once had with Dulles. 'He's like a lawyer. His analyses reflect a certain state of mind, but they lack commitment. You talk with him about arms for Israel and he says: "It's about time the State of Israel, which is so close to us, whose existence is in our interest, had sufficient arms to constitute a deterrent. We will examine this question with an open mind." If you ask him, "What does that mean – an open mind?" he gets angry and snaps, "I spoke perfectly clearly." ' Peres summed up acidly: 'That is the leadership of the Western world.'

Almost two years were to pass before a crack appeared in the solid wall of American resistance – and then it was as a result of developments only obliquely related to Israel. In 1958 a military *coup* in Iraq deposed the pro-Western Nuri Sa'id and replaced him by the pro-Nasserite General Kassem. As a result, King Hussein's regime was also placed in jeopardy, and it was only thanks to the intervention of the British, aided by Israel, that the Jordanian monarch was saved from a hapless fate. These events sparked the American realization that Israel was, in fact, the most stable ally in the Middle East. As the Italian Defence Minister, Paolo Emilio Taviani, put it to Peres: 'The Americans are eating their hearts out. In a talk with Italy's Foreign Minister, Dulles admitted the error of American policy regarding the Suez Campaign and underlined that Nasser seemed an ingrate.'

At any rate, following a visit to Washington in July 1958, Peres could finally report ecstatically: 'In the United States, for the first time, I received weapons which shoot! I got 100 pieces of recoilless artillery with shells. Of course, that's less than the 350 we asked for. But as I see it, the very fact that a modest but new source of arms like the United States has opened up to us is of genuine significance.'

One of the immediate consequences of the Sinai Campaign was the Security Council resolution imposing a general embargo on the shipment of arms to the Middle East. So far as Israel was concerned, the fidelity of the Western countries to this resolution was linked to the degree to which they identified with America's policy. Canada, for example, knuckled under to the pressures from its formidable neighbour. A few months before the Sinai Campaign, Israel had signed a contract with Ottawa for twenty-six F-26 fighter planes. Formally speaking, the supplier was the private aeronautics firm Canadair, and at the end of September 1956 the two sides agreed on the means of transferring the planes to Israel. The deal was closed secretly, one of its conditions being that the role of the Canadian air force would never be mentioned in any way. As the Chief of Staff of the Canadian air force, Air Marshal Slemon, cautioned: 'For God's sake, the Israelis mustn't say that the Canadian air force is flying planes for Israel!'

To Slemon's credit, it must be said that he had a sixth sense about these things. He 'suggested that everything be done to get the planes out of Canada as quickly as possible by sea and not to wait for the renewal of flights in March [1957], because not even he can be relied upon not to appropriate the planes when conditions change.' Israel was in no rush, however, partly because she was not entirely convinced that she wanted the planes. Then, after the Suez Campaign, Slemon informed Israel 'that the planes would not be delivered'. The loss was, admittedly, a minor one, but it was the Canadian attitude which hurt.

Other countries contented themselves with paying lip-service to the embargo resolution and kept up their arms shipments to Israel – sometimes at an accelerated pace. For all intents and purposes, when the profit-and-loss statement was drawn up in Jerusalem, the conclusion was that Israel had little reason to be upset by the embargo. It made life far more difficult for the Arab states.

A case in point was the experience with Belgium. On 4 November 1956, the French Ambassador in Brussels phoned the Israeli Minister there and tipped him off that in another three or four weeks Belgium would impose an embargo on the shipment of arms to the Middle East, in accordance with the Security Council resolution. His advice was that Israel take possession of all the arms she had ordered and get them out of the country immediately. First, however, the Israeli Minister, Yosef Ariel, wanted to clarify to what degree the Belgian decision would actually affect Israel. He approached Robert Rothschild in the Belgian Foreign Ministry and received the following explanation: 'A Syrian order for 5,500 rifles has been approved and is ready for shipment. The Syrians may call for the arms to be released to them at any time. When they do, the Belgians will declare an embargo to prevent the shipment from going out.' If it does not work, Rothschild promised, 'the Belgians will inform the French and the British, so that they can stop the ship'.

Belgium did indeed declare an embargo, and the shipment of Syrian arms was indeed held up. On the other hand, the embargo had no effect whatsoever on Israel, for on 3 December 1956, Peres visited the Belgian Foreign Minister and reached an understanding whereby everything that had been and would be purchased in Belgium would be transferred to Israel via a third country in the Caribbean.

Britain fell in line with the policy of her sister countries on the Continent during the post-Suez era, which brought changes in her political leadership. Anthony Eden's clumsy and inefficacious handling of the Suez crisis cost him his job. In his place as Prime Minister came Harold Macmillan; and if any hard feeling remained between Israel and Britain following the Sinai Campaign, it dissolved, for the most part, with the change over at 10 Downing Street.

But the dissolution of bitter feeling does not necessarily imply a relationship of trust. Peres's attitude towards the British was a combination – typical of Israelis – of profound admiration for their efficiency and no less profound distrust of their political ethics.

For the time being, the English were far less perfidious than Israel anticipated. After he visited London at the end of August 1958, Peres could report that on the day of his arrival, 'I found an article in *The Times* reporting that I had come to conduct negotiations on the purchase of arms. At the close of the negotiations, a joint communiqué was issued, and I think this is the first time in the history of our relations with Britain that this has happened.' He was also impressed by the way in which the British execute things – when they want to.

> One of the things that amazed me during the negotiations was the extraordinary communication between the heads of the Ministries. Within two hours of any talk, everyone concerned with or likely to be concerned with it or having any interest in it whatsoever knows exactly what took place during the conversation: what we said, what replies we received, when additional answers were promised for. At one cocktail party I buttonholed Sir John Paul about this. He explained that the system was fairly simple. After every talk, they write a memorandum and distribute it among all the parties concerned. The important part, he said, is that everyone knows they must write such memoranda – and even more that everyone knows they must *read* them.

Peres added wistfully: 'I dream of the day when we will achieve something like that.'
Other British mores, however, were inexplicable to him.

> We went to lunch with the First Lord of the Admiralty. Our host was the impeccably dressed Earl of Selkirk. He brought along Sir John Lang, the Permanent Secretary, and I witnessed a typically British oddity. Even though the First Lord was sitting right there, the only spokesman was the Permanent Secretary. He kept on saying: the Lord believes, the Lord agrees, the Lord will consider, the Lord prefers not – and all that time his Lord is sitting at his side and not a syllable passes his lips.

The yield of these talks in Britain amounted to, among other things, two submarines and sixty Centurion tanks. The sole condition that the British placed upon the supply of the tanks also testifies to the change in their attitude towards Israel. At that time, rumours were afloat about a possible Israeli action against Syria in reprisal for acts perpetrated by saboteurs who crossed the border into Israel. Traditionally, Britain was opposed to these reprisal raids. But now Peres heard a different tune from the head of the Middle Eastern desk of the British Foreign Office. 'If you intend to carry out a reprisal action against Syria,' he said, 'do it after receiving the Centurions, not before. Because after a reprisal action, you won't get them.' In other words, do whatever you please – just don't embarrass us.

The inroads that Israel was making in the Western countries led Ben-Gurion to the conclusion that the time was ripe to implement an idea that had been on his mind for years. He had always believed that, to shore up her security, Israel should become part of a military and political alliance with the West. His first preference was for some form of treaty with the United States; but since the Americans were not interested, his second choice was to join NATO.

The Foreign Ministry was charged with making the major effort towards this end, but this did not discourage Peres from taking action on his own. On the recommendation of Guy Mollet, he met (on 28 May 1957) Jean Monnet, father of the idea of a United Europe. 'I presented the idea to him, brash and rash as it was, meaning the prospect of Israel joining a United Europe. At first he was rather surprised. What had Israel to do with Europe? Later, in a second talk, he began to grasp the notion and said that if we can work quietly, he would be prepared to investigate the best way to have Israel join.'

Peres discussed the same subject with Paolo Emilio Taviani in a secret meeting in Rome on 30 November. He was pleased to hear from the Italian Defence Minister

> that five years ago, when he served as Deputy Minister of Foreign Affairs, he pursued a pro-Arab line and was opposed to strengthening ties with Israel. But over the past few years, he feels developments in the Arab world have taken a course that is quite unpromising for the West. That obliges him, as Italy's Defence Minister, to view affairs from an international standpoint and consider them from the vantage of global security. He checked, investigated, pondered and found that if a third world war breaks out, as far as the Middle East goes, the West can rely – in addition to its ally Turkey – only on Israel.

As to her joining NATO, however, Taviani had mixed feelings. He agreed that it would be profitable to establish a direct or indirect tie between the IDF and the NATO forces, but he believed that any such link should remain informal and highly secret.

Bourgès-Maunoury was, as usual, genial towards Peres. 'He really took to the idea and even volunteered to talk to [Belgian Foreign Minister] Spaak this week so that the latter can elicit the reactions of the other European states.' That same spirit of volunteerism was not evidenced by the British Foreign Secretary, though. 'When I tried to sell him the idea of a united socialist Europe that is not gluttonous for oil and represents a fusion of workers' needs, he snapped that a united Europe will never arise; it's just a dream.'

The Foreign Secretary was undoubtedly right about Israel's chances of merging into the European scene. Her envoys won a polite hearing, but were repeatedly sent away empty-handed. Then Peres had a new idea, which he shared with the senior echelon in the Defence Ministry on 9 April 1958: 'Three European Defence Ministers [French, British and West German] are meeting for the third time to hold nego-tiations. Their objective is to forge the unity of the European armies, parallel to their economic union. As I see it, Israel must strive to establish ties with this body, since at the present time we have no chance of doing so with NATO.'

But Italy's Foreign Minister soon poured cold water on this idea, though he did consent to 'you [Peres] meeting, before or after each conference, with each one of the three Defence Ministers. We'll tell you what has taken place, and you'll tell us what you have to, and we'll draw the appropriate conclusions.' Then and there, Peres came up with a more modest proposal: 'We won't be partners, but we'll be a department. Make us into a Department for Middle Eastern Affairs. He liked that formula very much,' Peres reported.

Yet that turned out to be a very sanguine assessment, for the countries of Europe had no intention of bringing Israel in on their thinking and planning. On the contrary, they looked upon the efforts towards that end as irritating pushiness. This campaign was hardly among the more glorious initiatives of Israeli diplomacy.

All attempts to establish a formal alliance with France similarly ended in frustration. But what did come out of the 'French Connection' surpassed even Peres's wildest expectations. His faith, shared by Moshe Dayan, that the Sinai Campaign would serve as the adhesive to strengthen the bond between the two states was fully vindicated. The friendship between France and Israel reached heights that Israel had not dared dream of. Politicians, journalists, poets all sang the praises of the unwritten alliance, and people of all walks of life in both countries went out of their way to demonstrate friendship and affection.

Peres would shuttle between Tel Aviv and Paris a few times a month. He would arrive in Paris with arms lists and leave with contracts for equipment – everything that Israel desired. 'Assistance to Israel has become an integral clause of French politics,' he exulted upon returning from one of these trips. 'Every political figure is measured by his aid to Israel. For example, on New Year's Day I sent greetings to the former Minister of Defence. One day [former Prime Minister] Edgar Faure turned up in the Israeli Ambassador's office and complained that he found himself in an uncomfortable position because he had not received a New Year's card.' In time Peres's work became easier from a technical viewpoint, too, for the Israeli Defence Ministry was provided with a room and all necessary services in the French Defence Ministry building. Israel reciprocated with an identical gesture.

The extent of the co-operation with France is illustrated by the following incident. A small Israeli airline owned by Leo Gardiner (one of the founders of the aeronautics industry in Israel) was conducting negotiations with Morocco to fly spare parts for tractors from Zagreb, Yugoslavia, to Rabat. These negotiations were top secret but came to the knowledge of Arthur Ben-Natan, head of the Israeli defence mission in Paris. He reported to Peres that 'they're talking about ten flights for much more than the price of a regular hop and there's no question that it's the air-freight of arms'. Now comes the interesting part. Gardiner claimed that he had received the IDF's permission for the deal, and his claim was confirmed. But Peres was very troubled by the affair, for he had the feeling that the arms, in whole or in part, would ultimately make their way to the rebels in Algeria. He therefore approved Ben-Natan's recommendation 'to report this immediately to friends [the French] so that they can sabotage the deal'.

On the morning of 27 May 1957, a black Chevrolet drove through the gate of the *Bedek* plant adjoining Israel's international airport at Lod. It approached the runway and stopped alongside a DC-4, whose engines were already warming up. Once again it was de Gaulle's private plane (which on an earlier occasion had flown Ben-Gurion and company to the Sèvres Conference). One by one, senior members of the Israeli defence establishment emerged from the car, headed by Chief of Staff Moshe Dayan and Director-General Peres. They bounded up the stairs and were swallowed up by the plane, which took off immediately. So began an operation that marked another breakthrough in Franco-Israeli relations.

The plane's first stop was the Istress airfield near Marseilles, where the entourage transferred to a French aircraft for its final destination: Colomb-Béchar, France's missile-testing site in the Sahara Desert.

During their stay there, the Israelis witnessed the launching of ground-to-ground guided missiles of the 1,000 and 1,100 type; 103-type air-to-air missiles (the standard armament on Votoure planes) and 4,500-type ground-to-ground missiles. After the display, talks were held with Generals Challe, Levaud and Martin.

In the wake of the discussions at Colomb-Béchar a consultation was held with Ben-Gurion (on 1 August 1957) and Peres argued that 'the French are not marking time. In another two or three years they'll be making sophisticated guided missiles. And if they won't sell them to us, we have to have an infrastructure in Israel that can manufacture missiles.' With overt impatience, Dayan retorted: 'I would rather not talk about the civilian electronics industry right now.'

'I'm raising the subject to round out the picture,' Peres insisted.

'I'm not sure about what you're basing it on. If it forces us into providing subsidies, I am not prepared to get involved,' Dayan pronounced.

But Peres would not yield. Of subsidies he understood very little – and wished to understand even less. He went ahead and introduced the missiles into Israel's aircraft industry, which has become the IDF's chief supplier of this item. Moreover, when the special relationship with France came to an end, Peres's foresight was seen to have a decisive impact on the IDF's might.

The focal project which occupied Peres's time and attention was the small atomic reactor, whose construction had begun in the interim. After achieving this objective, he came to the conclusion that conditions were ripe for taking another step, which he had been contemplating from the outset: the construction of a large, 24-megawatt reactor. A number of qualms were expressed in the Cabinet, but Ben-Gurion's unequivocal stand again outweighed his colleagues' reservations, and soon Peres was heading for the French capital, where he encountered many obstacles. The French, for all their feelings of friendship, had qualms of their own. Peres received a particularly chill response from Pierre Guillaumat, the head of the French Atomic Energy Commission. 'I went to have a private talk with him and asked him the reason for the coolness. His answer was that it stems from the enormous financial burden involved.' But Bourgès-Maunoury, now Prime Minister (following the fall of Guy Mollet's Government), was prepared to sign a contract, though he made it conditional upon the agreement of the Socialist Party. The head of the Party, Guy Mollet, had serious reservations and wavered over the issue. Once he actually expressed his consent to Peres, but immediately afterwards, at a meeting with Foreign Minister Golda Meir, asserted 'he's against this thing'.

When Golda reported Mollet's comment to Jerusalem, the consensus leaned towards abandoning the idea, for it seemed hopeless. The only one who refused to accept that judgment was Peres, because 'dropping the matter will destroy any chance Israel has of entering the age of atomic reactors'. At the end of September 1957, therefore, he returned to Paris to take another stab at getting the French to agree.

It is difficult to imagine less propitious circumstances for holding such negotiations than those obtaining in France at the time. Once again the Government was about to fall (this time Bourgès-Maunoury's Cabinet), and once again Peres found himself in a race against the political clock. He reached the French capital on a Sunday only to meet with the ubiquitous belief that the Government would fall by Monday night. Obviously 'whatever can be done by Monday must be done,' he wrote. 'Afterwards there may not be anyone to talk to.'

Peres's first meeting, with the Foreign Minister, was also his most difficult. For despite his warm feelings for Israel, Christian Pineau was the principal opponent of Israel's request. Before the meeting he sent Peres a letter spelling out the reasons for his opposition:

* There was no French precedent for the kind of aid that Israel was requesting.
* An agreement might prejudice the French position in the field of atomic energy.

'Those reasons were not easy to dismiss,' Peres admitted, but that did not stop him from trying. 'You know that our only purpose in building a reactor is for scientific research and development,' he said, adding additional explanations.

Stopping a moment to reconsider the point, Pineau conceded that 'he was convinced by the arguments'. Peres had others in his bag, but acted 'as they do in the Foreign Ministry. I didn't insist that he allow me to air all the other reasons I had. I contented myself with the fact that he agreed.' But Peres didn't really let up. 'The French Government is in the grips of a crisis,' he now noted. 'If it falls, what will we derive from your agreement? Perhaps you will be good enough to call Bourgès and tell him of your consent?' 'Of course,' replied Pineau and picked up the receiver. Since Bourgès was not in his office, however, Peres pressed again: 'Let me have your agreement in writing and I'll pass it on to Bourgès.' Once again, Pineau complied. He wrote out everything that had been agreed upon and called in his secretary to type it. After she had finished and left the room, Pineau destroyed the copies and kept only the original, which he signed together with Peres.

With Pineau's agreement in his pocket, Peres went out to look for Bourgès. The Prime Minister still wasn't in his office, but a message from him was waiting there. It said that he was in the National Assembly, making a desperate effort to save his Government, but he would try to recess the debate and meet with Peres at 6.30 to sign the agreement. When Peres returned to the Premier's office at the appointed hour, there was still no sign of Bourgès. Seven o'clock, eight, ten. Meanwhile, Peres had put away a healthy amount of the whisky proffered to make his wait more pleasant – and still no Bourgès. And with every passing moment, the fall of the Government drew nearer. He decided not to wait any longer and went to the National Assembly building. When he arrved, Bourgès emerged from the Cabinet's conference room and apologized; the critical debate had gone on longer than expected. Peres replied that he understood it was a fateful moment for the Government and would agree 'to put the matter off till tomorrow morning – if Bourgès agrees that the Government will approve the agreement before the day is out'. Bourgès consented, returned to the Cabinet meeting and received the Ministers' agreement. A meeting with Peres was set for nine the next morning.

At the appointed hour, Bourgès arrived at his office

after a sleepless night, with red eyes and without a Government, which he had lost during the night. He immediately took out his pen, saying, 'I understand that my friend the Socialist [Pineau] has agreed.' Then he wrote a letter to the Energy Minister [Guillaumat] stating that the French Government, in a meeting on the previous day, had ratified the agreement to construct the reactor in Israel and, accordingly, the Minister is being asked to implement that agreement.

Peres left Bourgès's office feeling light-hearted. His first inclination was to report to Jerusalem on the triumph, but 'something on high told me not to cable home until the papers were in my hands'. 'Something on high' was right. For when he presented Bourgès's letter to Guillaumat, the Energy Minister was dissatisfied. 'I wish France had a few people like you,' he said to Peres, then added: 'The pressure you've exerted has turned the Quai d'Orsay against you.

When Jaquet found out about the agreement with you, he was livid.'

'What does it have to do with the Foreign Ministry?' Peres asked.

'I am not prepared to sign,' Guillaumat snapped.

With amazing speed, Peres arrived back at Bourgès's office and reported on his conversation with Guillaumat. Then and there, Bourgès summoned Pineau and Jaquet, his assistant for energy affairs, and reprimanded them both: 'We have an agreement and nothing is coming of it. Why did the Government bother to decide?' He ordered them to act in accordance with the Cabinet's decision.

The next morning Peres met Jaquet and they agreed that the two Atomic Energy Commissions would sign the technical agreement stating France's commitment to give Israel the necessary plans and technical and material aid for building the reactor. As a condition for this aid, Jaquet demanded a promise in writing that Israel would consult France with regard to all matters related to the reactor.

Four days after Peres arrived in France, at 1 p.m. on Thursday of that week, the technical agreement was signed. But the political agreement remained to be endorsed by the Foreign Minister at 2 p.m. that day – and Pineau was nowhere to be found. Not at two, not at three and not at four.

While he was waiting for Pineau to arrive, Peres discovered that at 5.30 the Israeli Ambassador, Ya'akov Tzur, was scheduled to meet Jaquet on another matter. 'We'll go with Ya'akov,' Peres said to Arthur Ben-Natan, who was accompanying him. 'Jaquet will pour all his anger out on Tzur, because we have not behaved according to the dictates of protocol – an offical of a foreign country carrying a letter from the Foreign Minister of France to the Premier of France regarding an internal French matter without the bureaucracy of the French Foreign Ministry even knowing about it – and it worked! Jaquet will probably haul Tzur out on the carpet, chiding him: You're Ambassador to France. You know what procedures are. How can you let a thing like this happen?'

In the end, however, Peres decided to keep waiting for Pineau because 'I wasn't sure whether all these delays weren't just a pretence. In fact, I wasn't at all sure about that right up to the last moment.' But he briefed Tzur that 'when you walk into Jaquet's office, start out immediately by thanking him for the help he has given us, because then it will be more difficult for him to be evasive. Tzur did just that, and Jaquet confirmed that he had helped considerably.' After that reassuring beginning, Tzur was able to ask

Jaquet for additional help, namely, obtaining Pineau's signature on the political agreement.

Jaquet called in Martin, the Deputy Director of the Atomic Energy Commission, who said that the agreement was on Pineau's desk. Surely Dreiden, the Political Director of the Foreign Ministry, knows about it? They called in Dreiden, who said that he had the letter; in fact, he produced Pineau's letter, but it was unsigned. When Jaquet tried to discover Pineau's whereabouts, he was told that the Foreign Minister was in a secret meeting. Now the race against the clock began in earnest, since a new government might be formed at any moment. Martin said that he was willing to interrupt Pineau in the middle of the meeting and have him sign the letter, but Jaquet scoffed: 'I know Pineau's secretary, and she won't let you past the doorway.' Finally it was Dreiden who went in and secured Pineau's signature. Some ten minutes later, the letter was in our hands, and five minutes after that our letter was in theirs.

Only then, with all the documents in hand – signed by the heads of the Government that had already fallen – only then did Peres make his way to the Israeli Embassy in Paris to cable Ben-Gurion (on 3 October): 'Agreement signed this afternoon.' Ben-Gurion cabled back, 'Congratulations on an important achievement'. Nehemiah Argov joined in: 'We have just passed your cable on to the Old Man at Sdeh Boker. I have no doubt that there is no greater holiday gift than the one you have given him on the eve of Yom Kippur. Keep up the good work.'

The French believed that Peres's work had earned him the highest mark of distinction that can be accorded to a non-French citizen, and at the beginning of February 1957 they decided to award him the *Légion d'Honneur*. He accepted, but the news infuriated some people in the Israeli Foreign Ministry. Walter Eytan complained in a letter to David Rosolio, head of the Civil Service Administration, that 'when the French Government wanted to award the *Légion d'Honneur* to the Israeli Ambassador, it was told that an Israeli official is not permitted to receive a medal of honour. What will the French Government think now?' Rosolio immediately wrote to Ben-Gurion, bringing his attention to the Government's decision of 22 January 1956, that 'a man in the service of the State of Israel may not accept any foreign decorations'. Ben-Gurion felt that spurning the French gesture might be taken as an affront to its proponents, and he brought the matter before the Cabinet – which decided, as an extraordinary gesture, to let Peres accept the medal.

For all France's tremendous contribution to Israel's security, the almost unprecedented friendship between the two countries and the extraordinary measures which Peres initiated together with French government leaders, Peres never viewed France as the be all and end all of Israel's international relations. He was sure that like all good things, this special relationship would come to an end some day. He also foresaw something else: Europe was moving further and further along the road towards unity. Co-operation between the various countries was on the rise, and mutual dependence began to be the order of the day in Europe. Thus in order to make progress with one country, it was necessary to have the understanding of the others.

This mutuality was especially true of the Franco-German axis, around which European co-operation had coalesced. At the time, however, the mere mention of Germany in Israel was tantamount to playing with fire, for the wounds inflicted on the Jewish people during the Holocaust were far from healed. In 1952 Jerusalem and Bonn signed an agreement establishing a large sum as reparations to the State of Israel and the surviving victims of the Holocaust. When word of the agreement got out, Israel was rocked by street riots which threatened to burgeon into a civil war. Ultimately tempers cooled, however, and with a pronounced lack of desire most of the Israeli public accepted Ben-Gurion's argument that it would be unjust, if not downright irresponsible, to release Germany from having to pay reparations.

But there is a great difference between the acceptance of reparations and active co-operation. It was not easy for a young Jew with roots in Poland to reach the conclusion that it was time to inaugurate a new era of relations with a country whose citizens had slaughtered six million of his own people. 'How do I feel here as an Israeli?' Peres once asked after a visit to Munich.

Objectively speaking, [the Germans are] not a people that excite my imagination. Subjectively, everything I do is marked by a feeling of reserve, almost a physical fear that a German will touch me, a feeling of guilt if I like something. We live here in an atmosphere of insulation, not just being isolated but also constituting the insulating material. At the same time, everything remains on a human level. It almost hurts to see how human, how like ourselves, the Germans are. Can it be that this people harbours the seeds of evil and cannot be altered? Is it inexorable that this people bear forth hatred and arrogance, oppression and murder? Or can it be that if one repents, his contrition is thorough, determined, considered?

Given the choice, Peres would undoubtedly have been happy to eschew the Germans. He was always aware that 'six million Jews live in America, six million Jews are buried in Germany – and that is a substantive difference, from an historic viewpoint'. But he didn't have that choice, and so 'I don't see any reason to release the Germans from their moral obligation towards us. We may curse it in the Knesset, but I never saw curses create armoured divisions.'

Here, then, was the justification: the security of the State of Israel was the supreme imperative of the Jewish people, the answer to the Holocaust. And to achieve this end, one may – one must – enter into an alliance with anyone. Even the devil. Even Germany. Perhaps especially Germany. At the close of 1957, Peres raised the subject with Ben-Gurion and found him open to the idea from both a personal and a pragmatic viewpoint. Their talk concluded with the decision 'to approach Germany in the way we started with France – by making direct contact between the Defence Ministries'.

So it was that on 3 July 1957, Peres met secretly for the first time the West German Defence Minister, Franz Jozef Strauss, who was to become a key figure in the evolving relations between the two states. They shared a sense of understanding from the outset, and Strauss no doubt won Peres's heart, for this is how Peres described him: 'He is a mountain of a man, 100 kilos plus, with blue eyes that radiate energy. He loves to eat and is a brilliant polemicist.' The two men exchanged views on the world situation and the Middle East, in particular. Strauss agreed that Israel was the main obstacle to a deeper Soviet penetration of the Middle East, and that was always an excellent foundation on which to build ties of co-operation.

Peres's tangible request of Strauss was modest at first:

We have been approached by a German firm from Hamburg with a proposition to sell us two refurbished submarines of about 260 tons apiece. We have discussed the matter with our friends in the French Defence Ministry and navy, and they are prepared to buy the submarines for us. For public consumption, then, it will be the French navy that is buying the subs, but in fact they will be turned over to us.

Strauss promised to consider the matter sympathetically. He also had a request of his own: 'We want to learn from Israel's experience fighting against Russian weapons.'

This first meeting was reminiscent of the early rounds of a boxing-match: the two men exchanged light intellectual punches to assess each other's strength. Their conclusion was that they had what to talk about.

The turning-point in their relationship came during their second meeting – which was almost cancelled. It was set for 27 December 1957, and Peres was supposed to be accompanied by the Chief of Staff, Moshe Dayan. The travel arrangements were made in utmost secrecy, but somehow the matter became known to the Ministers from *Mapam* and *Ahdut Ha'avodah*, who objected to maintaining ties of any kind with Germany. They brought the matter before the Cabinet, asking the Prime Minister to report on the purpose of the Chief of Staff's trip to Germany. When Ben-Gurion replied that the trip was scheduled to wrap up negotiations on the purchase of submarines, the rebellious Ministers demanded that it be cancelled. In the subsequent vote, however, Dayan's trip was approved by a margin of one vote.

On 17 December, ten days before the scheduled date of the meeting, the daily *Lamerchav*, published by *Ahdut Ha'avodah*, leaked innuendos about the affair. Soon afterwards, a spate of articles and items appeared expressing strong opposition to ties of any kind with Germany. The resultant public outcry forced Ben-Gurion to make a change in plans. He announced that 'the Chief of Staff will not go to Germany'. At the same time, he demanded the resignation of the *Mapam* and *Ahdut Ha'avodah* Ministers. When they refused to comply, he himself resigned, bringing the Government down, so that he could form a new Government without them. Peres was not in the country during the days preceding Ben-Gurion's resignation (31 December 1957), for he was already on his way to the German capital. The only change in plan was that he was accompanied by the Deputy Chief of Staff, Chaim Laskov, instead of Dayan.

Strauss's first question related to the leak in Israel. 'He was less concerned about the consequences of the leak than the source, that it might be in Germany. "On my end, a total of three people knew: myself, the head of my bureau and my private secretary, and if we can't keep a secret between us, what have we come to!" he said.' Peres did not bother to calm the anxieties of the German Minister. 'We refrained from commenting on the source of the leak and contented ourselves with his remark that the incident had not jeopardized the specific matter under discussion.'

Much was said about regional and global strategy at that meeting. From a pragmatic viewpoint, the scope of their discussion expanded. No longer were they talking about submarines alone. Once Strauss accepted the principle that Germany should help arm Israel, they began to talk about the joint development of armaments, the purchase of Cobra anti-tank guided missiles, the M-47 hydraulic system for tank turrets, medium tanks – and, on the other side of the coin, the export of Uzi submachine-guns from Israel to the German army. Oddly enough, it was the sale of the submarines, over which the contacts had been initiated, that was ruled out in the end – though not by Germany. At that time, Israel was holding contacts with Britain, as well, and it was decided to purchase higher quality submarines there. Yet this fact did not interfere with the scheduling of another meeting – the third – between Peres and Strauss.

It took place, again under a heavy cloak of secrecy, on 28 March 1958. This time Peres found Strauss 'tired after a most difficult week under constant fire from the opposition in the Bundestag over the question of arming German military forces with atomic weapons'. To illustrate Israel's role in the Middle East, Peres told Strauss that 'Iran is seeking ties with us. This fact impressed Strauss, who was surprised that Iran had turned to us.'

Strauss, for his part, related that 'by chance he had heard that very morning that according to Jordanian officers studying at French military schools, their Government's assessment is that if Jordan joins the United Arab Republic, Israel will invade and conquer it. This prospect daunts the Jordanians. He also told of a conversation between Russian Ambassador Vinogradov and a number of French personalities.'

Later at the meeting Strauss told his guests that

von Brentano [the German Foreign Minister] had complained that he didn't know about the meeting in December and was at a loss to cope with the uproar in the papers, and by the German public at large, over the matter. Strauss agreed that in the future the Foreign Minister would be informed about his meetings with Peres, that is, there would be no formal obstacles to the coming meetings, but they must remain as secret as possible.

Peres asked about the veracity of press reports that Strauss was a candidate to succeed the ageing Konrad Adenauer as Chancellor. 'To that he replied: "I also read that in the press, and I am not so foolish as to deny it. But only young people die in Germany; the old go on forever." '

Back in Israel, Peres felt he could say in all frankness to his top aides, 'though it is not easy for a man involved in security to admit it, we have never been in such good shape as we are today, in every sense and in every sphere. There has been a vast improvement in our political posture and our consolidation socially, while economic opportunities have opened up as well.' The situation was so good, in fact, that Peres wafted into a state bordering on giddiness, which came out when he spoke of 'our national aims'. The first and primary one, he said, is a change in the country's borders. 'We must strive to change the borders of the State of Israel.' He did not mean that Israel would instigate any action to reach this goal. Rather he distinguished

> between a *war* to change the borders of Israel and a *desire* to change the borders. I would not suggest, and do not mean to suggest, an invasion of the West Bank or Sinai or Lebanon to capture the Litani River – which is perhaps the foremost national objective, because Israel's greatest lack is water, not land. I do not propose war and expansion. What I do suggest is that this idea remain part of our primary nationalist thinking; that in the event of various convulsions in the Middle East, we will be prepared to deal with the political need – or perhaps the military opportunity – to reconsider the borders of the state.

During the course of 1958, two events proved how tenuous was the political premise on which Peres had based his assessments. In the early months of that year, the domestic scene in France underwent a series of upheavals. Governments fell one after the other, as each proved no more stable than the last. The army, influenced by the political right, began to intervene in politics – especially on the question of Algeria – and the French public longed for an authority figure who could get a grip on things. All eyes turned towards Colombey, where General Charles de Gaulle was ensconced in splendid isolation. Called back into the service of his country, on 31 May the General was sworn in as Premier of France.

Israel was extremely concerned by this development. The old French leadership had been a reliable ally with which strong ties had been established; de Gaulle was an unknown quantity. Peres had met him once, following the Sinai Campaign. After hearing of the general course of the war, de Gaulle expressed his surprise that the Jews were 'both good farmers and good soldiers'. Now the question of his future position towards Israel and whether or not he would continue the policy of his predecessors received priority attention in Jerusalem.

Immediately after the turnabout in France, Peres went to Paris to try to evaluate the situation. When he returned to Israel, he submitted a memo to Ben-Gurion on 'Relations with de Gaulle's

France' (29 June 1958), based on the talks he had held with members of the new Government. He believed that although de Gaulle would attempt to restore France to a position of influence in the world, including the Arab world, he would perpetuate the policy of friendship with Israel 'because de Gaulle is an honest man and truly admires Israel as a political, military and social dynamo'.

Peres concluded that 'de Gaulle is a man with an open mind but susceptible to a certain type of argument. He has reached a high level of experience and wisdom, but his development is limited to a single direction. This fact is appreciated not only by us but – and to a far greater degree – by a large number of people in France.' Therefore 'parties operating from a variety of vantages will try to influence him'. On the one hand, there is 'the French Foreign Minister, whose Middle Eastern desk never reconciled itself to the friendship towards Israel'. On the other is 'the group of French defence people who have tasted the flavour of friendship with Israel, and whose individual and collective inclination is to maintain ties with the country whose strength and sincerity they have come to know.'

'The conclusion is that we must act vigorously and as soon as possible to make contact with de Gaulle personally, before his final point of view congeals.' Such contact must be conducted 'in the language of French interests, not just Israeli interests'. And what are those French interests? 'A Middle East that is anti-Russian, anti-Nasser, and in which Israel holds the key to France's *entrée*.'

The opportunity to establish direct contact with de Gaulle would present itself in time. Meanwhile, the situation was far from hopeless. 'We have a man who will serve as our ambassador within the new French Government,' Peres reported after a visit to Paris. 'Until [the formation of] de Gaulle's Government, our "ambassador" was Bourgès-Maunoury, and he deserves to be blessed for what he has done on our behalf. In this Government we have a sincere advocate and, in my opinion, a great leader as well – Guy Mollet.'

Peres's relations with Guy Mollet were doubtless very special indeed, for the French socialist leader would open his heart to Peres and consult him about a wide range of subjects. He viewed Peres not just as the representative of a friendly country, but as a personal friend. Mollet was also one of the people who played a decisive role in bringing de Gaulle back to power – and now he was having serious second thoughts. He told Peres in one conversation:

Throughout the world, there is a political élite. For most of recorded history, the élite has risen to the top as a result of legacy, the consolidation of power. In the twentieth century, quite by chance and wholly unexpectedly, the élite is evolving as a result of democratic processes. De Gaulle is part of the élite, but on his way to becoming so, he had to belong to a party, to be chosen by the party.

Suddenly he turned to Peres with an abrupt question: 'Tell me what you think. Did I do the right thing about de Gaulle or not?' Peres replied:

I am prepared to tell you what I think about you, but not about de Gaulle. I have been sitting here facing you today for six to seven hours and thinking what I would have done in your place. If you agree to my being impertinent, allow me to finish. A man in power lives under stress. One event follows on another. One minute he's on the phone, the next he takes off in his car, and after a while he wakes up one morning and asks himself: What have I done throughout my life? As I see it, great men are really able to break free from the world of drama at the proper moment and move into the world of history, of national memory. If the people remember him for generations, that's what history is. Napoleon wasn't great because of thirty or forty victories, but because he gave the French the Code that established equal rights for Jews, that touched the nation at the heart of its problems.

You're always telling me that you're a friend of Israel. Fine, give us another twenty tanks, another forty cannon. But that's not history. Do something historic now: find a way to break free of the world of dramatic dealings and move into the realm of historic decisions in the Middle East. Perhaps I'm a chauvinist, but there is only one serious country in the Middle East; and the state that displays an appropriately serious attitude towards it will, in the final analysis, be doing something historic. Within ten years we'll be four million people. Make an open pact now; a Franco-Israeli alliance, for better or for worse, in which both peoples pledge that if either is attacked, the other will come to its aid.

After concluding his description of this conversation, Peres added his impression that 'Guy Mollet was enthused by the idea'. But even if that assessment were accurate, it was irrelevant. For the man who had decisive authority in such matters was now Charles de Gaulle, not Guy Mollet. Peres knew that, of course. But at the time he was convinced, for a number of reasons, that 'de Gaulle will probably not remain in power for more than a year and a half'. It was on the basis of this prediction that he told Guy Mollet: 'Chances are that you will be the Premier of France in another year and a half, for a period of four to five years.' That assessment was well off the mark, perhaps because it stemmed more from emotion than from level-headed analysis.

The main difference between the de Gaulle era and those preceding it, as Peres saw it, was that 'until de Gaulle there was a single, blanket decision by the French Government regarding all Israeli matters. During the de Gaulle era, it was necessary to get a new decision made on every last thing.' To a certain degree this change made things difficult; however, 'since de Gaulle is making positive decisions, there's no cause for concern'. Indeed, Peres returned from his trip to Paris in October 1958 with a considerable haul. An agreement had been signed on the supply of the Super-Mystère combat plane equipped with air-to-air missiles. This put paid to the inferiority Israel suffered *vis-à-vis* the MiG-17, which the Soviets were supplying to the Arabs. Nord transport planes were also purchased in France, as were helicopters and seacraft – and all this on credit for a period of three years, without interest, 'when the interest alone is worth $1.5–2 million'.

Another friend of Israel in the de Gaulle Government was Jacques Soustelle, and Peres was on close terms with him as well. In the French elections held according to the new constitution, Soustelle's right-wing party emerged with a victory. Afterwards, on a trip to Paris in December 1958, Peres had lunch with Soustelle and 'asked him why he doesn't want to be Premier. I knew, of course, that it wasn't dependent on him alone. . . . But I couldn't ask him why de Gaulle thought he should not be Premier. He said he has no personal ambitions to be Prime Minister. But because I come from a party in which every Minister claims he lacks personal ambitions, I couldn't take his answer very seriously.'

Peres also talked to Soustelle about the idea of a pact between France and Israel, but here he came up against a problem. His relations with Guy Mollet were natural from an ideological standpoint, for both men belonged to socialist parties. The same was not so with Soustelle, who was associated with the right-wing in Israel and was personally close to the leader of the Herut Party, Menachem Begin. Peres laid his cards on the table. 'I have a simple question: With whom would you be prepared to make a pact? With the opposition in Israel or with the Government? "I would be prepared to make a pact with the Government of Israel," he replied, "but I still need time to think about the subject." "Take as much time as you need," I told him, "but if you reach a conclusion, you'd better tell me first, before you tell the opposition."'

Once the misunderstandings were settled, the relationship between the two men grew stronger until it blossomed into a personal friendship. And it was because of their closeness that Peres approached Soustelle with one of the most imaginative proposals he ever had – and there was no dearth of these. It all began during the visit of a French delegation to Israel at the beginning of 1959. One of the members of the delegation was the representative of French Guiana, France's colony in South America. In his boundless enthusiasm for what he was seeing in Israel, he remarked to Peres: 'Listen, if we were tied to Israel, instead of France, we'd be in a different situation.' Peres later mentioned this to Soustelle, adding: 'Do you really need Guiana? We could do wonders there!'

If Soustelle could do without Guiana, why should Peres want it? He envisioned an area of 90,000 square kilometres, rich in natural resources with a total population of some 30,000 people, and could not bear the thought of such waste. But there was also another, more important reason for Peres's attraction to Guiana. It was associated with the EEC, and Peres hoped that through it Israel would be able to make inroads into the European community. Another reason was that Guiana was rich in cypress trees, from whose wood orange-crates were made, and oranges were Israel's leading export.

Peres therefore suggested to Soustelle that Israel lease Guiana from France for a period of thirty to forty years, or, alternatively, establish a joint development company with France. Who would do the developing? A few thousand Jews, who would be sent there to establish a Jewish society linked to Israel – something like a branch of the Jewish state.

Before raising the idea with Soustelle, Peres naturally solicited Ben-Gurion's permission to do so. It's odd that the elderly statesman did not reject the notion out of hand, even though he viewed it with more than a touch of scepticism. 'Won't that be at Israel's expense?' he asked. 'And how do you know that the Jews of Guiana will want to remain associated with Israel? I advised Shimon not to go overboard in his talks with Soustelle, but to discuss joint projects. When he returns I will find out the reason why the country is a wilderness and whether there really is a point in settling there.'

To 'find out the reason why the country is a wilderness', a seven-man delegation headed by Hillel Dan was sent to Guiana, and it returned with a report and a film. When that film was screened for the Cabinet, most of its members were aghast. Pinhas Sapir told Peres that the idea was 'a catastrophe, colonialism, imperialism. It will bring about a holocaust in Africa and stir up opposition in South America. Golda will let it pass only over her dead body. The Old Man promised that as long as she's Foreign Minister, nothing will come of it.'

In the end, Ben-Gurion joined Sapir in concluding that he had enough problems with one country and didn't need another. The idea was buried in the files, which was undoubtedly the most fitting place for it.

On the day he presented the Guiana plan to Ben-Gurion, Peres could not have known that a mishap which occurred a few days earlier would snowball to proportions ominous enough to threaten the future of relations between Israel and France – as well as his own political and personal status. At the beginning of March 1958, on what was to become far from a routine flight, the Israeli pilot Leo Gardiner noticed that one of the engines of his DC-4 Constellation was not running smoothly. He switched off the faulty engine and continued the flight on the remaining three. A short while later his gauges indicated another hitch – this time an oil leak – and he decided to land for repairs.

Just then the plane was over the city of Bône, some 400 kilometres east of Algiers. Gardiner contacted the control tower of the French military airfield there and asked for permission to land. The French complied and, when he landed, welcomed Gardiner and his crew warmly. But the trouble began the next morning, in the person of the airfield's security officer. 'What's in the plane?' he wanted to know.

'Arms,' Gardiner replied without hesitation.

'Where are they destined for?'

'South America,' he again replied openly, adding with complete aplomb: 'We have a special arrangement with Paris regarding this plane.'

'Fine,' said the security man. 'We'll check it out.'

He called his headquarters in Algiers, and they telephoned to Paris. But no one had ever heard of the pilot, the plane or any arrangement, special or otherwise. The security officer was rightly suspicious. Peres recalls:

And then things began to unfold like *A Thousand and One Nights*.

Each member of the crew was interrogated individually, each was asked for his *curriculum vitae*. They asked the pilot what he had done for the past eleven years. And the pilot didn't realize that they suspected him, and he started to tell them everything. 'In 1947 I smuggled planes from America to Israel; in 1948 I flew arms from Czechoslovakia to Israel and bombed

Cairo; in 1953 I flew Spitfires from Israel to Burma; in 1956 I flew arms from France to Israel.' To Israelis that's a heroic saga, but to a French security officer it was proof that he had nailed a seasoned smuggler.

They asked each of the crew what language he spoke and in what language he chose to be interrogated. One youngster said that he had emigrated to Israel from Rumania. That's all they had to hear! They didn't ask him a thing; they just held him aside, because the word Rumania conjured up unimaginable suspicions.

Then they took the third man, a British pilot married to a Jewish woman, and started interrogating him. He said that he had taken part in the War of Independence and the Sinai Campaign. When the security officer heard that one guy is from Rumania, one is from America, one is from England, and they claim that there's a special agreement about their plane, and he has Paris contacted and no one ever heard of them, as far as he's concerned, they are one very suspect bunch.

And then there was the matter of the arms. They were wrapped in a blanket, and when the men were asked, 'Why did you pack them like that?' they said, 'To save space and packing crates.' 'We pack parachutes that way,' the security people observed. And our boys said: 'Maybe you pack that way for parachuting, but we didn't do it for that reason, and we don't have parachutes in the plane.' That led the security officer to believe that there were no parachutes because they had already parachuted the arms down to the Algerian rebels!

The whole affair got out to the press, and a public outcry naturally ensued, in both Israel and in France. Israel was suspected – even by parties within the French Government – of helping to smuggle arms to the Algerian rebels, against whom France was conducting a bitter, bloody war. And this was at the height of the Franco-Israeli amity, when France was going out of her way to help Israel!

What actually happened? Why did Gardiner think that the whole matter had been arranged with Paris?

Anyone who has ever flown to the State of Israel in the cabin of a plane knows that there is nothing more difficult than that maneuvre. As you approach Israel, you're surrounded on all sides by the enemy's radar beams. So it turned out that the best route to South America was via North Africa, but we knew a war was going on there, so we turned to a key figure in the French bureaucracy – and I must say a number of things to his credit, without mentioning his name. If there are special relations between France and Israel, this man is responsible for them. And he has not enjoyed any material gain from his help to us; he does it for idealistic reasons. [This 'key figure' was a close aide of Premier Bourgès-Maunoury.]

Naturally we approached him and consulted him as to whether it was worthwhile to fly over North Africa. His reply was affirmative and he volunteered to inform the proper authorities about the flight. Naturally we told the crew that if they ran into any problem along the way, they would be flying over friendly territory and that we had an arrangement with [the French]. And here's where the hitch occurred. The 'key figure' failed to keep his promise and pass on the information to the people he was supposed to. He simply forgot.

Then why didn't Peres simply put the affair to rest by telling the French Government about the oversight?

When we found out that he hadn't passed the matter on to the appropriate people, he said to us: 'If you wish, I'll take full responsibility upon myself. But you must know that this will be the last time I can do so.' I went to Ben-Gurion, and he decided that we would take responsibility for it. What's more, he ordered our representative in Paris to tell our friend that he was relieved of all responsibility, both because of his past services and because of our need of his services in the future. If you sacrifice a friend in a difficult hour, you never make another friend again.

The matter got out of hand because 'in this case we fell victim to the give-and-take between various Ministries and the tension between various members of the French Government and the bureaucracy'. Be that as it may, the affair was certainly exploited by various parties in France for whom the special relations with Israel were anathema. Peres told Ben-Natan: 'It's ridiculous to claim that the arms were prepared for parachuting. The story is absolutely groundless. There were no such arrangements, and no parachute was found in the plane.' Israel's friends in Paris accepted this explanation, and there were still enough of them in key positions to see to it that the affair was brought to a satisfactory close. First the crew was released, and some time later, after the commotion died down, the plane itself, with all its cargo, was returned as well.

Then a new affair surfaced and, from Peres's personal standpoint, it bore even graver consequences than its predecessor. If the weapons in Gardiner's plane were not destined for the rebels in Algeria, for whom were they destined? Peres said that they were on their way to Latin America, but that continent was not politically monolithic. It contained countries with which Israel was eager to maintain relations and others from which she kept her distance because of their despotic regimes. One of the worst offenders from this point of view was the

Dominican Republic – and that was precisely the destination of the weapons.

Israel's arms deals with Latin American countries began long before Gardiner's plane landed in Bône. In February 1957 a delegation from Nicaragua came to Israel to investigate the possibility of purchasing arms. It was composed of Nicaragua's chief arms agent, an American called Irwin Davidson, and two military officers. In Israel the delegation was guided by Yitzhak Shapira, Deputy Director of the Defence Ministry's Armament Division, who wrote to Peres that: 'The delegation arrived without a clear idea of what it wished to buy. In fact, they expressed enthusiasm about almost every item we suggested to them.'

Peres had no intention of dampening that enthusiasm. Moreover, he felt a profound sense of obligation towards both Nicaragua and the Dominican Republic, stemming from the fact that during Israel's War of Independence, when many countries failed to help the fledgling state in any way at all, those two Latin American countries supplied her with generous quantities of arms. For this reason Peres wrote to Colonel A. Somoza (on 20 February): 'Out of an awareness of the excellent and friendly relations between our two countries, we have tried, within our limitations, to provide every possible assistance to the success of your mission.'

The mission was indeed successful, and Israel received orders amounting to $1,218,850. After a part of the deal had been implemented, the other Latin American states learned about it and responded with an indignant hue and cry. Walter Eytan, Director-General of the Foreign Ministry, wrote to Peres on 5 July 1957:

> We really put our foot in it with the Nicaraguan arms deal. All the countries of Latin American shun [Nicaragua] because of its foreign policy and domestic regime. It's a shame that you failed to consult the Foreign Ministry before going through with this deal. You know as well as I do that we are very dependent on the Latin American bloc in the United Nations, which includes twenty countries. We cannot disregard their feelings. Therefore, I am asking you immediately to order that any new deal with Nicaragua be cancelled and that shipments which have not yet gone out be held up.

Some four months later it appeared as though Peres had accepted the inevitable. He wrote to Eytan (on 13 November 1957): 'Recently a number of South American countries have displayed an interest in purchasing weapons from us. Naturally we are most interested in deals of this kind. But considering past experience (the Nicaraguan deal), we wish to co-ordinate the matter with the Foreign Ministry, so as to avoid any political embarrassment.' In reply, Eytan sent Peres a list of the countries to which it was permissible – and forbidden – to sell weapons. The Dominican Republic was at the head of the list of boycotted countries.

And then came the flap over the plane. Before long, it came out that the latest deal with the Dominican Republic was one which Peres had made on his own cognizance – and in contravention of explicit directives from the Foreign Ministry. The press came down hard on him and, in a subsequent meeting with the editors of the country's dailies (on 13 March 1958), he attempted to explain his motives by saying that the arms sold to the Dominican Republic were taken from IDF surpluses and were worth about $15 million. Disposing of these arms would enable Israel to purchase new weapons needed by the IDF. 'I see it as the Defence Ministry's task to transform old weapons into new ones.'

He went on to tell of a discussion with Ben-Gurion – at which Foreign Minister Golda Meir was likewise present – regarding the sale of arms to the Dominican Republic. Israel received an order for Uzi submachine-guns, bazookas and a frigate, and the decision was to turn it down because it would be possible to identify the source of the sale. Peres accepted that ruling insofar as the Uzis and the frigate were concerned. But his story implies that he decided, on his own, that it would be impossible to trace the bazookas back to Israel. So, once again on his own cognizance, he proceeded with the deal, primarily because he had his own ideas about the prohibition of arms sales. 'By not selling an Uzi to a certain state, we're not imposing an embargo on that state; we are boycotting ourselves. It's sheer idiocy to boycott ourselves on an item that can be obtained elsewhere.'

Yet all these explanations did not lessen the fact that Peres had disobeyed unequivocal orders. Had it not been for the plane mishap, he might have won praise for his initiative at some later date. But when it happened, it caused grave political damage. Here was an opportunity to square accounts which many people in the Foreign Ministry had been waiting for. And most eager of all was Golda Meir herself.

From the day she replaced Moshe Sharett as Foreign Minister, Golda had been opposed to Peres's activities and *modus operandi*. The friction between the two became almost habitual and often required

Ben-Gurion's intervention. One reason for these tense relations was the objective situation which Golda found when she entered the Foreign Ministry. For many years she had been cut off from fluent contact with foreign affairs. She had relatively little experience in this sphere and her links with personalities around the world were limited. Facing her she found a young man of thirty-three who had built a ramification of connections throughout the world. What could not be achieved through standard diplomatic channels, because of pressure from the Arab countries, Peres achieved in back rooms by unconventional means. For the most part, it's true, he used back doors and side entrances; but these were the doors to the men in key positions of power.

Peres had very decided views on this subject. 'I know that you think I spend too much time on politics,' he said with disarming frankness to his Ministry's senior officials in a session on 13 May 1957. 'But defence and foreign policy go hand in hand, and the fact that the Ministry of Defence did not concern itself with these matters in the past is not proof that it was right in the past.'

What infuriated Golda more than anything was the generous backing Peres received from Ben-Gurion. As Premier and Minister of Defence, he understood that the kind of contacts Peres maintained could be exploited effectively only if they remained secret – even from the Foreign Minister. And even when he felt that Peres had gone overboard in keeping things from Golda, he never went out of his way to rectify the situation.

Because most of Israel's diplomatic and defence activities were related to France during that period, France became the heart of the problem. In July 1957 Golda went to Paris to meet Jean Monnet, one of the principal leaders in the crusade for European unity. Her objective was to win his support for bringing Israel into NATO, or at least integrating her into the European community in some other way. But the day before the meeting was to take place, Golda discovered that Peres had beat her to it by four months. She 'responded trenchantly about your talks with Monnet and the fact that she did not know about them', Arthur Ben-Natan cabled Peres on 10 July 1957. 'I explained that it was impossible to tell her since the meeting was organized at the last moment, and we intended to tell her afterwards but it didn't work out because of objective circumstances. Golda did not accept that explanation and decided to cancel her meeting with Monnet and return home immediately.'

After returning to Israel, she poured her heart out to Ben-Gurion. He wrote in his diary:

I told Golda that I am concerned and regret her suspicions (which are not entirely unfounded) about the Defence Ministry butting into foreign affairs. When she said that she has already despaired of the matter, I said that I could not accept her being 'beyond despair'. Golda said she had no complaints against the Chief of Staff, but Shimon does things without her knowledge, and she agreed to hold a comradely clarification of the matter.

That session placated her somewhat, but not for long. When Peres was about to leave for France on an arms-purchasing mission, Golda demanded that he report to the Israeli Ambassador there and include him in the talks. The matter reached Ben-Gurion again, and he accepted the part about reporting to the Ambassador but rejected the notion of bringing him along to the talks. The essence of his verdict was expressed in a letter he sent to the Paris Embassy on 18 March 1958:

The Director-General of the Defence Ministry is going to France on an arms-acquistion mission. He will inform you of the people he intends to meet, but the interests of secrecy require that he see them alone. A number of things have been done – and will yet be done – with France in an unorthodox manner. Sometimes they have involved bypassing one Minister or another, including the Minister of Finance, and therefore the members of the French Government choose to talk alone and informally. I am sure that you value the interests of arms-acquisition above ceremony, and just as the French forgo protocol, so will you.

In the case of the Dominican deal, however, Peres outdid himself and earned a rebuke from Ben-Gurion. 'No sale of arms should be made to any country without my prior knowledge and consent,' the Prime Minister wrote to Peres in a formal letter dated 5 March 1958. 'The information should be provided only when one of the countries has asked to purchase arms. I will not decide before consulting the Foreign Ministry.' After slapping Peres on one cheek, however, Ben-Gurion saw fit to caress the other. 'This order is not intended as criticism for past [behaviour]. I wish that all the government Ministries were run with the talent, accomplishment and reliability that the Defence Ministry is under your direction. But at this grave hour, we must have complete co-ordination of our policy; and the sale of weapons is a diplomatic fact, not just a financial and economic one.'

He could also have added that it was a political fact, for the confrontation between Peres and Golda expressed itself not only in differences of approach regarding foreign affairs and defence but in the power struggle within *Mapai*. The rule of the Old Guard, of which Golda was one of the principal representatives, was under attack at the time. Leading the challengers were Moshe Dayan and Shimon Peres, who drew around them a group of dynamic and talented people. The press dubbed them the 'Youngsters'.

Youngsters they were, but they owed their power, in fact their very existence, to the 'Old Man'. Ben-Gurion had aways found himself attracted to young people. He considered them the future of the state, and this affinity grew stronger following the Sinai Campaign. Ben-Gurion ascribed the success of this war first and foremost to two people: Moshe Dayan, the man who prepared the army for the crucial test; and Shimon Peres, the man who equipped the army and provided it with the necessary diplomatic and military backing.

At the same time, other young men were coalescing into a group around Ben-Gurion, and their power and influence were steadily on the rise. On the level of officials and aides were Nehemiah Argov, Yitzhak Navon and Chaim Yisraeli. Within the Party Ben-Gurion drew around him Abba Eban, Giora Yoseftal, Yigael Yadin, Ehud Avriel and Shlomo Hillel. He knew very well that the veterans would not easily be reconciled to the promotion of the Youngsters. 'There will be opposition to this change in the Party, and it must be withstood,' he told Yoseftal in May 1958.

This forecast proved chillingly accurate. Though they were relatively advanced in age, the Old Guard displayed a fighting spirit equal to that of the Youngsters. Golda Meir, Levi Eshkol, Pinhas Sapir, Pinhas Lavon and the others had absolutely no intention of vacating their positions, and they offered a taste of things to come in November 1958, a few months before the elections. Ben-Gurion intended to bring a number of Youngsters – Eban, Yadin, Dayan and Peres – into the Party leadership. But the Old Guard rebelled, leaving the party in a furore. Ben-Gurion decided to convene the two sides and arrange a 'reconciliation' between them. When one of the Party veterans told Ben-Gurion that Pinhas Lavon (then Secretary-General of the *Histadrut*) might boycott the convention if Peres took part, his response was quite unequivocal: 'I'll regret if Lavon doesn't come, but Shimon must not be ostracized. No one has done as much as he has in the Defence Ministry.'

In addressing the so-called reconciliation convention on 22 November 1958, Ben-Gurion adopted the strategy of the carrot and the stick. He promised the Old Guard that he would not promote the Youngsters at their expense, but he also adopted a vigorous stand in favour of opting them into the Party's leadership. 'Only if [*Mapai*] remains the most youthful [of all the other Parties] will it fulfil its mission in the future,' he admonished. 'Throughout history young peole have done great things. A youngster does not deserve a prize for being young, but neither should he be punished for it; and if he is deserving of a mission and of leadership, his youth will prove a blessing.'

The Old Guard was not reassured at all. Lavon, in fact, called the meeting the 'coronation assembly' of Dayan and Peres. More fuel was added to the flames by Dayan, who meanwhile had retired from the army after completing his term as Chief of Staff. He attacked the veterans at almost every opportunity, deliberately provoking and irritating them. And they had a hard time handling him, for by then Dayan was already draped in the aura of a military commander, the hero of the Sinai Campaign. His fresh, youthful image, to which the black eye-patch added a touch of mystery and magic, had become the symbol of Israel's renewal. Certainly it was daunting to take up the cudgels against Ben-Gurion, the leader of unimpeachable authority. So there remained the powerful senior official who did his work behind the scenes, the figure of the young, ambitious, unbridled 'executor'. All the Old Guard's rage and bile were directed at Shimon Peres.

Peres's opinion of the *Mapai* veterans was not much higher than theirs of him. He spoke obliquely of their determination to survive when describing the leader of another country: 'De Gaulle says: I am sixty-seven years old today. But in contrast to the members of *Mapai*, he believes that sixty-seven is not the age at which the exuberance of youth begins, but rather the age at which one retires from political life.' In a letter to a friend written in June 1958, he elaborated on the subject:

Undoubtedly you've heard about the war of the Youngsters and the Old Guard. According to the press, the Youngsters want to get rid of the veterans. That is only natural, but at present it appears hopeless. However, the truth is that the Youngsters (and I as one of them) are tired of Mozart's *Eine Kleine Nachtmusik* and the Russian *rubashkas* [blouses] that are still considered the height of modern Israeli originality. We have always

86

thirsted for a kind of art that contains the energy of life, exhilaration, levity, and even a little provocative irony about the mores that have taken root in our lives and seem tiresome, grey and outdated.

Thus the clash of generations was not just a struggle over positions of power. It was a struggle between opposing ways of life, outlooks, ways of thinking and doing things. To Peres and his colleagues, the veterans symbolized everything that was outmoded – the Diaspora, the mentality of the Jewish ghetto. The Youngsters viewed themselves as the 'new Israelis', perhaps the true Israelis. The ideology of the Old Guard was regarded as prattle that had long since had its day. They believed in creativity, in achievement. It was not by chance that the word 'executors' stuck to them

Dayan clashed with the Old Guard head on, unabashedly, publicly. It was more difficult for Peres to do so because he was in the Procrustean bed of the Civil Service. This fact was becoming particularly irksome to him, and on 3 May 1958, he spoke of it to Ben-Gurion, who asked him, '*Quo vadis?*' Peres replied: 'I can not go on being an offical. I am forbidden to speak out, and the Civil Service Law will restrict me even more.' When Ben-Gurion said, 'I can't see anyone else running the Ministry of Defence', Peres suggested that he resign and take part in the elections. Once in the Knesset, he could be appointed Deputy Minister of Defence and continue running affairs, but he would be free to speak, like every other Knesset member.

Ben-Gurion readily consented, and a few weeks after the elections in November, when the new Knesset convened, Peres took his seat in the plenum among the delegates from *Mapai*. Nearby sat his political partner, Moshe Dayan, for whom this was also a début in political life. After the session 'I drank tea with Moshe Dayan. He asked me if I felt anything special and without waiting for an answer commented how strange it was that his entry into the Knesset and the Government were void of any feeling of celebration or the sense of a special event. I told him I empathized with that.'

In addition to appointing Peres Deputy Defence Minister, Ben-Gurion intended to fill other senior positions in the Government with three other Youngsters: Dayan, Eban and Giora Yoseftal. But the Old Guard, and especially Golda Meir, Pinhas Lavon and Zalman Aranne, opposed this move with a barrage of arguments. At this stage Ben-Gurion was not interested in a direct collision with them, so he opted for a series of concessions. He appointed Dayan to an economic (rather than defence- or foreign-affairs-oriented) post – Minister of

Agriculture. Abba Eban, for whom Ben-Gurion had earmarked the post of Minister of Information, was forced to make do as Minister without Portfolio. Yoseftal was appoined Minister of Labour.

It wouldn't have taken much for Peres to have been left without any Cabinet post at all. To take some pressures off the veterans, and especially Golda, at one stage Ben-Gurion floated the idea of having Peres run as *Mapai*'s candidate for Mayor of Tel Aviv – a very respectable position, though on the fringe of the real work of government. It is difficult to imagine how things would have unfolded for Peres had this suggestion been taken up. It was turned down, however, by the powerful Tel Aviv branch known as the 'Gush'. And this time Peres was not disappointed by the opposition. Neither, it appeared, was Ben-Gurion. It may well be that he advanced the suggestion only to prove his readiness to compromise with the veterans, not because he really wanted it to be accepted.

In any event, when Ben-Gurion presented his Cabinet to the Knesset, Peres was included as Deputy Minister of Defence. On the day the Ministers were sworn in (17 December 1959), he was present in the Knesset plenum, but when he returned home to his diary that night, he had nothing to say about himself. He was completely under the spell of the man he was growing to admire more and more: 'Moshe Dayan looked very formal in his dark suit, spruced up by a red tie. He is very handsome and once again his personality stands out, though under completely different circumstances. For him this is not the high point of his life, but rather a major turning-point.'

It was not until two days later that Peres sufficiently recovered from the impression made by Dayan to mention his own appointment: 'In the morning I saw Ben-Gurion. He congratulated me on my new position and said: You're a deputy before you become a Minister.'

3
Conflicts and Loyalties

The transition from the halls of officialdom to the political realm afforded Peres the room for maneuvre he so desired and enabled him to advance his own position within the party, as well as take a more active role in the power struggle which continued to rack it. From this point of view, he had no complaints. But he was disturbed by the fact that his new title had not been translated into new authority within the Defence Ministry. This was the first time Ben-Gurion had had a deputy, and the Old Man found it difficult – or was simply unwilling – to see the difference between a Deputy Minister and Director-General.

But Peres was eager to and did see a substantial difference. He had no intention of being just Director-General by another name. In one of their talks on this subject he told Ben-Gurion:

> With a deputy, you can work according to one of two systems. Either you delegate part of the work to him or you delegate him part of the responsibility. That is, either he takes over some of the Ministry's affairs or he deals with all the Ministry's affairs solely from the administrative viewpoint. I suggested to [Ben-Gurion], in the event that he prefers a division of labour, that I will deal with financial and economic matters and with the whole complex of armament: research, the military industry, acquisitions and the General Security Service. He wanted to think it over.

Added to Ben-Gurion's reservations about this shift in responsibility was a disagreement – likewise over authority – with Chief of Staff Chaim Laskov, who had succeeded Dayan. In his diary Peres described the day when he 'went up to Jerusalem with a heavy heart. I ate lunch with Yitzhak Navon and told him about the difficulties I'm having with the Chief of Staff and about the trouble defining the division of labour with the Old Man. I complained that consultations were held – admittedly at random – without me.'

Ben-Gurion sensed his deputy's discontent, and one evening,

after a discussion, the Old Man called me in. 'I feel that you're dissatisfied,' he said. 'What's happened?' I told him that I have problems, some of them with the General Staff. When he asked why I hadn't told him, I replied that I didn't want him to intervene, that I wanted to solve them, not force them to a crisis. 'But I sense that it's not just the Chief of Staff,' he said. So I told him that it's very difficult to define what a Deputy Minister of Defence is. He conceded that he was likewise having a hard time with that point. He said that he trusts me completely, and his friends get angry whenever he says that I was a better Director-General than Sapir or Eshkol. When he asked for advice, I suggested a division of labour that I thought was pretty good.

Peres wrote that in his diary on 9 February 1960. But Ben-Gurion also kept a diary, and it allows us to see that Peres's assessment of his scheme left something to be desired. 'Eight days ago Shimon proposed to me a division of labour,' Ben-Gurion wrote. 'I rejected it.'

Much as he appreciated and respected Peres, Ben-Gurion had trouble yielding authority – even over the smallest matter – in the realm of defence. He regarded the country's security as the most important of the many responsibilities entrusted to him. It was all but sacrosanct in his eyes. Nevertheless, he ultimately granted Peres broad powers which were spelled out in a detailed paper. The final sentence of this document speaks of the Deputy Minster's right to 'meet with any officer', and it was designed to solve Peres's other problem: the Chief of Staff.

Chaim Laskov was the polar opposite of Moshe Dayan. Most of all, he sorely lacked the imagination, daring, vitality and resourcefulness with which his predecessor was so amply endowed. Laskov had received his military training in the ranks of the *Haganah* and the British army, but it was from his British instructors that he adopted his way of thinking and behaving – even his physical appearance. For better or for worse, Chaim Laskov looked, conducted himself and functioned like a model British officer.

As long as Peres was the Director-General of the Defence Ministry, the relations between the two men were satisfactory, even friendly. Both accepted that their positions within the defence network were parallel. But when Peres was appointed Deputy Minister, Laskov refused to accept his superiority in the Defence hierarchy. As Chief of

Staff he considered himself responsible to the Defence Minister – and to him alone. This is why he was against allowing Peres to meet IDF officers at will, and this point became the subject of a dispute in principle over the Deputy Minister's authority *vis-à-vis* the IDF.

At first they attempted to solve the problem peacefully, with

> Chaim and I closeting ourselves in a room (in the Prime Minister's Office in Jersulalem). But a dismal discusssion which lasted three hours got us nowhere. I told him that I want to maintain contact with the officers corps, and it didn't go over with him. He said there's no point in changing anything in the army or the system of reporting to the Old Man. He appreciates me, admires me and is interested in seeing me succeed. But it's out of the question for senior officers to meet with me.

Two weeks later another attempt was made.

> After the weekly meeting [of the General Staff], the Old Man asked Laskov and me to remain behind and tried to conciliate us – without success, I'm afraid. I pointed out to Chaim the absurdity of his proposal: Anyone under me will be free to see the generals, but I won't. Chaim insists that he knows all and reports all – his personal opinion and that of others. He intimated that if I have meetings with the generals, he will resign. The Old Man told me that, of course, I can see any general I choose wherever I choose.

As matters turned out, Peres was not the only one with whom Laskov was having communication difficulties. The complaints of senior General Staff officers, such as Ezer Weizman and Chaim Bar-Lev, were even more caustic. Major-General Yitzhak Rabin was in the habit of expressing particularly sharp criticism of Laskov in private conversations and even resorted to abusive language.

Laskov's views did not mellow with time. On the contrary, he seemed to become more adamant and repeatedly demanded that his officers not have meetings with the Deputy Minister of Defence except with his prior permission. Peres, for his part, continued to summon them, and the officers, caught in the middle, were at a loss. This absurd situation forced Ben-Gurion to take the unusual step of approaching the General Staff officers directly, over their commander's head. 'I have been asked by the Defence Minister to inform you', Ben-Gurion's military secretary, Chaim Ben-David, wrote on 5 May 1960, 'that the Deputy Defence Minister is authorized to meet with any IDF officer or employee of the Defence Ministry as he requires and is further authorized to receive any written material necessary to fulfil his duty.'

A copy of this letter was sent to Laskov, who was quick to pen his reply. In an injured tone he said that the order would

> place before every officer two channels of approach. One – the channel of command; the other – the channel leading to the Deputy Defence Minister. The result of such a situation will be that the choice of subject, the channel through which it will be pursued and the manner of raising it will be left to the officer, on the one hand, and the Deputy Defence Minister, on the other. Under such conditions, co-operation is void of any practical meaning.

In the final paragraph of his letter, Laskov made it plain that he considered the satisfactory resolution of this issue a *sine qua non* of his continued service: 'Knowing myself and knowing the IDF, after considering the implications of your order as far as I myself am concerned, I must inform you with regret that I cannot fulfil the conditions that this order establishes and I am forced to request that another Chief of Staff be appointed to execute the working arrangement you have formulated.'

Ben-Gurion read the letter with 'regret and astonishment'. That very day he wrote back to Laskov

> not as Minister of Defence and not to the Chief of Staff but as a colleague to a colleague and as one friend to another. I don't see the damage caused by allowing the Deputy Defence Minister to meet with officers. He is not authorized to issue orders to anyone in the army, and I don't see contact between the Deputy Minister and officers as detracting from the supreme authority of the Chief of Staff. I am particularly grieved by the final paragraph of your letter – both its content and its reasoning. I am quite taken aback. At the end of the week, I shall come to Tel Aviv and we shall discuss the matter.

Actually, there was nothing more to discuss. Ben-Gurion was convinced that relations within the General Staff had deteriorated to a perilous nadir. Most of all, he was influenced by what he heard from Yitzhak Rabin, who complained that the General Staff officers had lost faith in the Chief of Staff. After that talk with Rabin, Ben-Gurion asked Peres: 'What's the best way to relieve Chaim of his post without offending him personally?'

So it was that Chaim Laskov backed himself into a corner from which there was only one exit. Even in the eyes of his rivals, he was a talented soldier and a man of the utmost integrity. But he was destroyed by his own inability to get along with people or to back down from an untenable position. He failed to understand that Peres's superior status was not a personal matter but a corollary of the elementary principle of civilian authority over the military. So rather than yield, he resigned and was succeeded by Lieutenant-General Zvi Zur. Major General Yitzhak Rabin was appointed Deputy Chief of Staff.

'As I see it, this is one of the most important scientific endeavours that the State of Israel has even taken upon herself.' That was how Shimon Peres described the atomic reactor at Dimona. It was also, without doubt, his greatest love. Every advance in the construction of the reactor and its facilities signified a step closer to manifesting an impressive Israeli scientific achievement. It was only natural that the construction of a plant of this size would attract attention. Many people wondered about all the activity near the small desert town of Dimona. Someone ventured to suggest that a textile plant was being built, and somehow this notion developed a life of its own. The legend of the Dimona textile plant prevailed among the people for years.

Few people in Israel had any idea what was actually going on in the 'textile plant'. Those in the know included the members of the Atomic Energy Commission and, of course, the people actually handling the operation in Dimona. And the Jordanians almost found out.

During a visit to Eilat, Peres was accompanied by Elhanan Yishai, his friend from Alumot, and Yishai's eight-year-old son, Dudu. They returned to Tel Aviv in a small plane, and Peres and Yishai promptly fell asleep immediately after take-off. Suddenly Dudu woke his father, asking, 'Where are we?' Yishai looked at his watch and mumbled drowsily, 'At Avdat', in the Negev highlands. But the child would not let up: 'Then where are the lights of Sdeh Boker?'

Yishai peered out the window. The boy was right. There were no lights, just the bright white sand that was ominously reminiscent of the Judean desert. 'What's going on?' he asked, half in alarm, half in indignation. 'We've strayed off course and I've lost contact with Lod,' the pilot confessed. There were some tense moments before he managed to raise the control tower at Lod airport and was directed to the Sdeh Dov airfield just outside Tel Aviv.

Peres did not wake up until the plane was landing. As he disembarked, he was very surprised to see the Commander of the Air Force, Ezer Weizman, and his Deputy, Motti Hod. Even more puzzling, they were wielding a bottle of cognac and four glasses.

Barely suppressing his laughter, Ezer bellowed: 'Didn't you know that you were in Jordan? We saw you on the radar, but there was nothing we could do about it!' Shimon Peres shuddered as he glanced at the file of documents gripped in his hand.

In May 1960 French policy on the matter of the reactor took a sharp turnabout. Peres wrote in his diary on the 16th of that month:

> Disturbing news from France. [French Foreign Minister] Couve de Murville called in [Israeli Ambassador] Walter Eytan on Saturday and informed him orally – and then in writing as well – of the French Government's decisions regarding the reactor. First, the time has come to make the Dimona matter public. They appreciate the fact that we have kept it secret, but now it must be disclosed. Second, foreign, perhaps international, supervision must be assured. Third, until then, they will not be able to supply the uranium they have promised.

Years later, de Gaulle mentioned the French change of heart in his memoirs: 'We halted the aid for initiating construction near Beersheba of a facility for transforming uranium into plutonium from which, one fine day, atomic bombs might emerge.'

Ben-Gurion decided that the matter was grave enough to ask for a meeting with the French President – the first since de Gaulle had returned from Colombey. France assented to the Israeli request and the date was set for 13 June 1960.

Peres preceded Ben-Gurion to France to prepare the groundwork for the summit. At his meeting with the French Energy Minister, Pierre Guillaumat, on 8 June, he learned of the official reason for demanding disclosure. Circles in Paris were arguing, Guillaumat explained, 'that the project can't be kept secret anymore. A leak can occur any minute now because of the scope of the project and the number of Frenchmen already employed in Dimona. Their employment contract states that they are being sent to "a warm climate and desert conditions" – and it's not difficult to figure out where that is.' Guillaumat was surprised that 'we have been able to keep the matter under wraps'.

Afterwards Peres went to meet Couve de Murville, 'the man whom everyone depicts as the source of the coolness towards Israel'. This impression was reinforced by General Levaud, the Chief of Staff of the armed forces. 'I'm warning you about something you've known for a while,' he said. 'You mustn't talk to Couve about concrete matters. We get along and we'll try to continue getting along without him.'

But there were matters on which one could not sidestep Couve –

and the reactor was one of them. As he walked into the office of the French Foreign Minister, Peres thought wistfully about 'how thoroughly conditions have changed. For reasons of secrecy, I would meet Pineau in his private apartment at the Quai d'Orsay. We knew that a friend was awaiting us. This time we were received in the Minister's official bureau.' There Peres found Couve sitting 'in the dim light . . . impeccably dressed, extremely polite, tense and attentive'. Peres told him that Israel did not reject the notion of disclosure on principle, but she would like to have a say about the timing. To Peres's surprise, Couve promptly agreed, saying that the date of the disclosure was secondary and definitely open to negotiation.

Peres did most of the talking at this session, Couve the listening. But at their second meeting, on the following day, the situation was rather different. France had never helped another nation to establish a reactor, and it was out of the question to keep such a matter secret.

Peres replied that Israel was now caught in midstream: to swim back would be just as difficult as to go forwards. Contracts existed, millions of dollars had already been expended. Couve doggedly aired all the opposing considerations, but stopped short of pronouncing negative conclusions.

From Couve's office, a depressed and anxious Peres went to greet Ben-Gurion. The state visit came off successfully, with de Gaulle sparing no effort to demonstrate affection and friendship for his guest. An official luncheon was held in the garden of the presidential palace with 'little tables and chairs set up for drinking coffee. De Gaulle, Ben-Gurion and [Prime Minister Michel] Debré sat at the first table. Emile Rauche [de Gaulle's aide] came up to me and said that General de Gaulle wishes me to join him at his table. When I approached the table he remarked, "You undoubtedly know Paris and its suburbs well." I replied that that was so.' Obviously de Gaulle had been well-briefed about Peres's activities and wanted Peres to know it.

De Gaulle and Ben-Gurion were steeped in animated conversation – on Algeria, philosophy, the world situation – and the *raison d'être* of the visit came up in passing, almost by chance. In the midst of discussing another subject entirely, de Gaulle suddenly leaned towards Ben-Gurion and asked *sotto voce*: 'Tell me frankly, what do you need an atomic reactor for?' Ben-Gurion promised not to develop a bomb. De Gaulle, on his part, promised to reconsider the

French attitude and suggested that Guillaumat and Peres stay in close touch.

The reassessment did not yield the coveted results, however. On 1 August Israeli Ambassador Walter Eytan was summoned to Couve de Murville's office and told unequivocally that if Israel maintained its opposition to disclosure and supervision, France would suspend its aid in building the reactor. Couve added that France would be prepared to compensate Israel for the financial loss that would result from the cancelled assistance.

Now Israel could take one of two courses, which Peres spelled out for Ben-Gurion. One was to accept the compensation from France and acquiesce in the cessation of assistance. The other was to insist that the assistance continue. Peres himself inclined towards the latter option. He realized that it would mean a bitter debate with the French, but contended that Israel would not be the loser on that score. 'Well then,' Ben-Gurion pronounced, 'we'll spar with them and not agree to international supervision.'

It was to conduct this debate that Peres went to France again in November 1960. 'I knew that this time delicate, almost hopeless negotiations awaited us.' He readily admitted to his diary that 'in his opposition, Couve de Murville represents true French interests'.

To prepare for a meeting with Couve, Peres took Isser Pen (the head of the Defence Mission in France) along with him 'to a small hotel in Barbizon, near the Pont Bleu, to escape the din of Paris and work in peace. A few minutes after arriving there, the head waiter told us that a car from the DST [French Intelligence] had arrived and the men were asking about a colonel [Pen] accompanied by a minister. It's very nice of them to be concerned about our well-being,' Peres recorded drily, 'but how in the world they found out about this out-of-the-way place is beyond us.'

Peres arrived at the meeting with Couve and Guillaumat with clearly formulated plans in hand. Insofar as disclosure of the reactor was concerned, he was already resigned to the fact that it could not be avoided. So he arrived at an agreement with the French whereby Israel would continue building the reactor on her own while France would drop her demand for foreign supervision.

Back in Israel, on 20 December Peres held a briefing for aides and officials who were in on the secret of the reactor. He said:

It may well be that in the coming days the Prime Minister will issue a statement confirming that we are building another 24-megawatt atomic reactor. It may be tomorrow, the day after, or next week.

The main points are:

* That the reactor in Nahal [Sorek] does not suffice, and the Dimona reactor is for learning purposes.

* The Dimona reactor, contrary to rumour, is a long-range programme and is designed for the development of the Negev.

* The reactor exists for peaceful purposes.

* The precedent of building this reactor has to do with ourselves.

* No country in the world is subject to international supervision, and those who suggest that Israel should be the first are the same people who advocate the internationalization of Jerusalem.

After the constitution of the Fifth Republic in France, a dispute again erupted between Peres and Golda Meir over the best means of dealing with the administration in Paris. The Foreign Minister argued that the days of 'anarchy' were over in France and were never to return. The habit of people doing whatever they pleased no longer obtained, and the time had come to abandon the ways of secret diplomacy and return to the conventional manner of doing things. In other words: let the Foreign Ministry conduct the contacts with the ruling circles in France.

Peres disagreed with both Golda's assessment and her conclusion. One can discern cracks in the new order, he argued, 'and there's room for manoeuvre via the Defence Ministry'. When they failed to see eye to eye, they at least concurred 'on bringing the dispute before Ben-Gurion'. But before they went to see the Prime Minister, Peres wanted 'to tell Golda two things: I can't require you to act pleasantly towards me, but I wish to avoid giving the impression of acrimony or rivalry. I allow myself to disagree, and what's more I may well make mistakes. All I ask is that you point them out to me immediately, because I don't want to make them. She agreed and promised to do so.'

But it is highly doubtful that she believed his profession of sincerity. 'Afterwards we met at Ben-Gurion's, and Golda and I laid out our positions. He accepted mine.' Nevertheless, to a large degree Golda was right. Peres's great friends, those same people who were prepared to help Israel at almost any price and in almost any way, had already been eased out of the inner circle of power. Peres did not forget them. He made an effort to see them on almost every one of his visits to Paris, even if his schedule was very tight. Bourgès-Maunoury, Abel

Thomas and Louis Mangin came to one such meeting on 22 February 1960.

> It was a reunion tinged with memories, even though their fortunes had changed considerably. Bourgès is now the manager of a large bank. He doesn't believe in de Gaulle or his doctrine. He's in good spirits, though, and good physical condition, because Gentiles have a way of taking sports seriously and dealing with policy amateurishly. Abel Thomas is working in the French Development Ministry. Louis Mangin has been at a loss for work, though not for a living (the Government pays its employees even if they don't work). Today he received an appointment to the Cabinet of the Minister of Demobilized Soldiers. We've all grown a little older, even aged. But the memories of the past are sweet; the phenomenal personal trust makes meetings like this á particular joy.

His visit in February 1960 was to settle a number of vital issues, including the immediate supply of sophisticated Super-Mystère planes which had been agreed upon earlier. This time, however, problems arose. The planes were supposed to be supplied from French air force stocks, and suddenly France claimed that doing so would disrupt the air force's training programme. Peres turned directly to the Commander of the Air Force, General Johue, one of Israel's last outstanding friends. After a short exchange, the General said: 'Now, what did you want? For you, we'll do anything!'

The French General also had a request of his own – proving not only that secret diplomacy had not departed this earth, but it was a two-way affair. The General was not happy with the guided missiles used to arm his planes 'because of their low ceilings'. He believed it was possible to develop a missile 'with a really long range, suitable speed and very high ceiling. But the Government is reluctant to do so.' Yet Peres could help the Government overcome its qualms, the General suggested. How could he do that? By hinting that Israel might be interested in such missiles. He didn't have to commit himself, Johue explained, just express interest.

Peres complied willingly – and Johue was right behind him in complying with Israel's request. Shortly afterwards, on the afternoon of Friday, 11 March 1960, the first six Super-Mystères reached Israel.

> They arrived with French markings and French pilots. The flight went well except over Greece, where Greek planes took off after them. That led one of the planes to break away from the formation and come in six minutes after the rest. The delay might have turned into a disaster, because the delinquent aircraft was about to land in [the Sinai coastal town of] El

Arish! That's all we needed – to have a French Super-Mystère with a French pilot on his way to Israel fall right into the lap of the Egyptians! At the last minute, the pilot realized his mistake and landed his plane at Ekron [in Israel].

The other purpose of Peres's visit was the negotiation for the latest French combat plane, the Mirage. The course of these negotiations reflected the change that Israel's standing had undergone in Paris. For the most part the talks had their ups and downs, because all those who believed that the French connection with Israel was still too strong – particularly quarters in the Quai d'Orsay – exploited the issue to try to weaken that bond. Quite unexpectedly, and in a manner which caused Jersualem great satisfaction, it was none other than President de Gaulle who decided in favour of closing the deal.

Nevertheless, signs of opposition to the sale caused Israel great concern. So much so that, at his meeting with Couve de Murville on 25 February 1960, Peres saw fit to ask 'whether he thinks Israel can rely on France's sustained aid'. Couve was prudent in his reply. Essentially, he reiterated the policy set by de Gaulle: 'Israel's plight must concern the entire Western world, and, most of all, the United States. Naturally, France is part of the Western world and will contribute her part.' But Peres was not satisfied with that rendition. 'Does the Minister object to proclaiming the fact that France continues to stand behind us, as she has for so long?' he pressed. Again Couve was cautious in formulating his reply. 'What do you want to proclaim? The truth about the Mirages?'
Peres: 'No.'
Couve: 'The fact that we're supplying you with arms and planes?'
Peres: 'No. Just the fact that cordial relations continue to exist. A statement of that kind will serve as a deterrent to the Arabs and calm people at home.'
Couve: 'I understand your reasoning, and from your point of view you're right. But we're against it. An announcement of that nature would have an undesirable effect on North Africa. The King of Morocco has just returned from a visit to the Arab countries. We must be careful.'
Peres: 'But his mission failed.'
Couve: 'Quite. But we must nevertheless take into account the Moslem reaction in North Africa.'
Peres: 'Then there are contradictory needs here. What do you do when you come up against a contradiction?'

Couve: 'In political life, when you come up against a contradiction, you speak with two voices.'
Peres: 'Well then, we'll take the tenor. . . .'
About two months later, on 11 May 1960, 'we met in the Defence Minister's office with representatives of three large French companies who had come to sign on the first sale of Mirages. We had arrived at the hour of formally signing a $24 million agreement for twenty-four planes that flew twice the speed of sound.' The era of the Mirage had begun for the Israeli air force. Its predecessor, the Mystère-4, played a key role in defeating the Egyptians during the Sinai Campaign; the swifter and more efficient Mirages would decide the fate of the Six Day War.

One of the most complex deals Peres handled during this period had to do with the purchase of a large quantity of Centurion tanks. The objective was to buy the tanks from a friendly country that was prepared to sell them out of her stocks at a particularly low price. The stumbling-block was that country's refusal to sell directly to Israel.

To overcome this obstacle, Peres went to London, where a change for the worse had likewise taken place in the posture towards Israel. He expressed Israel's concern about this shift in attitude in a talk with Mr Fraser, the Under-Secretary of Defence, on 3 March 1960. 'We have the feeling', he said, 'that London has decided to pander to Nasser again and is ready to play a game based on two sets of rules.' Fraser, a member of the anti-Nasser lobby in the House of Commons, did not deny Peres's reading of the situation. 'Try to understand my problem,' he implored. 'My hands are tied, and I can speak to you only in noncommittal language.'

Peres nevertheless made his bid for Britain to supply Israel with 100 Centurions or to purchase them for her from another, friendly state. Fraser replied that 'the British are willing to buy the tanks for Israel but the Foreign Office has limited the number to thirty tanks.'

'I understand your fear that word may get out,' Peres commiserated, 'and there's always that risk. But I can tell you that it's easier to keep the number of tanks secret than the fact of the sale. A smaller serving of pork will not make the affair any more kosher.'

Fraser understood his reasoning, but stood his ground. 'I should like to make a commitment, but I cannot.' He promised only to have further consultations.

From Fraser's office Peres went to see Deputy Foreign Secretary John Profumo, and the impression he had of his colloquist was telling: 'His black hair and temperament give away what he might prefer to conceal. A man of polished manners and pleasant demeanour, it seemed that he preferred genial relations to unpleasant decisions. His personal connections and many talents – *perhaps more than his character* – are what led him to such a lofty position in England's holy of holies – the Foreign Office.'

'What will happen if Nasser finds out that we're giving you so many heavy tanks?' asked Profumo in a tone of alarm. Peres replied that 'perhaps it will be difficult to keep the existence of the tanks a secret, but the number will not be known, not even to the British military attaché [in Israel] – if his Government wants it that way.'

When Profumo likewise promised no more than to consult further, Peres realized that his salvation was not to be sought in Britain. This led him to another European state in which popular support for Israel was a byword. He met the Defence Minister and made the same request that had fallen flat in London: the purchase of tanks on Israel's behalf.

The Defence Minister had a number of practical questions: 'How would he explain the purchase of Centurions without the permission of his Parliament? Secondly, if he keeps the matters secret, how would he explain the considerable outlay? And what happens if word gets out? How would the Arabs react? Of course they were assuming complete secrecy, but how could this secrecy be assured at the source? And at the final destination?'

Peres offered him the following solutions:

The tanks could be purchased by a local company, rather than by the Government, thereby obviating the need for parliamentary approval. The company would purchase the tanks under the guise of 'spare parts'. If word got out at the start of the journey, it would hardly be a sensation that a private company was buying spare parts for tanks. If it became known while the ships were in the Mediterranean, the story would be that Israel had sent a number of Centurions for overhaul and the company had purchased spare parts for this purpose. Since the Centurions had been refurbished, they were returning home. The loading would be done all at once, on two or three large 'Liberty' boats destined for the European country. Once in the Mediterranean, they would change course and make for Israel. As to the port in Haifa, we are experienced in unloading at night. All the arms from France came in after dark.

The scenario rattled off by the young man from Israel evidently astonished the Defence Minister somewhat, for he remarked: 'We are innocent babes when it comes to such things.' Peres therefore suggested that Israel send 'one of our people to supervise the whole operation'. This suggestion was accepted. Afterwards Peres wrote in his diary of his admiration for 'this friendly people prepared to take risks for a distant friend – and not for the sake of winning a prize'.

A new initiative on Nasser's part went a long way towards escalating the tension between Israel and her neighbours: the Egyptian President signed an agreement unifying Egypt and Syria into the United Arab Republic. The more popular Nasser became, the more he stepped up his verbal and operative belligerence towards Israel. The rising tension obliged Israel both to maintain a state of constant readiness and to adopt measures designed to gnaw away at Nasser's power. One such initiative testifies to Israel's unusual role in the life of the region.

On 4 May 1960, Slade Baker, the correspondent of *The Times* of London, came to Peres's office. When Baker had asked for the meeting, Peres naturally assumed that it was for journalistic purposes. In fact, his guest came bearing a request that one does not hear very often from a newsman. Baker said that in London he had recently met General Shihab, the Commander of the Lebanese army. Elections to the Lebanese Parliament were scheduled to take place on 12 May and, fearing disturbances, the Government had decided to have the army supervise the balloting. But Shihab knew that the army was riddled with pro-Nasserite officers, and he feared that they would use the opportunity to propagandize and otherwise stir up trouble.

How could Israel help? Actually, it was rather simple. A few days before the elections, Shihab wanted the IDF to create an atmosphere of disquiet along the Lebanese border. This would provide him with the necessary pretext to send part of the army – and he would make sure it was the pro-Nasserite part – down to the border, thereby getting it out of the way. All that was needed was for Israel to fire off a few shots, and she would be doing a great service to the Christians of Lebanon.

Baker did not ask Peres for an answer and didn't get one – at least not right away. The Defence Ministry's reply became evident in a practical manner a few days later and served as the first link in a chain which ultimately led to close co-operation between Israel and the Christian section of the population in Lebanon.

The flow of weapons into Israel did not distract attention from the aim of building a local industry to provide better arms at a lower cost than purchase from abroad. The most significant step in this direction was taken on 1 July 1960, and Peres was unable to conceal his excitement when he described it in his diary:

A ceremony took place in the afternoon, the culmination of many debates, efforts, hopes and difficulties over many years. At 4.30 I went to the aircraft industry with Ben-Gurion. Some 4,000 people were seated in the plaza, including employees, Ministers, foreign diplomats and represent-atives from all walks of life. Within a painted circle, modest but lovely, stood the first Fouga-Magister manufactured in the country. Last night I was still looking for a name for it, and *Snonit* ['Swallow'] caught my fancy. Planes must be named after birds, just as submarines are named after fish. It is the first swallow, and I was also taken by a verse from the Talmud: 'A swallow may frighten an eagle.' More than 50 per cent of the jet is manufactured in the country, and that is a major achievement. The Old Man seemed very excited, and he began his speech by saying, 'If I were a religious man and wore a *kippah* [yarmulka; skull-cap], I would take my hat off to Al Schwimmer.' Al was very moved and read his Hebrew speech in a pronounced American accent. He was very gracious in describing me as 'the pillar of the aircraft industry'.

The ceremony marked the end of a long and bumpy road along which Peres had found himself up against almost wall-to-wall opposition. The Government's Economic Ministers groused that the plan to assemble and manufacture sophisticated weaponry in Israel was wasteful and profitless. Others feared the prospect of diplomatic complications. Even the army was against it! In a memorandum to the Defence Minister, written in response to Peres's recommendation in favour, Chief of Staff Chaim Laskov wrote, with more than a hint of sarcasm, that it would be best if the faith Peres had expressed in the industry were based first on its ability to supply spare parts for weapons such as bazookas, flamethrowers, new mines and the like.

But Peres refused to confine the purpose of *Bedek* to servicing aircraft. He wanted to establish a plant that would manufacture the entire range of products in the aeronautics field – particularly planes, but missiles as well. The first locally manufactured missile was inaugurated about three months before the Fouga-Magister's first flight. As we can see from Peres's description, it was not a particularly formidable weapon, but his pride in it was no less for that fact.

At two in the afternoon [on 2 April 1960], I flew by helicopter to the Negev, where the test of the G-25 missile was being held. The missile can be launched from a plane, ship or command car to a distance that reaches up to 30 kilometres. Three missiles were fired in that breathtaking landscape of tattered mountains and plateaus. The first one got off the ground, but immediately plummeted down for reasons unknown. However, the other two missiles – light, magic creatures – flew a distance of 16 kilometres and hit the bull's-eye whitewashed on one of the facing hills. The impact was superb. And the two officers who directed the missiles – a navy man and an air force man – did so with considerable skill and confidence, despite the excitement all around. Scoring that target brought to a successful conclusion an uninterrupted effort of four years of work, perseverance and research. And it provides the IDF with both a new weapon and an entrée into the complex world of guided missiles. Other nations have invested tens of millions of dollars just to reach the initial stage, and what we couldn't achieve with money we achieved through the talent and devotion of our workers. It was a fine and promising day for Israeli science, the defence effort and the project's management.

The name *Bedek* was changed to the Israel Aircraft Industry, and henceforward it soared to heights that even Peres had not dreamed of during those freezing nights in Newfoundland. A daughter company was established alongside the main plant, and together they produced planes for a variety of needs, including the Arava STOL plane, which was a big seller in the developing countries, and the Westwind Executive Jet, which has become a very popular model in the United States and Europe.

The manufacture of missiles enjoyed a terrific impetus, which climaxed with the sea-to-sea Gabriel missile mounted on gunboats and the Reshef- and Keshet-class seacraft. In its wake came sophisticated air-to-air missiles. Meanwhile, the production system had expanded to include a wide variety of communications equipment, radar systems, computers, testing equipment, electronic equipment used in medicine and a series of control systems for use in the air, at sea and on land. In fact, the Israel Aircraft Industry has become the largest industrial enterprise in the State of Israel.

The *pièce de résistance* of local manufacture was the Kfir fighter-bomber. Some fifteen years later, on 14 April 1975, the first model was turned over to the Israeli air force as a gift from the aircraft industry on the twenty-sixth anniversary of the State of Israel. On that day, Shimon Peres had occasion to recall the swim he had taken in the Sea of Galilee twenty-four years earlier. Schwimmer and he had manufactured a jet, as they said they would.

In mid-1960, quite out of the blue, the old affair of the 1954 sabotage operations in Egypt came up again and ominously inched its way to the centre of the stage.★ It had seemed that the incident was over and done with, and it might have been if new information had not now come into Pinhas Lavon's hands. It was supplied by Colonel Yosef Harel, formerly a member of the IDF's Intelligence Branch, and consisted of material implying that Benjamin Jibli and others had forged Intelligence documents to clear Jibli of all responsibility for 'the unfortunate business' and place the blame squarely on Lavon, thus forcing him to resign as Defence Minister.

Lavon took the new evidence straight to Ben-Gurion and demanded that his name be cleared. Ben-Gurion managed to put him off by promising to look into the matter and charged his Military Secretary, Chaim Ben-David, with the task. When Ben-David's conclusions (submitted to the Prime Minister some two months later) indicated that forgery and the destruction of documents had indeed occurred, he ordered Chief of Staff Laskov to appoint a new board of inquiry (this one headed by Supreme Court Judge Chaim Cohen and including two army officers). But this latest step infuriated Lavon, who wanted a full exoneration without further ado. Ben-Gurion turned him down flat.

At this point the press began to publish items about the revival of the affair and almost without exception demanded that the injustice to Lavon be remedied forthwith, without waiting for the results of the Cohen Commission's investigation. Ben-Gurion stood his ground by explaining that, present evidence notwithstanding, the Prime Minister was not authorized to exonerate anyone without an investigation. He had nothing against Lavon, he said, but the matter must be examined in an organized and legal fashion.

Drawing encouragement from the press and supportive public opinion, Lavon decided to challenge Ben-Gurion head on. He asked for the opportunity to testify before the Knesset Foreign Affairs and Defence Committee and was permitted to do so. His testimony, which extended over four sessions, was subsequently leaked to the press and had the entire state in a dither – *Mapai* and Ben-Gurion included.

At these hearings Lavon related his version of 'the unfortunate business' and placed responsibility for the abortive action on Jibli and his men. He also told of the forgeries and other underhand doings. In fact, he attacked the entire defence establishment, charging that it

★ See pages 32–4.

suffered from 'economic imperialism', waste and faulty organization. Speaking of military operations which had ostensibly been executed behind his back – and had therefore taken a toll of unnecessary victims – he pointed an accusing finger at Dayan and Peres. While conceding that they were not parties to the sabotage operations in Egypt or the forged documents, Lavon none the less charged that they had exploited the affair to get him out of the way. To illustrate how he had been subverted, he claimed that in 1954 Peres had testified against him – his own superior – before the Dori-Olshan Commission. The proof was that when asked what he had told the commission, Peres refused to say!

Peres was abroad at the time of Lavon's appearances before the Foreign Affairs and Defence Committee, but on his return he consulted Ben-Gurion and made an appearance of his own to give his version of events. With the aid of documents, he demolished every one of Lavon's claims about the defence establishment. As to his own testimony before the Dori-Olshan Commission, Peres said that he had been admonished by the committee chairman to 'keep the entire matter secret, even the fact that he had testified'. He had, therefore, refrained from telling Lavon about it. He firmly denied Lavon's allegation that he had spoken against his superior. (Several years later, in his memoirs, Judge Olshan confirmed Peres's version of that testimony.)

Peres also addressed himself to another of Lavon's charges, namely, that he and Dayan had regularly met Ben-Gurion behind Lavon's back.

> I see no need to justify my consultations with Mr D. Ben-Gurion on any matter on which he is prepared to give his advice. After all, is there anyone in this country whose advice on a defence matter is more valuable than Ben-Gurion? Has the state willingly waived such advice, or has Mr Ben-Gurion asked to be relieved from providing it? Obviously you can view this negatively, if your Minister considers it an invasion of his jurisdiction. But Mr Lavon not only failed to prohibit such contact, he personally told of one or two meetings that he held with Mr Ben-Gurion, *inter alia*, on the subject of 'the relations of the Defence Minister with his subordinates'. It was never intimated to me that such contact was forbidden or undesirable. It was Mr Ben-Gurion who imposed restrictions on the matter of contact with him.

But all the protestations were to no avail. Lavon became the public's darling, Peres its black sheep. Once again the press adopted a double standard. Lavon told the Knesset committee that it was beneath his dignity to consult Dayan and Peres; the press mentioned only Peres – and added, in complete disregard of the facts, that Dayan had been loyal to Lavon and Peres had not.

Ben-Gurion fiercely defended his deputy in articles, letters to editors and personal letters, speaking of Peres as the one 'who ran the defence network with rare talent', as a man 'whom few have matched in working for the country'. His support touched Peres very deeply. 'Throughout the debate, I never turned to Ben-Gurion or ever asked him to stand up for me,' he told the senior officials of the Defence Ministry. 'I was moved by the extraordinary friendship that he displayed towards a man whose "case" seemed pretty wretched. He did it without saying a word. I don't know of any example of such a busy man finding time to defend the honour of his disciple, friend or official – and so unpretentiously – the way Ben-Gurion has. I cite it as a paragon of conduct.'

But for all that, Ben-Gurion's defence did not help much, especially since his own prestige was beginning to suffer. The damage done to values he cherished above all else and to men he admired and respected had roused him out of a position of neutrality. Embarking on a frontal attack against Lavon, for the first time since the establishment of the state Ben-Gurion found himself in the position of the underdog.

In the interim, the Cohen Commission wound up its work by concluding that there had indeed been forgeries as well as pressures leading to perjury. This verdict strengthened the hand of those calling for Lavon's full exoneration. But now Ben-Gurion insisted that only a legal investigation would bring out the truth. The press pronounced this latest claim as wanting in sincerity: not a thirst for truth and justice were behind Ben-Gurion's crusade, but a desire to conceal the failures of the defence establishment and those running it.

The leaders of *Mapai* could no longer stand idly by. Indeed, Finance Minister Levi Eshkol attempted to hammer out a compromise that would settle the dispute. But he was already too late to salvage the situation, for Ben-Gurion no longer considered Lavon's sin as merely having tarnished sacred values. After studying the matter thoroughly, he was convinced that Lavon, not just Jibli, was to blame for 'the unfortunate business' – and this conclusion made him all the more obdurate about a legal investigation.

On 30 October 1960, the Cabinet decided to establish a committee of seven Ministers, chaired by Justice Minister Pinhas Rosen, to examine how the affair should be handled. In the course of its work, however, the committee exceeded the bounds of its competence and delved into the question of who gave the order. This excess of zeal came to Ben-Gurion's attention, but curiously enough he did nothing about it.

What brought on the sudden quiescence? Had Ben-Gurion lost interest in the affair? Was its outcome a matter of indifference to him? These questions vexed the 'Youngsters', so much so that when Peres met Yitzhak Navon on 18 November 1960, 'we were both distressed about what was going on. We decided to go into action within the Party and *vis-à-vis* the press to elevate Ben-Gurion's prestige and raise the subject of the committee [of Ministers] again. But we were no longer sure that we were representing something and someone who wanted it.'

The next morning Peres met Dayan privately. 'I argued that we can't remain indifferent to the [latest] developments. Moshe again warned that we mustn't interfere.' But the state of uncertainty could not go on. In the afternoon Dayan and Peres met Navon 'and Yitzhak suggested that we go to Ben-Gurion and talk to him frankly'.

> At 3.45 we went up to Ben-Gurion and found him dressed in a robe, pale and calmer than he has been of late (he looked very depressed during the past week). He expressed surprise at the match of Moshe Dayan (agriculture) and myself, but I think that this time he heard frank, basic Hebrew, the likes of which he may never have heard before.

Moshe Dayan started out by telling Ben-Gurion in no uncertain terms that if the present situation continued he would cease to be anything more than a figurehead. If he intended to fight, he had to lay things on the line and say: either Lavon or me. If he did so quickly, there was still a chance of winning a majority; but if he dragged his feet, people would stop taking him seriously.

Peres added his impression that everyone was terrified by the idea of an investigation because of what it might uncover. It was not a static situation, he warned.

> If, through blackmail and fear, one can get whatever one wants out of the leadership, there will be increasing use of these means, and we will turn into a sick society. Postponing the inevitable doesn't solve anything. The closer we come to the elections, the more the fear will grow. What's more, fear won't remain inside the Party. And once it gets out, everyone will know the truth. This is no longer a Party that has a vision and a path; it is a Party in which no one believes anyone else.

Ben-Gurion's indecision had already prompted a certain degree of tension between Peres and Dayan. A few days after the meeting with the Old Man, the two returned to the subject of how to proceed.

He [Dayan] warned that we must not interfere in the dispute with Lavon, lest everyone else turn tail and leave the two of us alone in the ring. I argued that it's risky to leave a hiatus of inaction that might be interpreted as fear or evasiveness. But Moshe countered that there's no getting round it. The decision is in the Old Man's hands, and as long as he fails to exhibit a fighting spirit ('he really has got old'), there's nothing to be done. I noted that he [Ben-Gurion] remains alone in the field.

While the Youngsters agonized, the committee of Ministers pulled the chestnuts out of the fire for them. On 21 December 1960, they submitted their conclusions: 'We hereby determine that Lavon did not give the order and that "the unfortunate business" was not executed with his knowledge.'

The days of wavering were over. Ben-Gurion erupted like a volcano, calling the committee's mode of operation 'biased and [based on] half-truths' and its conclusions 'devoid of truth and justice'. Once again he appealed for a legal investigation, 'which is the only possible way to get at the truth. Witnesses are cross-examined, people are pitched against each other, both sides have lawyers, lawyers interrogate and sum up.' In even tones he asked the members of the Cabinet: 'What is this fear you have of a legal board of inquiry?'

But by now the Ministers, and especially the veteran *Mapai* Ministers, were fed up with the affair and their only desire was to remove it from the national agenda. Arguing that continued preoccupation with the affair would cause incalculable damage to the Party, they insisted that the conclusions of the Rosen committee be accepted as the end of the matter. Ben-Gurion retorted that the truth came before the Party.

When the Cabinet, none the less, voted to accept the conclusions of the Rosen committee, the *Mapai* Ministers were confident that Ben-Gurion would accept their decision. But Peres knew him better. 'Those conclusions will force Ben-Gurion to resign,' he recorded in his diary. 'It is obvious that unless Lavon goes, Ben-Gurion will not stay.' Equally clear was the fact that Peres was dismayed by that prospect, and he tried to reason with the Old Man.

But Ben-Gurion was past persuasion. On 31 January 1961, he submitted his resignation to the President – which meant the resignation of the entire Cabinet. There can be no question that viewed from the vantage of moral standards and the desire for truth, his demand for a legal inquiry was justified. But he lumped it together with a personal vendetta against Lavon, thereby weakening his position on grounds of principle and rendering his cause unpopular.

Mapai was in the throes of panic. Rattled by the extreme step which Ben-Gurion had taken, its leaders embarked on an hysterical scramble to find some compromise and reverse the mean decree. But Ben-Gurion would no longer settle for anything less than Lavon's head.

And they gave it to him. Cynically, hideously, brutally. On Saturday, 4 February 1961, when the *Mapai* Central Committee met behind closed doors, Levi Eshkol stood up and proposed that Lavon be dismissed as Secretary-General of the *Histadrut*. After a debate, the committee accepted the proposal. Ben-Gurion had his way, but he paid a high price for it. The Old Guard would not easily forgive him for forcing it to yield so abjectly to his dictates. No longer could he rely on the automatic support of Levi Eshkol, Pinhas Sapir, Golda Meir, Zalman Aranne or their associates. Ben-Gurion had set in train a process that would grind on inexorably until the end of his rule.

For the present, however, he agreed to rescind his resignation and form a new Government. Then another obstacle arose: he was unable to forge a coalition because *Mapam* and *Ahdut Ha'avodah* objected to his leadership. He therefore suggested to his own Party that a new Government be constituted without him and even proposed candidates for the post of Defence Minister. First priority went to Peres. 'I would suggest Peres for Minister of Defence, but if that arouses opposition among key comrades, I won't insist on it.' As a second choice 'you can take Dayan and appoint another comrade as Minister of Agriculture'. And in third place, 'perhaps you can turn to Yadin'. But *Mapai* was not exactly snapping at Ben-Gurion's offer to retire. So the only choice left was to go to the polls in a general election, which was held on 15 August 1961. The Lavon Affair cost *Mapai* five seats, but at least Ben-Gurion was able to form a Government. Peres was again appointed Deputy Minister of Defence.

In the course of a visit to France in February 1960, Peres 'dropped over' to Germany for another secret visit with Defence Minister Strauss, this time accompanied by Moshe Dayan. As in the past, their talk began with a direct question from Strauss: 'What can I do for you?' Peres had a three-part reply. First, aid in the development of a missile. (In return, Peres proposed showing the Germans, 'for their interest', the recoilless artillery which Israel had captured during one of the reprisal raids over the border.) Second, a small submarine. (To overcome the 'difficulties', Peres suggested that it be referred to as 'marine equipment and components'.) Third, the loan of Nord-Atlas cargo planes (which were built in Germany under French licence).

Strauss made it plain that he would have to report to Adenauer about the deal, but he assured his guests that the Chancellor 'is a discreet man'. Suppressing a smile, Peres asked whether the same could be said of von Brentano (the German Foreign Minister), and Strauss permitted himself to laugh. 'How right you are,' he said, and both of them understood that Adenauer would be the only recipient of the information.

At the beginning of March 1960, the historic meeting between the Premiers of Israel and West Germany took place at the Waldorf Astoria Hotel in New York. Ben-Gurion received confirmation of the Peres-Strauss deal and much more than that: a grant of $500 million for developing the state, in addition to the supply of armaments without remuneration. This agreement consolidated an arms-supply triangle which Peres described to the IDF's General Staff as follows: 'If America gives us funds but not arms, and if France gives us arms for cash, the Germans give us arms without remuneration. This German policy has now been confirmed subject to a number of limitations – the most important of which is secrecy. If word of it gets out, there's no hope of it lasting.'

Peres met Adenauer for the first time on 8 June 1962. 'We left . . . for Bonn by car and at 4.30 were in the Chancellor's office. A surprise awaits the visitor immediately upon entering that room. From behind a small desk rises a tall man with a light step and excellent hearing who reads without glasses and whose movements are free of any sign of fatigue or age. Whoever has not seen this with his own eyes will not believe that he is the eighty-six year old Adenauer.'

After exchanging views on various subjects, Peres spelled out Israel's security needs. 'Adenauer said: "We've helped you up till now and we'll help you in the future. We have common problems and a common enemy [Communism]. But I also consider it a debt we owe to Israel, and there's no need to go into the reasons why." '

Peres went on to enumerate Israel's requests to Defence Minister Strauss, whom he saw again about a month after meeting Adenauer (11 July 1962). Now, however, he found the dynamic, buoyant Bavarian in a melancholy mood, smarting from political wounds. The German press was hounding him and had published a number of muckraking articles which were very damaging to his image. 'He nurtured plans to retire from office, and so – and perhaps also out of a desire to place aid to Israel on a broader governmental footing – he was eager to receive the final confirmation from the Chancellor, the approval of the Foreign Minister and support from the socialist opposition.' The list of items discussed in the framework of the German grant was both impressive and unprecedented in the history of relations between the two countries: twenty-four helicopters; twelve Nord transport planes; six Nasti Norwegian torpedo-boats; fifty-four Bofors anti-aircraft guns; fifty-six Brist mobile cannon; three 350-ton submarines; 1,000 Cobra anti-tank missiles.

The next morning Strauss sent Adenauer a letter to the effect that in accordance with the Chancellor's instructions, he had discussed Israel's requests with Peres and now enclosed a list thereof. From a military and technical viewpoint, the requests could be fulfilled. However, there were certain difficulties pertaining to secrecy, and for that reason Strauss asked that the number of people let in on the deal be kept as small as possible. In the light of past experience, he wrote, there was no question of the Israelis' ability to maintain secrecy. As to the Occlides (a new tank), there were still certain doubts, which were brought to Peres's attention. Finally, from a financial standpoint the matter could be arranged by exploiting a certain clause in the existing budget and by a special allocation, which could be arranged in one of two ways. Moreover, there was nothing to fear from the opposition's reaction.

Strauss saw Adenauer on 17 July and Peres subsequently reported to Ben-Gurion on the agreement reached at that meeting:

> The upshot, relayed in veiled language, is that the Chancellor approved the items of German manufacture and, as in the past, they will be transferred via France. This decision places the submarines in question. Taking into consideration the fact that it is no simple matter for any country to decide to give arms to Israel – not to mention providing them without financial remuneration – and considering Strauss's special position, the effort that has been made to meet our requests, while not overwhelming, is nothing to sneeze at, either.

Yet co-operation between Israel and Germany extended beyond the sphere of arms supplies. Strauss was about to visit Communist China and conceded to Peres's request that he talk to Chairman Mao about establishing diplomatic relations with Israel. One day, when Peres was on a tour of the navy, an excited secretary ran up to him and spluttered that he had a call from China. On the line from Peking was none other than Strauss, reporting that Mao's reaction had been negative. His reason: 'How can we do that when they get arms from America and soldiers from Russia?' What did he mean, soldiers from Russia? It turned out that the venerable Chinese leader was referring to the Jewish emigrants coming to Israel.

On the occasion of another meeting with Strauss, in the Minister's home (9 February 1962), Peres brought along a visitor, the thirty-two-year old Tom Mboya, one of the most prominent leaders of Kenya. Dressed in a tailored suit, the guest seemed somewhat ill at ease, but full of gratitude to Peres for having arranged the meeting with Strauss and in such a homely atmosphere. As they sat sipping Madeira, 'Mboya lectured Strauss on the situation in Kenya and warned of the danger of a complete Soviet takeover by means of local communist groups supported by Moscow. He spoke animatedly of his visit to Israel and of the assurances he had received regarding aid in training a group of officers.'

To Strauss's question, 'How can I help?' Peres answered that what Israel was giving Kenya in terms of training, Germany should provide in the form of equipment. Then and there Strauss ordered his aide to work in consultation with Israeli representatives in preparing 'a list of the equipment that independent Kenya needs to fight the subversive forces. Tom was delighted, and Strauss was also pleased with extending the scope of his activity.'

Thus the co-operation between Israel and Germany extended into many spheres and continued to branch out. But at the height of its florescence, an event occurred which almost brought it to an abrupt end.

Four days after Peres's meeting with Strauss on 21 July 1962, President Nasser used the occasion of an impressive military parade to unveil four ground-to-ground missiles of two types. The first, e-Zafar, had a range of 28 kilometres; the other, el-Kahar, a range of 560 kilometres. Bristling with pride and arrogance, the Egyptian ruler told an exultant crowd that his country could now hit any target in Israel.

This news struck Israel like a bolt from the blue (it was one of the worst failures of Israel's Intelligence network), and the first question was, how had Nasser managed to get his hands on such weapons. A hasty probe revealed that the missiles had been developed in Egypt with the aid of German scientists hired specifically for that purpose, and Egypt intended to build 500 of the short-range missiles and 400 of the long-range ones. The only solace was that the scientists were having problems with the guidance system, so the missiles were not yet operational.

Peres had returned to Israel and to the strident debate about how to proceed. Foreign Minister Golda Meir argued that the German authorities knew about the work of their scientists in Egypt, and, if they didn't encourage it outright, they certainly hadn't taken any steps to impede it. Her accusations received considerable support from Isser Harel, the head of the *Mossad*, and together they led the lobby which demanded that vigorous and uncompromising action be taken against the German Government.

But Ben-Gurion scoffed at the charges of collusion or involvement of any kind on the part of the German Government. The information at his disposal convinced him that the German scientists were working in Egypt without Bonn's knowledge and against her will, and he resisted any action that might disrupt the programme of co-operation between the two countries. Instead of making an official approach to the German Government, he instructed Peres to turn to Strauss directly and personally. Peres sent a cable to the German Defence Minister informing him of Israel's findings and urging him to exercise his influence to halt the scientists' activities in Egypt. When Strauss replied that the German constitution denied the federal government any authority over the actions of her citizens abroad, his answer only added fuel to the debate. Ben-Gurion and Peres accepted it at face value; Golda and Harel considered it an evasion and even proof of the German Government's complicity.

Strauss added in his letter, however, that if Israel supplied proof of the scientists' activities in Egypt, he would try to do something despite the constitutional restrictions. This rider prompted Peres to order Major-General Meir Amit, the chief of IDF Intelligence, to double-check Harel's findings. The conclusions of Intelligence Branch were that things weren't really as bad as they had been made to seem. Actually, the Egyptian venture was closer to science fiction than to science.

It was not until later that Ben-Gurion's reason for distinguishing between the flap over the scientists and the issue of relations with Germany came to light. At the time secret negotiations on the constitution of full diplomatic relations between the two countries were entering an advanced stage. At their New York meeting,

Adenauer had promised Ben-Gurion that relations would be established before he retired from political life, and the time of his departure was looming closer. Ben-Gurion was eager to conclude the negotiations successfully. Peres, however, was markedly less enthusiastic: 'I do not regret that there are people in the State of Israel who object to relations with Germany. It would be a tragedy if they didn't.'

This was an emotional sentiment, but his lukewarm reaction had a pragmatic side as well: 'If I were asked which is preferable, relations between the two Defence Ministries without diplomatic recognition or diplomatic relations without defence ties, it seems to me that the answer is obvious. Diplomatic relations are not always preferable.' Undoubtedly this outlook was influenced by his experience in working with France. Diplomatic relations, by their very nature, lead to the institutionalization of ties, usually through the two countries' Foreign Ministries. Peres believed that the more official the channels, the poorer the results. At the same time, he feared that Germany would come to regard full diplomatic recognition as a form of paying its moral debt to Israel, in place of military and financial aid. In time, Israel would have occasion to see that this fear was well-founded.

At the start of 1963, there were signs of a possible shift in the United States' policy of military assistance to Israel. The item the Israelis wanted most from the United States was the Hawk anti-aircraft missile. When he visited Washington in June 1961, Ben-Gurion asked President Kennedy to allow Israel to purchase the missiles, and about a year later he received the reply that the President had decided to comply with his request. But there was a price attending that decision: Israel's approval of an American plan to solve the problem of the Palestinian refugees. The programme called for the refugees to decide whether they wished to return to Israel or settle permanently in the Arab countries in which they were presently living. Ben-Gurion considered the price exorbitant and decided to forgo the plan together with the Hawks.

Despite Ben-Gurion's rebuff of his plan, Kennedy did not relent on the refugee issue. In January 1963 he announced a new proposal calling on Israel to take in 20 per cent of the Palestinians. At the same time, he revived the negotiations for the sale of the Hawk missiles and, as in 1961, the issue of the reactor was drawn into the affair.

The refugee proposal was quickly disposed of, primarily because of opposition from the Arab states and the Palestinians themselves. But the residual linkage between the Hawks and the reactor brought the old debate in Jerusalem to life again. The Americans called on Israel to allow them free access to and full supervision of the Dimona reactor. Peres thought that their price was too steep, even considering the return, and, during a consultation at the Prime Minister's Office on 16 January 1963, he mused aloud that if it wasn't possible to obtain the Hawks from the United States, 'What about getting them from Europe?' The very notion sparked Golda's anger. 'We're back to where we were a few years ago,' she growled. 'We must have some kind of allergy to America. The moment that she – with great effort – starts to take a baby step in our direction, suddenly we recall that actually we can get the same thing elsewhere. That's exactly what happened with the radar.'

Peres: 'It took them a year to check [the radar] out.'

Golda: 'When did we discover that it was possible to get it in Europe? When the Americans were willing to provide it.'

Peres: 'No one is suggesting going elsewhere.'

Finally, Ben-Gurion pronounced, 'We're not breaking off negotiations with America on this matter. That much is certain.' And it's a good thing they didn't. In fact, Peres himself went to Washington at the beginning of April 1963 to conclude the deal. At an informal dinner-party, he had the opportunity to gauge the change in the American attitude towards Israel's reactor. During a conversation on the subject, the highly influential Senator Stuart Symington admonished him: 'Don't be a bunch of fools. Don't stop making atomic bombs. And don't listen to the administration. Do whatever you think best.'

Even the administration had become less sensitive about the issue, as Peres found out from the President himself. After a meeting with presidential assistant Mike Feldman, he was ushered into John Kennedy's office for a brief greeting. Harold Wilson was waiting in the adjoining room, so that Kennedy could not accord Peres more than a handshake. But that afternoon, Peres was with McGeorge Bundy, another presidential assistant, when Mike Feldman called to say that the President was sorry he could not talk to Peres that morning and was inviting him to come over immediately. As they walked over to Kennedy's office, Feldman told Peres that at the last minute the President had cancelled a meeting with congressional leaders to make time for a chat with him.

> We entered the President's room (a fairly nice room, nothing extraordinary; we've seen nicer) and then the President came in. I was surprised to see

that he has such a small face – a small forehead, dark blond hair mixed with a lot of grey, lines on his brow. He looked pretty tired, and his large grey eyes reflect a semi-sardonic smile. He has a quick grasp of things, really telepathic, and an extraordinary familiarity with the subject. An up-to-date man who reads the papers, he knows what's going on in the world and the region and has an excellent memory. Nevertheless, he conducts himself pretty informally. You don't get the feeling that here sits the President of the most powerful country in the world, a man whose very name arouses excitement. He speaks very fluently, and you can immediately see that here is a man who can't stand being bored. He's succinct and quick and expects you to be so, too; to ask a direct and pointed question and give a clear answer. Our conversation began without any games. Actually it was his conversation. He interrogated me throughout that half-hour.

Kennedy tried to get at the subject of the reactor indirectly, beginning with the question: 'What missiles have been introduced into the area?'

Peres: 'There are four types of missiles in Egypt today. Recently, missiles have been mounted on torpedo-boats.'

Kennedy: 'What? They have Komar boats?'

Peres: 'Yes. They received them recently.'

Kennedy: 'How many?'

Peres: 'By now, four.'

Kennedy: 'They have a range of 16 miles, don't they?'

Peres: 'Correct. That's 30 kilometres with a 750-kilogram warhead. In addition, they've got air-to-air missiles and ground-to-air missiles from the Russians. The fourth kind is ground-to-ground missiles.'

Kennedy: 'They didn't get those from the Russians.'

Peres: 'We have no evidence that the Russians supplied them with those missiles. They are being developed with German assistance.'

Kennedy: 'West Germany helping them?'

Peres: 'Not the Government; German scientists and technicians. At present that missile is the most accurate. It has a range of 500 kilometres.'

Kennedy: 'How many do they have and when will they become operational?'

Peres: 'They have thirty today, and they will be operational within a year and a half.'

Kennedy: 'Can you explain to me what brought about the resignation of the man who resigned during the past twenty-four hours [Isser Harel, the chief of the *Mossad*]?'

Peres: 'I must explain that any subject touching upon Germany is an especially sensitive and delicate matter in Israel. The debate is over a question of proportion, nothing else. No one forced him to resign, but because of the sensitivity of the issue, the man felt that he should submit his resignation.'

At this point Kennedy began to press a little. 'On this subject of the missiles, the danger is that there's no point in having missiles unless you place nonconventional warheads on them. Don't you agree that the warheads are more dangerous than the missiles?'

Peres: 'Let me say that a missile with a conventional warhead is very different from a bomb released from a plane. The main feature of the missile is that it is unmanned. It sows terror and enhances the sense of power of those who employ it, because there are no effective means of defence against it.'

Kennedy: 'That's true. But as you know, the atomic warheads are more dangerous than the missiles.'

Peres: 'The missiles exist already, while the atomic warheads won't be around for a long time – if at all.'

Now Kennedy began speaking more explicitly. 'You know that we follow with great interest every indication that an atomic capability is being developed in the region. It would create a very perilous situation. That's why we have been diligent about keeping an eye on your effort in the atomic field. What can you tell me about that?'

'I can tell you forthrightly that we will not introduce atomic weapons into the region. We certainly won't be the first to do so. We have no interest in that. On the contrary, our interest is in de-escalating the armament tension, even in total disarmament.' (This affirmation that Israel would not be the first country to introduce atomic weapons into the area became the official statement of policy for all Israeli Governments to come.)

Kennedy contented himself with this answer on the atomic issue and went on to a series of other subjects. 'How would you suggest dealing with the matter of the missiles and the arms?'

Peres: 'As I see it, handling it through diplomatic means is preferable to force of arms. I don't see how you will be able to persuade the Soviets to hold back weapons while the Egyptians are clamouring for them. If it depended on us alone, we would be willing to renounce arms altogether. You must remember that we are a democratic country. . . . We face pressures to move forwards in the fields of development, education, socal integration. And there's a natural inclination to deal with these problems instead of building up weapons stocks. So when we speak of the diplomatic approach having preference, it's not because it's more desirable for us but because it's more realistic.'

Kennedy: 'What are you getting at?'

Peres: 'I'm referring to a declaration accompanied by the means to keep the peace.'

Kennedy: 'Doesn't the declaration of the Three Powers apply?'

Peres: 'The declaration of the Three Powers was made long ago. It's out of date, full of loopholes, and it didn't stand up to the test in 1956. Relations between America, France and England aren't what they used to be, and so the formulation is also full of holes.'

Kennedy: 'Let me ask you two questions. First, don't you think that if we were to make a declaration like that, we would have to commit ourselves to the Lebanese, the Jordanians, the Saudis, etc.? Wouldn't that leave the impression that we are establishing ourselves as the final judge? What would we ourselves think, for example, if Russia made such a declaration? There's also another question, but answer that one first.'

Peres: 'There's a difference in the nature of the dispute between Israel and Egypt and between Egypt and the Arab states. The risk of war shadows these two countries, just as the prospect of peace attends these two most of all. The United States' great prestige would not suffer if she came out openly not in favour of someone but against something, namely, any attempt to alter the *status quo* by force.'

Kennedy: 'The second question. Does that also apply to Egypt, meaning, are you asking for a unilateral declaration in favour of Israel or a declaration that will protect Egypt as well?'

Peres: 'As an Israeli, naturally I am talking about Israel. We have no aggressive intentions, and I doubt that you will be able to reach any agreement with Nasser, as you can with us. This time we're talking not about limited intervention in time of war, but intervention to avert a war.'

Kennedy: 'What formulation would you suggest?'

Peres: 'Words can be found. It's the principle that must be agreed upon.'

Kennedy: 'What will you do in the event of a *coup* in Jordan that ousts Hussein or if something else happens to him?'

Peres: 'There are three possibilities. (1) An Egyptian invasion. (2) A military *coup* that will invite Egyptian intervention, as in Yemen. (3) A local *coup*. In the first case, Israel will immediately find herself in a complex situation and will not be able to stand idly by. In the second case, as well, we won't be able to stand by and may have to thrash it out with the American Government. In the third case, it will be difficult to decide. But as usual we take into account three possibilities, and there could be a fourth we haven't considered. We will have to decide according to the nature of the development.'

Kennedy (with a smile): 'You certainly never imagined that one day you would pray for the safety of Hussein and Feisal. How long are you staying here?'

Mike Feldman: 'He has come to wind up the negotiations over the Hawks, and tomorrow he'll be at the Pentagon handling it.'

Peres: 'I represent a country of doves which has come to get Hawks.'

The actual negotiations were conducted with the President's advisers and representatives of the State Department and the Pentagon. In the end Israel got what she so sorely needed: five batteries of Hawk ground-to-air missiles. The significance of this agreement went far beyond its immediate terms. Its principal importance was in breaching the American wall of refusal to sell Israel sophisticated weapons. From here on, the 'breakthroughs' would multiply until the United States became Israel's principal arms supplier.

The successful conclusion of the American arms deal was the event for which David Ben-Gurion had been waiting. Now he would act on an idea he had been contemplating for months. The spate of political flaps – the Lavon Affair, the German scientists and the incessant squabbling within *Mapai* – had begun to leave their mark on him. He felt tired, and his closest associates sensed him growing more distant, almost oblivious to the reality surrounding him. On 16 June 1963, he submitted his final and irrevocable resignation as Prime Minister. As usual, some Party activists pleaded with him to recant, but their cries fell on deaf ears. One of the people to whom he explained his move was Dr Dov Yosef, the Minister of Commerce and Industry. 'The burden was more than I could bear, especially as Minister of Defence. And when I saw that there were two comrades who could be relied upon, Eskhol and Shimon [Peres], I felt free to unburden myself and become a man beholden to no one but himself.'

On Ben-Gurion's recommendation, Levi Eshkol was chosen to replace him as Premier and Defence Minister. The Old Man liked and trusted his former Finance Minister, but the same could not be said of Moshe Dayan. Immediately after Ben-Gurion's resignation, he announced his own intention to follow suit. In a conversation subsequently reported to Ben-Gurion by Peres, Dayan explained that 'there are five important portfolios: finance, foreign affairs, defence, industry and the premiership. All of them will be concentrated in the hands of three people: Eshkol, Golda and Sapir. None of those three has any notion of foreign affairs.' Dayan added that 'if Shimon were proposed for defence, he would stay on' as Minister of Agriculture. Peres, for his part, suggested to Eshkol that he appoint Dayan as Minister of Defence, but 'Eshkol said that he couldn't agree to that'.

Later that day, after Ben-Gurion had recorded these developments in his diary (19 June 1963), he added: 'Meanwhile, word has come from Eshhkol that Moshe agrees to stay on.'

A few days earlier, at the meeting of the *Mapai* Central Committee confirming him as Ben-Gurion's successor, Levi Eshkol sent Peres a note on a piece of paper torn out of his small notebook: 'Will you agree to work with me as Minister of Defence if I retain the portfolio permanently or temporarily? Naturally I will want to be involved in affairs. I'll try to patch things up with Golda.' Peres did not reply immediately because he wanted a few points cleared up before deciding. For this purpose, he met Eshkol on 18 June and, after the meeting, sent a document to the new Prime Minister:

> In the talk we had on 18 June 1963, we discussed and agreed upon the following matters:
> (1) You stated that military matters related to foreign affairs will be discussed by a small forum composed of yourself, the Foreign Minister and myself.
> (2) The special relationship with Germany will continue and be extended.
> (3) Although you wish to make greater use of the Ministerial Committee for Defence Affairs, its jurisdiction will not be enhanced, but will remain as delineated in the coalition agreement.
> (4) You will try to clear up any misunderstandings between the Foreign Ministry and the Ministry of Defence and strive towards defining a division of labour and jurisdiction between them.
> (5) I will be invited to Cabinet meetings at which military affairs are discussed.
> (6) I will be made a member of the Ministerial Committee for Defence Affairs.
> (7) The chain of command in the defence establishment will be Premier and Defence Minister, Deputy Defence Minister, Chief of Staff.

Eshkol confirmed receipt of the document and its conditions. But when he tried to implement Clause 6, a storm broke out. The

Ministers from *Ahdut Ha'avodah* absolutely refused to accept Peres as a member of the Ministerial Committee for Defence Affairs. Yigal Allon, who led the rebellion, argued that according to the Government's bylaws, only a fully-fledged Minister was eligible to be a member of the committee.

Behind the legalistic reasoning lurked the enmity which *Ahdut Ha'avodah* and its kibbutz movement, *Hakibbutz Hameuchad*, retained for Peres from as far back as his days in *Hanoar Ha'oved*. It had gained fresh impetus during the clash over relations with Germany, to which *Ahdut Ha'avodah* was vehemently opposed. In the eyes of this rival labour party, Peres, like Dayan, epitomized the unprincipled and unrestrained 'executor' who had turned his back on socialist ideology.

At first Eshkol was determined to honour his commitment to Peres. But the members of *Ahdut Ha'avodah* were equally determined not to yield, and they took their struggle to the public. Before anyone knew what was happening, the affair had been blown up out of all proportion and took on the dimensions of a crisis. This was the last thing Eshkol needed in his opening days as Premier. Buckling under the pressure, he asked Peres to forfeit membership of the Ministerial Committee 'in light of *Ahdut Ha'avodah*'s opposition'.

Peres thought the matter over and gave his reply in a letter dated 18 July 1963:

> I hereby inform you that I waive full membership on the Ministerial Committee for Defence Affairs, despite the commitment you made on the eve of my appointment in the present Government. I appreciate your resolution that the Cabinet vote unanimously to allow me permanent participation in the committee's meetings (rather than membership). I don't need that. I prefer to have my participation determined by the demands of the work, rather than with an eye to the factor of prestige or coalition politics.

At this point something curious, but not uncharacteristic of public life, altered the equation. The publication of his letter generated a wave of public support for Peres. His office was flooded with thousands of letters and telephone calls praising him for his concession. For one of the few times in his life, he even had a supportive press.

One of those many letters came from Sdeh Boker:

> I was pleased to read this morning in *Davar* [the *Histadrut* daily paper] that you waived full membership on the defence committee. It was a wise

and brave decision on your part and lends you more prestige than any presumed right to vote. Your opinion carries far more weight than any raised hand. The committee needs your expertise and advice on defence affairs – which can match that of any other member of the committee or the Cabinet.

I should note that this Government will not collapse before new elections, and Eshkol must be helped over all the obstacles. He has more goodwill than some comrades in the Party and the Government, though one is not always bound to accept his opinion. Best of wishes to you.
Yours,
D. Ben-Gurion

And so it was that nothing Peres had ever done before brought him as much admiration and support as this concession to pettiness.

On the face of it, there was no reason why his work with Eshkol should encounter difficulties of any kind. After all, it was Eshkol who had recruited Peres from Alumot and guided his first steps. In fact, Eshkol had brought him into the secretariat of *Hanoar Ha'oved* and thereafter into the field of defence. But many years had passed since then. And even if Peres still had a warm spot in his heart for Eshkol, his undivided loyalty belonged to Ben-Gurion. What's more, the rivalry between the Youngsters and the Old Guard had inevitably stirred up friction between them. Despite their disagreements, however, the personal relations between the two men were satisfactory, even warm. Undoubtedly they were influenced by the fact that Ben-Gurion accorded full support to his successor – for the time being, at least.

To everyone's surprise, Eshkol became a very popular Prime Minister. After the turbulent years of Ben-Gurion's leadership, it seemed that the public was delighted with a populist leader, a man with a ready smile and a rich sense of humour – a man given to compromise, not battle. Eshkol's popularity soared when, at the end of May 1964, he was invited for a state visit to the White House, now occupied by Lyndon Johnson. 'This was the first time that an Israeli Prime Minister was formally received [in the White House], through the front door, with all the pomp and circumstance. A nation like all nations?' Peres asked his diary with unabashed satisfaction.

Peres accompanied Eshkol on the trip and never ceased to be impressed by a multitude of details. He had already been to Washington a number of times, and meetings with presidents and heads of state were not new to him. Nevertheless, this visit was different. It had a sense of the historic about it.

A trace of irony found its way into Peres's description of the official guest-residence, Blair House.

> The temporary quarters of American presidents and the guest-house for VIPs is located across the street from the White House. Its walls are covered with silk. Its ceilings sport very expensive chandeliers. It is furnished in French and Early American décor and filled with art works and knick-knacks from China, France and America. Eshkol commandeered the first floor and I was given two enormous rooms on the second. We are provided with everything from fruits and whisky to a box of shaving-soap whose cover gleams so that it seems to be gold-plated. The carpets are lush, the towels magnificent, though the floor quakes like a wooden train station when a locomotive chugs by.

Indeed, 'a standard fit for a king', he pronounced, adding ruefully that 'we don't have a free minute'.

When he accompanied Eshkol into the Oval Office, Peres was fascinated by the presidential telephone.

> On the desk alongside Johnson's chair was a telephone with a set of buttons. That was the 'hotline'. From here you can 'call up' the most destructive force the human race has ever known. Nothing symbolizes more vividly the power, limitations and responsibility of the American president than that telephone. Evidently it is relatively new, or at least it's in a new spot, for the line runs under the red carpet and in order to install it someone cut an improvised hole in the rug.

Practically speaking, very little was accomplished during that visit to the United States, just as the expectations about it were modest from the start. Before leaving for America, Eshkol had consulted Ben-Gurion, who (as Peres recorded it)

> gave him the most important political advice: as long as Israel is perceived as an accessory to the Arab-Israeli conflict, she is in a losing position. On the other hand, whenever Israel appears as a power in her own right and directs the spotlight on herself, her position and the course she has chosen, she comes out ahead, with her enterprise having value and purpose.
>
> Our problem was how to present Israel detached from the context of the Arab-Israeli conflict. We snapped at the idea of focusing on the scientific field. Today that is the prime drama in the world.

The scientific venture which Israel raised for consideration was co-operation in the field of water desalination. 'If we can really desalinate sea water and dig a canal in the Negev, we can rectify a geopolitical error made by Moses and make science a supplement to the Torah,' Peres wrote in his diary.

Eshkol raised the subject in a talk with President Johnson, while Peres reached agreement with administration officials that Israel and the United States would find the research and application equally. (Eventually the project was dropped because the production costs made the process unprofitable.) The Americans seemed just as happy as the Israelis to talk about desalination instead of armaments. 'The difference between America and France', Peres noted in summarizing the visit, 'is that the Americans took us to Cape Kennedy, but told us that Israel doesn't need missiles, while the French give us missiles but won't take us to their equivalent of Cape Kennedy (Vernon).'

On the surface, it appeared that Ben-Gurion was party to the widespread admiration enjoyed by Levi Eshkol. Yet behind this façade, the choler of the elder statesman began to churn within him, once more in connection with the Lavon Affair. After receiving new material on the subject, he was totally convinced that Lavon was the one who had given the order for 'the unfortunate business'. Armed with these new findings, he descended on Eshkol to request – practically demand – that he appoint a legal board of inquiry. The very thought of raking over the affair yet again made Eshkol blanch and, after consulting his colleagues, he denied Ben-Gurion's request. This created the first rift between them.

Not the last, though; for Eshkol added two sins to his crime (at least that's how Ben-Gurion saw it). The first was his decision to permit the remains of Ze'ev Jabotinsky to be interred in Israel, complete with a state ceremony on Mount Herzl. Throughout his years in office, Ben-Gurion had consistently denied every request from the members of *Herut* to honour the memory of their mentor by this gesture. Jabotinsky was the father of the Revisionist movement and, as such, Ben-Gurion considered him anathema. Eshkol, on the other hand, felt the time had come to settle the historic but antiquated feud between the two camps. And perhaps he also wanted to prove his independence.

When Ben-Gurion got word of the decision, he concealed his reaction – but he was outraged. What's more, he had no inkling – and Peres never undertook to tell him – that it had been he, Peres, who had given Eshkol the idea.

At this time, Eshkol and his allies in the Party were also conducting serious efforts to merge *Mapai* and *Ahdut Ha'avodah*. Presumably, a move in this direction should have brought Ben-Gurion great satisfaction. A few months earlier (on 19 July 1963), he had written to Peres that 'everything possible should be done to promote a union with *Ahdut Ha'avodah*, for once that comes about, I have no doubt that, sooner or later, *Hashomer Hatzair* [*Mapam*] will be willing to join it.' But this letter was written before he received the new evidence on the Lavon Affair, before he had advanced his demand for a legal investigation and, most important, before *Ahdut Ha'avodah* had made it a primary condition of any union that Ben-Gurion's demand be rejected and, what was worse, that Lavon's dismissal be rescinded. After all this, Ben-Gurion did an about-face and fiercely denounced the proposed union.

This time, however, his political powers failed him. Eshkol surrendered to *Ahdut Ha'avodah*'s ultimatum and revoked the decision of the *Mapai* Central Committee dismissing Lavon (2 May 1964). This drove Ben-Gurion to even greater heights of fury and he declared open war on Eshkol and the senior echelon of *Mapai*. His house at Sdeh Boker was flooded with anxious *Mapai* functionaries pleading with him to lay the Affair to rest. He turned them all away empty-handed. Meanwhile, Eshkol had also assumed a more radical stance by proposing that Lavon be restored to an active role in Party affairs. The suggestion riled even Peres, who expressed his objection loud and clear. Moshe Dayan went one step further. On 3 November 1964, he submitted his resignation from the Cabinet because of 'the oppressive, hostile atmosphere I encounter within Eshkol's Government'.

Ben-Gurion enjoyed his first triumph when the Attorney-General, Moshe Ben-Ze'ev, graced the Cabinet with a legal opinion which endorsed the Old Man's contentions about the Lavon Affair. On the basis of this document, Justice Minister Dov Yosef recommended that the Government appoint a legal commission of inquiry. Left with no choice, Eshkol agreed.

Back at Sdeh Boker, Ben-Gurion gloated – but not for long. For under pressure from his Party colleagues and *Ahdut Ha'avodah*, Eshkol changed his mind – a mere three hours after acceding to the Justice Minister's recommendation. With the battle lines drawn, *Mapai* scheduled a meeting of its Central Committee for 13 December 1964 to decide between Ben-Gurion and Eshkol.

Then Eshkol showed that he had taken a page or two from Ben-Gurion's book. A few hours before the Central Committee meeting, he convened the Cabinet and announced his resignation, placing before the Party a clear-cut choice: either Levi Eshkol as Prime Minister or a legal investigation – and a government crisis. The Central Committee decided by a large majority in favour of Eshkol continuing his term. In other words, for the first time since Ben-Gurion had become the leader of *Mapai*, the Party expressed its preference for another man.

The final break between the two men occurred at the *Mapai* Party convention in mid-February 1965. Both camps came well prepared for the show-down. Essentially, the confrontation was over the generation gap, and the Old Guard put on an impressive performance. Moshe Sharett arrived in a wheelchair. Stricken with cancer, his days numbered, he delivered a vitriolic attack on Ben-Gurion which stunned the audience. Eshkol and Golda followed suit. Ben-Gurion was scheduled to reply to his opponents, but the vehemence of feeling against him, particularly Golda's speech, left him deeply shaken. He stood up and left the hall without uttering a word, and his call to establish a board of legal inquiry was voted down by a large majority.

When Ben-Gurion returned to his hut at Sdeh Boker, he began to contemplate a break with *Mapai* and the establishment of an independent Party. He envisioned it embracing previously unaffiliated people who favoured a change in the election system and members of *Mapai* opposed to Eshkol. Ben-Gurion believed that a Party of this sort could win between twenty and twenty-five seats in the Knesset, and he predicted that the alignment between *Mapai* and *Ahdut Ha'avodah* (which had come to fruition in the meantime) would get the same.

Soon Ben-Gurion began to seek out people willing to join him. As these contacts proceeded, Hillel Cohen, the director of the *Histadrut* construction company, Solel Boneh, telephoned Ben-Gurion's trusted aide, Chaim Yisraeli, to suggest that if Ben-Gurion talked to Aharon Becker (the secretary of the *Histadrut*) and Abba Houshi (the Mayor of Haifa), they would go along with him. It was a valuable tip, as both these men wielded considerable power within *Mapai*. But when Yisraeli rushed to bring it to Ben-Gurion, the Old Man was not impressed: 'That's not important to me,' he scoffed. 'What counts is whether Moshe [Dayan] and Shimon [Peres] will go along with me.'

Neither Moshe nor Shimon seemed particularly inclined to do so. Peres did not share Ben-Gurion's optimism about the electoral potential of the new list, and he also felt a certain emotional resistance to

the move. 'We were educated not towards division and obstruction-
ism, but to unity and construction,' he told a gathering of Ben-
Gurion's supporters, who now came under the heading 'The
Minority'. At a meeting of The Minority's leading figures on 27
June 1965, Peres tabled a draft resolution which proclaimed: 'The
majority of the participants concur that the best way to fight for what
we believe in is to do so within the framework of the Party [*Mapai*].'
He was confident that the declaration would put a stop to any drift
towards a split. So sure, in fact, that when Gad Ya'akobi called to
say that he would cancel his scheduled trip to Moscow if a new Party
were about to arise, Peres assured him he could go. 'There won't
be any independent list,' he vouched.

Ya'akobi went, but Peres's confidence soon proved unfounded.
Two days after the resolution was passed by The Minority's
leadership, Ben-Gurion called together his leading supporters – some
fifty people – in his Tel Aviv home. Peres opened the meeting by
enumerating the options open to the minority camp. No sooner had
he concluded than Ben-Gurion reduced the choices to one. He had not
convened the meeting to hold a discussion, but to inform his followers
of his decision to establish an independent list that would fight the
travesty of justice known as the Lavon Affair. He had even written up
the new Party's manifesto, which he proceeded to read out to his
stunned audience.

Ben-Gurion also gave vent to his anger with Peres, by ordering
someone else to assume the chairmanship of the meeting. Pale and
smarting, Peres remained mute. A few minutes later, he resumed the
chair, but he no longer referred to his proposals.

That same evening, 29 June 1965, a statement was issued on the
foundation of a new Party headed by David Ben-Gurion. It was called
the Israel Workers' List and came to be known by its Hebrew
acronym, *Rafi*.

Peres found himself in a difficult quandary, perhaps the sorest of his
life. He did not believe in the new Party, its manifesto or its chances of
gaining a substantial following. Moreover, he was deeply hurt by
Ben-Gurion's attitude – both towards himself personally and towards
his other comrades for serving them up a *fait accompli*. Neither did he
hold any personal grudge against Eshkol – and certainly nothing even
faintly resembling Ben-Gurion's smouldering hatred. Still, Ben-
Gurion was Ben-Gurion, his leader and mentor. Could he forsake him
now, in the hour of his greatest trial?

The morning after that meeting at Ben-Gurion's house, Peres was woken by the telephone. The Old Man was on the line saying that he wanted to come over immediately and apologize for his behaviour. It stemmed, he explained, from the fact that he was very tense. Peres assured him that it wasn't necessary to trouble himself. He would come to Ben-Gurion's house. As soon as he crossed the threshold, the Old Man embraced him warmly and again asked his forgiveness. 'You don't deserve that kind of treatment from me.' Afterwards he said that he knew Peres was opposed to a split, but 'I'm in a position where I can't go on without Moshe [Dayan] and you. *Certainly* not without you,' he stressed. 'If you tell me no, I'll drop the idea.' All of Peres's qualms vanished in a flash. 'I won't leave you,' he promised.

Two members of *Rafi* remained in senior Cabinet posts. One was Yosef Almogi, Minister of Labour; the second, Shimon Peres, Deputy Minister of Defence. Eshkol begged Peres to stay. Almogi wanted to resign, but only on condition that Peres go with him. He called several times a day, urging his fellow-maverick to resign. 'I don't want to die of dysentery,' he said, referring to the uncomfortable situation the *Rafi* people were subject to in *Mapai* and the Cabinet. 'We should bow out.'

Deep in his heart, Peres knew what he had to do. But he stalled – perhaps in the hope that something would miraculously 'come along' or that he would wake up one morning and discover that it had all been a bad dream. Finally, circumstances forced him to decide – though they were helped along by Yossi Sarid, then spokesman for *Mapai*. During that mad period, *Mapai*'s Executive used to meet even on Fridays; and at one of these meetings, called for seven in the morning, Eshkol remarked that whoever could not work with him for lack of trust had best leave the Cabinet. This was one of those statements which tend to slip out and, if confined to the bounds of the conference room, have no operative implications. Publishing them in the press, however, may accord them far more weight than was intended.

The moment Eshkol finished speaking, Sarid, a protégé of Pinhas Sapir, who believed that 'the partnership with *Rafi* destroys whatever good is left in the Party', stood up and left the room. 'Everyone sitting there – and who wasn't there? Ben-Gurion, Eshkol, Golda, Dayan, Peres – all knew where I was going,' Sarid recalled. He made straight for the Party secretary's office and telephoned the two afternoon papers. Both published Eshkol's remark as headlines and copies reached the Executive while it was still in session. Everyone knew that a crossroads had been reached.

As he explained afterwards, Eshkol had made the comment essentially for Almogi's benefit, but Peres understood that its publication made it impossible for him to avoid a decision. That evening two friends came to his home and begged him not to resign. 'Just because the Old Man has suddenly decided to set the world on its ear is no reason for you to destroy your future!' 'How can I go on working there?' Peres replied in a whisper, as if mumbling to himself. 'What will I look like?' Both men understood that his mind was already made up. When one of them asked, 'What will you do?' Peres smiled sardonically. 'Who knows? Perhaps I'll be secretary of some branch or another.' The next day he announced his resignation as Deputy Defence Minister, parting from the enterprise he so loved and to whose growth he had contributed so decisively.

There can be no doubt that without the backing from Ben-Gurion, Peres would have found it difficult to achieve what he did during his terms as Director-General and Deputy Minister of Defence. But the opposite is also true: an atomic reactor, guided missiles and a flourishing industry are not built with backing alone. Peres's talent was in knowing how to translate the support he enjoyed into concrete achievements. His partnership with Ben-Gurion was a rare match of two men who complemented each other: Peres, bubbling over with ideas, the innovator and executive; Ben-Gurion, the man of broad vision who created the parameters of endeavour which Peres needed in order to work.

From the standpoint of Israel's military strength, these formative years were a crucial period. Ironically enough, it was also a decisive period in terms of Peres's personal future – though not necessarily to his benefit. His style of operating championed the unprecedented growth of the IDF and the Israeli arms industry, but it was also the source of his controversial image. Herein lies one of the more tragic ironies of Israeli political life. The man who was a close confidant of premiers and senior ministers the world over was branded in his own country with the stigma of disingenuousness.

It was when Peres crossed the line from *Mapai* to *Rafi* that his personal makeup came out most clearly. He went along with the new Party not because he believed in it; quite the opposite was true. He joined it solely out of loyalty to Ben-Gurion. Yet from the moment he threw in his lot with *Rafi*, he not only identified with the Party, but became one of its pillars. Ben-Gurion was an old man obsessed with the Lavon Affair. Dayan behaved like Dayan: a prima donna waiting for things to be served up to him on a silver platter. But someone had to *do* something. The creation of a new Party from scratch needs money, members, branches, offices. Someone had to do the work, and it fell, as if perfectly naturally, to Peres.

First of all, he understood that the Lavon Affair alone could not constitute the basis for the new Party, so he expanded the manifesto to include reform of the electoral system; a nationally oriented approach, as opposed to a partisan socialist one; the goals of scientific progress, stepped-up industrialization and technological progress. Secondly, he assumed control of the organizational work and wholly devoted himself to it. Within a short space of time, Party branches had sprung up, thousands of volunteers had been mobilized and a substantial sum of money had been collected.

Another characteristic change was his volte-face from mild pessimism to unwarranted optimism. He offered Gad Ya'akobi the fifteenth place on the Party's Knesset list, telling him that 'it will be the tenth place before the last realistic one' – meaning that he believed *Rafi* would win twenty-five seats. Ya'akobi wanted a second opinion and went to talk to Dayan, who warned that 'the fifteenth place will be the eighth *after* the last realistic one' – meaning he envisaged a maximum of seven seats.

Peres's diligence did not escape the notice of *Mapai*'s leaders, who reacted in a typical manner. Despite all that had happened, they still felt uncomfortable attacking Ben-Gurion. Peres was the most convenient stand-in, so they went after him with a vengeance. He did not take it impassively, and this period saw the birth of an enmity which, after a long effort, would be allayed but never forgotten.

The subsequent election campaign was a brutal one. *Mapai* fought tooth and nail against those who had deserted it – and they matched its fervour in every way. Erstwhile friends went for one another's throats with a fury verging on hysteria.

The results proved that Dayan and, even more, Peres had erred in their forecasts. *Rafi* won only ten seats in the election of November 1965, compared to forty-five for the alignment of *Mapai* and *Ahdut Ha'avodah*. The outcome was a great disappointment. For the first time in many years, men like Dayan and Peres found themselves shut out of government work. They had been sentenced to a sterile sojourn in opposition, and no one could say how long it was likely to last. Tabling questions in the Knesset, attending the meetings of marginal committees, visiting the Party's branches – these were the things which occupied Peres's time now, not atomic reactors, missiles, tanks or deals with heads of state.

As for Ben-Gurion, when he failed to achieve his aims, he simply lost interest in *Rafi*. Rarely did he come to the Knesset, but the throne of leadership in the Party did not remain vacant. Though it was Peres who built up *Rafi* from the foundation to the rafters, he was not chosen to occupy that seat. Almost as if it were self-evident, to Peres as well as to all its other members, the leadership of the Party belonged to Moshe Dayan. He became the final arbiter on every issue. This was a natural relationship for the two men: Peres, the one who generated the power; Dayan, the man who wielded it.

Once they had become used to their new state of affairs, the *Rafi* people recovered their fighting spirit, and their parliamentary struggle against the Labour Government became as fierce as the election campaign. Only a common enemy could assuage the fevered feelings, and it was not long in coming.

At the end of 1966 a rash of serious incidents occurred on the Syrian, Jordanian and Egyptian borders. Especially grave was the situation along the border with Syria, and reports circulated about the possibility of an Israeli attack on Syria. President Nasser announced that he would stand behind the Syrians and even send military units to their aid. But he did not content himself with gallant gestures alone. On 16 May 1967 he demanded that UN Secretary-General U Thant remove the UN Emergency Force stationed on the Egyptian-Israeli border.

The deteriorating political situation reached its nadir on 21 May, when Nasser announced the closing of the Straits of Tiran to Israeli shipping. In effect, he had declared a blockade on Eilat, Israel's southern port, and for Israel the announcement was tantamount to a declaration of war.

Nevertheless, the Government did not despair of finding a way out. It decided to try and avert war by diplomatic means, and approaches were made to France, Britain, the United States and the UN. All these parties acknowledged the justice of Israel's case and the gravity of Nasser's move. After all, following Israel's withdrawal from Sinai in 1956, the Egyptian President had committed himself to allow free passage of Israeli shipping to Eilat. But as the days continued to pass, it became increasingly clear that except for a stab at diplomatic persuasion, the Powers and the UN were unwilling to do anything. Nasser stood his ground and even warmed up the atmosphere by deploying a large military force in Sinai near the Israeli border. On 19 May a general mobilization was declared in Israel, but still the Cabinet tarried.

Gradually the Israeli public began to show signs of impatience and, worse, flagging confidence. The bolder Nasser became, the more the public questioned Eshkol's ability as Minister of Defence and feared that the approaching war might prove the destruction of Israel. The people wanted the ship of state to be in the hands of a man who had steered it through earlier crises. In its time of trial, the nation remembered the old man on whom it had turned its back. The name Ben-Gurion was on everyone's lips.

In their despair, the Israeli people did not know, or did not want to acknowledge, that Ben-Gurion was no longer the man or the leader he had been during the early years of the state. The passage of time and the burden of struggle had taken their toll. Now the irrepressible activist of the 1940s and 1950s was alarmed by the prospect of war and forecast dire consequences if fighting broke out. He was viciously critical of Eshkol's handling of the crisis and accused him of responsibility for the deteriorating situation. He even suggested that *Rafi* would demand Eshkol's resignation (a proposal which was never taken up because of opposition from both Dayan and Peres).

The first concrete initiative towards a change of leadership came from the leader of the National Religious Party, Interior Minister Moshe Chaim Shapira. At a meeting with Peres, he announced that his Party would support the replacement of Eshkol by Ben-Gurion. Opposition leader Menachem Begin likewise backed this initiative and suggested that Eshkol vacate his place and allow Ben-Gurion to form a government of national unity. Eshkol refused.

At the time Peres still accepted Ben-Gurion's opinion that Israel should avoid a war unless she had a mutual arrangement with a friendly power – by which he meant the United States. Dayan also accepted this view, but he changed his mind after touring army camps in the southern part of the country. During his visits, he came round to thinking that Israel should take the bit in her teeth and attack Egypt. Thus Ben-Gurion's stand, coupled with the opposition of the *Mapai* leadership, made his candidacy for the premiership irrelevant. At the same time, however, the lack of confidence in Eshkol's ability to lead the fight was verging on hysteria.

In his contacts with the leaders of various Parties, it became clear to Peres that

> there's no majority for replacing Eshkol, but what can be achieved immediately is to have Moshe Dayan join the Government as Defence Minister. Eshkol has already asked Dayan in and offered him the post of commander of the southern front. Moshe agreed. He sent Avraham Ofer to me and suggested that I join the Government as a Minister without Portfolio. I refused. Dayan rang me that same day and said, 'Shimon, don't waste your energy. Nothing will come of it.' But I insisted that Dayan be co-opted into the Government as Defence Minister. I consider it a basic condition for forming a government of national unity, deciding to go to war and winning that fight.
>
> Facing me was one of the most difficult duties of my life: going to Ben-Gurion and telling him that there's no chance of him supplanting Eshkol and that we should make do with Dayan being taken into the Government as Minister of Defence. I knew his reaction would be furious.
>
> I went to see him on Thursday morning, together with a friend, and described the situation in detail. David Ben-Gurion blew up at me like a volcano: 'I thought you were a statesman and a friend. Now I doubt both. Don't you understand that Eshkol isn't intelligent enough to lead the fight? And didn't we decide together that our condition for joining the Government is the replacement of the Prime Minister?'
>
> I knew that the only thing to do in that situation was to fight back relentlessly. 'Ben-Gurion, when you say that we must place all the security considerations on one side of the balance – the decisive, defence side of the balance – does that statement obligate only the rest of us or you as well? Can't you see what kind of defence situation we've got ourselves into?'
>
> He simmered down just as abruptly as he had erupted. 'I'm sorry,' he said, embracing me. 'I've done you an injustice.'

Ben-Gurion agreed to have Dayan join the Government but only on condition that Peres tell Eshkol that 'we have no faith in him as Prime Minister'. Peres duly executed this unsavoury mission, though he felt that he was 'making things difficult for a man I like [Eshkol], deep inside, despite all that has happened recently'. Eshkol's reaction 'was mild, even apologetic: "I understand that's your position. Perhaps you will change it sometime." '

On 1 June 1967, Eshkol formed his government of national unity and turned the defence portfolio over to Moshe Dayan. That evening the leaders of *Rafi* convened in Ben-Gurion's home to celebrate the event. 'I know you have all worked for this thing,' Ben-Gurion said, 'but there's one man who has worked particularly hard and skilfully –

and that is Shimon.'

Four days later, on 5 June, the war broke out. It lasted for six days and climaxed in a victory greater than the most outrageous expectations. The Sinai desert, Golan Heights and West Bank were captured by Israeli forces. Jerusalem was liberated.

The aura surrounding Moshe Dayan began to reach the proportions of hero-worship. It was not affected in the least by the fact that he had taken over the defence post a mere four days before the outbreak of war, and so his influence over its course and outcome was marginal. The people wanted a hero, and Dayan was more than willing to fill the bill.

People are drawn to symbols with which they can identify. Rarely do they stop to think who made it possible for these symbols to emerge. It was the Mirages and the Mystères purchased in France by Peres which destroyed the Egyptian air force. It was the tanks he assembled from all over the world which rolled through the Sinai desert, up the Golan Heights, across Judea and Samaria. The stunning victory would not have been possible had it not been for the unique qualities of the Israeli soldier and his commanders. But it would have been equally beyond reach without the sophisticated weaponry which Peres provided for them. These facts were completely ignored at the time. As usual, the crowd bore Dayan on its shoulders while Peres remained on the sidelines, then joined the cheering throng.

The trauma of war and intoxication of victory placed the rivalry between *Mapai* and *Rafi* in a new perspective. In fact, the only obstacle to a reunion was Ben-Gurion, who did not forgive and would not forget, and whose refusal to consider *Rafi*'s return to the mother Party was adamant. His uncompromising position forced Peres to stand up to him again. Peres reiterated the call he had issued before the war – namely, to unite the workers' movement – and a convention of *Rafi* members was called for the middle of December to decide for or against the union of *Rafi* with *Mapai*.

Yet even before the convention met, an incident illustrated for Peres and his comrades the disarray that was already rampant in their own ranks. Prime Minister Eshkol, who was very interested in the union of the two parties, asked Yosef Almogi to join the Government. The offer was made not to *Rafi*, but to the candidate personally. Almogi, for his part, also made an unusual move: without turning to his Party's official bodies or consulting any of its heads, he agreed.

Once the deal was completed, Eshkol telephoned Dayan and asked for his approval. Dayan instantly replied that he had no objection. Only then did he call Gad Ya'akobi and report his conversation with the Prime Minister.

Dayan, like Almogi, had replied to Eshkol without consulting the Party at all. Evidently he understood that he had blundered, for a few moments after reporting to Ya'akobi he telephoned him again. 'I'm afraid that I've overstepped the bounds of my authority,' he said apologetically. 'I want you to tell Shimon and ask him to convene the Party bodies.'

Ya'akobi did as he was asked, and that was the first inkling that Peres, the Secretary-General of *Rafi*, had of the gambit. His reaction was vehement. 'Tell Moshe to call Eshkol and say that he had expressed his personal opinion and the Almogi matter must be agreed upon by Eshkol and *Rafi*, not between Eshkol and Dayan.' Ya'akobi phoned Dayan, Dayan phoned Eshkol, but by then the issue was essentially spilt milk. The appointment became a fact, and it was a brutal slap in the face for Peres. For the truth was that the Party in which he had invested so much effort had become a burden on its principal members. On 12 December 1967, *Rafi* held its last convention and decided, by a majority of 52 to 48 per cent, to take part in the constitution of the Israel Labour Party, along with *Mapai* and *Ahdut Ha'avodah*.

The principal achievement of the Six Day War was not the military victory – which was phenomenal in its own right – but the ability to keep a hold on it. The United States had learned a lesson from the Sinai Campaign and, although the principle of withdrawal from occupied territories continued to direct its thinking, this time the Americans linked the withdrawal to an Arab willingness to establish peaceful relations with Israel. And because such willingness was non-existent, the territories remained under Israeli control.

The irony is that what the United States learned, France seemed to have forgotten. For now President de Gaulle blamed Israel, in the strongest language, for the outbreak of hostilities. His outburst was so incontinent one was tempted to believe that he was personally insulted that Israel had gone to war despite his admonitions against it. He immediately slapped a total embargo on the shipment of arms to Israel, thereby ending once and for all the special relationship between the two countries.

It is hard to avoid wondering what role was played in this development by the fact that Peres was on the opposition bench during the critical period in question. Not that relations with France had soured when he left the Government, but they were bereft of the element of personal friendship and intimacy. It is no exaggeration to say that had Peres been in the Government in 1967, he would have pressed to let the French in on Israel's soul-searchings and ultimately her decision to go to war. More than likely, his special connections would have tempered France's opposition before the fighting broke out and her acid response thereafter.

Be that as it may, no one in Israel bothered to contemplate this question, for it was purely academic. Gradually the United States assumed France's place as Israel's chief arms supplier and, despite the regret over losing France as a close friend, many officials in Jerusalem preferred the United States, which was deemed more stable.

The boost which the Six Day War gave the State of Israel and its people was incredible. National pride and self-confidence soared. Economic development bounded forward, recession and austerity were superseded by industrial and agricultural development – and a wave of prosperity which meant a dramatic rise in the standard of living. Of course, there were problems too. President Nasser would not accept his defeat, and his artillery on the west bank of the Suez Canal relentlessly shelled Israeli positions on the opposite shore. In response, Israeli planes bombed targets in Egypt daily and even penetrated as far as Cairo.

It wasn't until the summer of 1970 that the guns on both sides were silenced by an American-sponsored cease-fire agreement. Shortly afterwards, the man who had cast his terror over Israel for so many years departed the arena. President Nasser died of a heart attack and was succeeded by his Vice-President, the little-known Anwar Sadat.

Even more difficult were the problems posed by ruling over a million Arabs in the West Bank and Gaza Strip. An immediate consequence of the occupation was a surge in the activities of the PLO, whose members initiated a spate of terrorist actions in Israel's cities and countryside.

During this period, Peres filled a series of Cabinet posts as Minister of Transport, Minister of Absorption, Minister of Communications and Minister of Information. Finding himself on the periphery of the main arena, in his own way he tried to accord these affairs a sense of vitality and sparkle – sometimes in an artificial and pretentious manner. When he was appointed Minister of Posts, he considered it important to change the name of his office to Ministry of Communications, which sounded more chic and sophisticated. When he entered the Ministry of Transport, he made statements which identified him with the fatuous slogan 'A car for every worker' – a motto that served his adversaries for many a year to come.

But alongside the penchant for flair was action. Under his direction, the Communications Ministry built the first satellite facility and decided to restructure the telephone services as a private company (a plan not implemented for reasons beyond Peres's control). On another plane, most of the new immigrants were channelled to housing in Jerusalem, which accelerated the development of the city and substantially augmented its population. Whatever free time he had from government work, he used for Party activities. As things turned out, the union of the three factions did not dissolve old barriers. Each element of the Labour Party zealously maintained its original framework, and mutual suspicion and rivalry became the norm.

When Levi Eshkol died in February 1969, his place was filled by Golda Meir. Like Ben-Gurion before her, she was not one to forgive or forget; and now, as Prime Minister, she had the opportunity to settle an old score with Peres – for the days when he ran his own foreign policy and ignored her; for the period of the struggle against *Rafi*. She could not dismiss him, because the agreement on the unification of the Party stipulated that the various factions chose their representatives in the Cabinet. But she could restrict his activities and at least ignore him – and this she did with relish.

In contrast, Golda learned to live with Moshe Dayan – and he with her. In fact, the two of them grew into the symbol of contemporary Israel: Golda, the proud and valiant woman, a mixture of Jewish mother and chiding Biblical prophetess; Dayan, the war hero. The people of Israel, who never had it so good, were confident that so long as these two figures were in charge, no evil would befall them.

Until another war came along to shatter this cosy situation. The fighting broke out on Yom Kippur, 6 October 1973, but for this round there was no waiting period, not even a warning of what was about to occur. After months of meticulous preparation which remained totally secret, the armies of Egypt and Syria launched a co-ordinated attack on Israel. The IDF was caught unprepared, both for the assault *per se* and for the notion of a war.

The first days of fighting were a nightmare for the citizens of Israel and their political leaders. The Egyptian army managed to cross the Suez Canal and dig in on its eastern bank, while the Syrian army invaded the Golan Heights. The country seemed permeated by an air of wholesale collapse, of standing on the brink of annihilation. After the opening days, however, the military situation steadily improved for Israel. Large quantities of arms were airlifted from the United States, the Syrian army was repulsed on the Golan Heights, and finally a sizeable Israeli force crossed the Canal, captured a broad salient on its western bank and was poised at the Egyptian heartland.

By the time a cease-fire had been called, the Israeli public was in the throes of prolonged trauma. Thousands of young men had fallen in battle. And equally shocking was the fact that the unbelievable had happened: the Arabs had managed to hoodwink Israel and prove – at least during the first days of the war – their military superiority. Most of the anger was directed at the god whose feet turned out to be made of clay: Moshe Dayan. But Golda, too, and with her all the other members of the Cabinet, were targets of trenchant criticism and the pangs of frustration. Her Cabinet began to be called the 'blunder government'. It looked as though its days were numbered.

Elections had been scheduled to take place in November, but because of the war they were postponed until 31 December 1973. The odds were that the Labour Party would lose its political hegemony. But then American Secretary of State Henry Kissinger arrived in the area to mediate between Israel and the Arab states. His talks produced a plan to convene a peace conference in Geneva, and the Labour Party portrayed itself as the only political force that could lead the country towards the coveted peace with the Arabs. Certainly there was no question of adopting the militant alternative offered by Menachem Begin. Thus, despite the unforgivable fiasco of October 1973, a shattered and war-weary Israeli public again placed its faith in the Labour Party.

About a month before the elections, another blow came down on Israel, though of a different kind. On 1 December Peres was at home when the telephone rang and on the line was Chaim Yisraeli, who uttered a single word: 'Ben-Gurion'. Peres later recorded:

I rushed to Tel Hashomer Hospital. His family was outside, and I asked for permission to go into the small room. He lay on his back, his high, pale forehead adorned by the shock of white hair, as if carved from marble. He was strangely, frightfully still. I thought that, for the first time in his life, he was finally, fully at peace. A rare phenomenon of nature had surrendered to the inevitable order of nature.

The room stood witness to the orphanhood of a people.

4
Reaching for the Top

By its ballot in the December 1973 elections, the Israeli voters created a paradoxical situation: they returned Golda Meir's Government to power, but then made it perfectly clear that they hadn't really meant to. There was no question that the electorate preferred the Labour Party to the *Likud*, but its opinion about the Government that had been responsible for the blunders of Yom Kippur remained in force. As Golda Meir went about trying to form a new coalition, the public demonstrations and press attacks grew more and more strident. The sharpest darts continued to be aimed at Defence Minister Moshe Dayan, who met with withering outbursts of implacable hostility wherever he went. It seemed that if he resigned, the public would content itself with his head and allow Golda Meir to constitute the Government of her choosing. The problem was that Dayan refused to go and Golda accorded him her full backing.

Throughout this period, which was unquestionably the most difficult of Dayan's life, Peres stood beside him and showed him unreserved support, though he knew that in doing so he hardly enhanced the value of his own political capital. But it was a losing battle. For even a man like Dayan, who was not particularly known for his sensitivity to public sentiment, could not hold out for very long against the waves of increasingly heavy pressure and open rancour. On 26 February 1974 he broke. 'Somewhere along the way we reached the point where a responsible man cannot go on being Minister of Defence,' he told a rally of *Rafi* people in Jerusalem, and went on to announce that he did not intend to join the new Government headed by Golda Meir. But Peres refused to accept the inevitable. 'Moshe has every reason to refuse to be Defence Minister,' he declared, 'but the people have every reason to want him to continue serving as Defence Minister!' This was not Shimon Peres's greatest hour, for it was not the welfare of the people which moved him to speak out. The people were clearly united in their desire to see Moshe Dayan go, but Peres was guided by a blind reverence which even the war had not managed to affect – yet. For this same reason, he had no doubt whatsoever about his own political future: if Dayan went, he, Peres, would go with him.

More to the point was the fact that Golda likewise refused to accept Dayan's departure. The stronger the public and internal Party pressure, the more she seemed to be caught up in an irrational process of growing identity with the Minister of Defence, who had once been the target of her hostility. The mere though of a Government without him sent her plummeting into a depression, as evidenced by a note she passed to Peres during the Cabinet meeting on 24 February 1974: 'Shimon, To my great regret, Moshe already considers himself out of office. I am in such despair that there are no words to express it.' At a subsequent meeting of the Party Central Committee, Golda turned to Dayan and Peres in an emotional appeal: 'You have no right to go. Not at this time, and not from your positions!' The inevitable stream of Party functionaries tried to persuade the two men to change their minds and, to the deep dismay of the public at large, their efforts bore fruit. Dayan announced his readiness to return to the Government – together with Peres, of course.

Now the public's fury was turned against not only Dayan, but Golda and the entire veteran leadership of the Labour Party. On Sunday, 3 March 1974, the Labour Party's Knesset faction met to endorse the line-up of the new Government. After a number of members had spoken, Golda exercised her right of reply, challenging the criticism that had been sounded throughout the meeting. Then, without warning, she shocked her audience by declaring: 'This evening I shall inform the President that I am finished with forming a Government and am returning to him my mandate to do so. I hope you will find a way to tell the President who the new candidate [to form a Government] is.'

No sooner had she said it then a parade of delegations began streaming to Golda's door begging her to relent. In the end, the Old Lady of Israeli politics yielded to their supplications and presented her new Government (including Moshe Dayan as Minister of Defence) before the Knesset, which granted it a vote of confidence. But the public did not follow suit. On the contrary, the call for Dayan's resignation began to take on the proportions of public hysteria. Golda understood that she faced the choice of sacking Dayan or resigning herself, and she opted for the latter. Her announcement to this effect was made at a meeting of the Labour Party's Knesset faction on 10 April 1974: 'I have come to the conclusion for myself – and without any relation to the parliamentary responsibility that does or does not apply to Moshe Dayan – that I must resign. I cannot bear this burden any longer.' This time the Party did not come to Golda on bended knee. There were no delegations, no entreaties. So it was that the 'Generation of Titans' in the leadership of the state came to an end, and the search for a new candidate for the premiership began.

For the first few days after Golda's announcement, no one in the Labour Party – not even Peres – challenged the traditional assumption that the leadership of the Party was the province of the *Mapai* faction. 'If [Minister of Justice] Chaim Zadok or [Minister of Labour] Yosef Almogi are candidates, I will support either one of them,' he said. But two other names were mentioned as well: Yigal Allon and Yitzhak Rabin. And where they were concerned, Peres's support did not automatically apply. In fact, he declared himself 'an alternative candidate to either one of them'.

The decisive factor was the possibility that Finance Minister Pinhas Sapir would advance his candidacy. Sapir was considered the strong man and kingmaker of the Labour Party. When it appeared that he was about to make his move, the members of the *Rafi* faction were in a disgruntled mood. Some of them went so far as to demand that if Sapir became Prime Minister, *Rafi* should pull out of the Government and the Labour Party. Peres wanted to avoid another split at all costs. To placate his comrades, he announced that he would be prepared to run against Sapir – an act which called for no little courage and which many regarded as political suicide. Peres's sole condition was a commitment from his colleagues that if he lost the contest, there would be no walk-out or split. When he forwarded his candidacy it was, therefore, against Pinhas Sapir. In the end, Sapir refused to assume the grave burden of the premiership, but like the other members of *Mapai*, he had no intention of leaving the field wide open to Peres. To sabotage his candidacy, the search for a counter-candidate began.

The chances were slim that Rabin's name would not come into the race. On paper, he had all the necessary requirements: experience in the field of defence as a former Chief of Staff; diplomatic experience as

Israel's Ambassador to Washington; and most important of all, he was wholly untainted by any connection with the Yom Kippur War – not even the slightest involvement. He did offer his help at the beginning of the war, but Golda turned it down. In dealing with the question of who to send to the front to straighten things out there, Golda had chosen Chaim Bar-Lev instead of Rabin, so that the former Chief of Staff spent the war acting as the chairman óf a voluntary fund created to help cover the costs of the war. During those days Rabin felt rejected and humiliated. The irony is that, for the purposes of the race for leadership, Golda's rejection of him then placed him at something of an advantage now.

All the same, Rabin's candidacy did little to excite the imagination of the Party leadership. Knesset member Yossi Sarid later related that when he brought up Rabin's name at a meeting of the Party's powerful Tel Aviv 'Gush' ('Bloc'), 'I could feel how the wind was blowing against me.' Sapir and his minions continued to try to persuade Golda to think better of her decision. And if Golda would not give in, the preferred candidate was Chaim Zadok. Peres evidently agreed, for he sent Gad Ya'akobi to see Zadok and persuade him to put forward his candidacy. But the Minister of Justice was as adamant as Sapir. So it was that the likelihood of Rabin's candidacy grew stronger. But in order for the Party's leaders to accord this 'saint' their ardour, they needed a villain to enhance his attractiveness by contrast, and this need was fulfilled in the person of Shimon Peres.

Once it had become clear that neither Zadok nor Almogi was going to enter the race, Peres had to make a difficult decision. He took a preliminary sounding of members on the Central Committee and found that most of them were not very pleased about Rabin's candidacy, for they regarded him as a Johnny-come-lately to the Party. At the same time, the press began to feature items which cast serious aspersions on Rabin's character. It seems that while he was serving as Ambassador to the United States, he regularly lectured for a fee. Then Ezer Weizman, who had been Chief of Operations when Rabin was Chief of Staff, asked for an urgent meeting with Sapir and revealed that in the tense period preceding the Six Day War, Rabin suffered a nervous collapse. When this presumed bombshell did not achieve the desired results from Sapir, Weizman made it public.

At the same time, Peres came to the conclusion that he simply had nothing to lose. He was presently Minister of Transport – a junior post of which he was assured in any case – and he believed that if Sapir allowed the members of the Central Committee to vote as they pleased, he had a reasonable chance of beating Rabin. Even if he didn't win outright, an impressive show of support could catapult him into second place in the Party.

The fact is that Peres was in need of a political manoeuvre of this sort from a personal, emotional point of view as well. Once the decision was firm, he talked to Gad Ya'akobi about it, explaining that 'this is the first time since the days of *Hanoar Ha'oved* that I can act on the basis of my own considerations and not the considerations of Ben-Gurion and Dayan. For the first time, I feel that I'm standing on my own two feet.' His reference to *Hanoar Ha'oved* was not arbitrary, for it was there that he had last won the only political victory that was solely and wholly his own. Now he returned to the paradigm which had served him then – a thorough, deep and uncompromising probe; not a single member of the Central Committee escaped, including those who had already pledged their support to Rabin. Sapir and Golda sniffed at his candidacy with a disdain that bordered on loathing, and when told that he was making his mark on the field, they were surprised. Once the extent of that mark became clear, they were almost in shock. Especially Golda, for the thought that Peres might take over the leadership of the Labour Party was anathema to her. To beat him back Golda was prepared to lend her support to Rabin – though he wasn't exactly her cup of tea either.

Under these circumstances, it was conceivable that the only votes for Peres would come from the *Rafi* people on the Central Committee. To win, or even lose respectably, he had to break the monolith of *Mapai*, which was susceptible to the pressure coming from Golda and Sapir. What he needed most of all was some development that would free him of the stigma of '*Rafi*'.

A development of precisely this kind occurred quite unexpectedly in the person of Abba Eban. The seasoned Foreign Minister had problems of his own, for his relationship with Rabin was in disarray and had been ever since the period of Rabin's tour as Ambassador to Washington, when he had refused to accept Eban's authority. Eban had no illusions that if Rabin became leader of the Party, he might well find himself without a seat in the new Government. Moreover, he believed that *Mapai* would naturally back him – as a veteran Party man – rather than throw its support behind a parvenu. But he was prepared to forward his candidacy only if Sapir supported it; and when he approached the Finance Minister on this subject, Sapir poured cold water on his plans. 'Why bother?' he told Eban. 'It's too late now. Peres has already got organized. You won't get more than 25 per cent in the Central Committee. And as far as Golda and I are concerned, the problem is to stop Peres. We need someone who has a 100 per cent chance of doing that.' Eban was stung to the depths of his being. He knew that if Sapir wanted to hand him the leadership, it was in his power to do so. From a political standpoint, he had reached a dead-end.

Following this mini-drama from his own corner of the stage, Peres quickly grasped the tactical advantage in the situation. He hurried to Eban's home and spoke to him in no uncertain terms: 'You can't live with Rabin. You couldn't when he was subordinate to you and certainly won't be able to when you are subordinate to him. With me, it's not just that we can get along; you'll be a senior member of the Cabinet.' As a result of this conversation, Eban came out publicly in support of Peres's candidacy. The announcement hit the *Mapai* chiefs like a bolt from the blue, and soon a host of delegations, individuals, pressures and threats began to issue from *Mapai* quarters. But Eban would not budge. Of all the political alliances Peres had made throughout his life, this was perhaps the most crucial. It accorded him the *Mapai* stamp of legitimacy which enabled him to move out of the narrow confines of *Rafi* into the broad expanse of the Israel Labour Party.

On Monday, 22 April 1974, the Party Central Committee met in an atmosphere of tension to decide between Shimon Peres and Yitzhak Rabin. The consensus in the press and among the delegates themselves was that Sapir's political machine would ensure Rabin a comfortable majority – something in the area of 65 per cent. When the results of the vote were announced, the shock was therefore all the more stunning. Rabin won, as expected, but by only a slim majority: 298 votes as opposed to 254 for Peres. Only 44 ballots stood between Peres and victory.

The outcome of the contest was considered a stunning accomplishment for Peres, for he had almost managed to out-poll the veteran *Mapai* leadership. Despite pressure from Golda and Sapir, close to half of the *Mapai* people voted for Peres! Thus, the vote spelled the end of *Mapai*'s long-standing hegemony within the Labour Party. From then on, the power of the veteran leadership would steadily erode until it, and *Mapai* as an institution in Israeli politics, would vanish from the political map.

From Peres's standpoint the gamble had been worthwhile. His rank as number two in the Party was unchallenged now. He and Rabin showered each other with compliments, and the public accepted their new leaders willingly, even eagerly.

With that much settled, Peres and Rabin were still forced to wait a few weeks before assuming their new posts, for during that period negotiations began on a separation of forces agreement with Syria and it was decided that Golda Meir and her Cabinet colleagues would see these talks through to their conclusion. Rabin and Peres were attached to the negotiating team, but they served more as observers than active participants.

In fact, Rabin dedicated most of his time to the task of forming a Government. Peres's place therein was, of course, assured, but for his part he still had an outstanding commitment which had to be dealt with one way or another. In a talk with Abba Eban, after thanking the latter for his help in the contest within the Party Central Committee, Peres had promised that 'I'll fight for you to be included in the Cabinet.'

'Rabin will never agree,' Eban warned.

'He didn't want me either. But he won't have any choice. We'll force you on him.'

Peres did demand of Rabin that he include Eban in his Government. Consequently, Rabin asked Eban to serve, but in a junior post devoid of all authority – Minister of Information – and Eban summarily rejected the offer.

When it was clear to all that Eban would not be asked to join the Government in a senior post, Sapir went to see him and taunted: 'So, where's Shimon's war on your behalf? He's entered the Government without you.' This time the unflappable Eban lost control of himself: 'You're the last person who can afford to talk. Shimon couldn't force Rabin to accept me. You could have!'

As for Peres, he justified his failure to Eban by claiming that he was helpless against Sapir, and to Eban's political logic it seemed a reasonable enough explanation. Nonetheless, the fact was that he had helped Peres attain his present position, and now Peres was in the Cabinet and he was out in the cold. Eban felt cheated, humiliated and abandoned – by Golda, Sapir and Peres, too. Gradually, however, his feelings towards Peres began to soften – a process abetted by the fact that Peres did not let Eban languish in the political wilderness. Throughout his term as Defence Minister, he met Eban regularly to provide him with information and seek his counsel.

On Friday, 31 May 1974, Israel and Syria signed a separation of forces agreement in the Palais des Nations in Geneva, and three days later, when the Knesset gave its vote of confidence to the Rabin Government, Shimon Peres became Israel's Minister of Defence. The Ministry that he found upon assuming office bore little resemblance to the one he had known during his long service as Deputy Director of the Ministry, Director and then Deputy Minister of Defence. The structure of the defence network had not changed, but over the years it had grown substantially and become considerably convoluted. The most noticeable difference was the prevalent bleak mood born of the Yom Kippur War: a loss of self-confidence, mutual mistrust and a sense of failure. Morale had reached a nadir. The Ministry was rife with gossip and smear campaigns regarding responsibility for the failures of the war. The overall feeling that everything was falling apart was met by a sense of helplessness which stopped just short of apathy. What should be done to overcome the rot? Some officers said that the first priority was to reorganize the entire system, including the army. Peres came to the conclusion that even if there were organizational defects in the system, they were not the root of the problem. The best solution was to run the existing organization properly by maintaining tight control over it.

This conclusion highlighted the differences in character and approach to work associated with Peres and Dayan. The previous Minister of Defence had focused his attention on the spheres of political and defence affairs, the administered territories and the IDF's operative programme. The remainder simply did not interest him. Peres certainly did not neglect these spheres, but he had a deep need to feel in control of the other parts of the defence network as well, right down to the last detail.

He didn't content himself with the answers to his questions from the generals, but asked to see things for himself. No less important, he wanted the officers and enlisted men to know that they might be exposed to his critical eye at any and all times and without warning. He began by engaging in a series of surprise visits to emergency stores (whose low level of maintenance had come in for sharp criticism following the war). 'On one of these visits he astounded the officers by climbing into tanks and checking their equipment. He asked the men in charge to open equipment bags and discovered that binoculars, signal flags and other vital equipment were missing from some of them. "It's inexcusable", he growled at the officers, "that binoculars are missing from a tank and a tankist hasn't got a sleeping-bag!" '

Another sore point for the Ministry during this period was the exodus of officers, including some of the most talented men in the army. Military service had always demanded personal sacrifices – in finance and family life; the compensation had been status and public admiration. But these compensations, like so many other things, had fallen victim to the Yom Kippur War. Suddenly a substantial body of officers began to discover that the whole business just didn't pay. From time to time someone would propose bringing retired officers back into the army. A few days before taking up his new position, Peres spoke to Dayan and found that the incumbent Defence Minister was opposed to this idea. 'I don't think the trend is a good one; the army should be made younger, not older.' Peres adopted this philosophy – an occasional exception notwithstanding – and if he accepted the services of retired major-generals, it was within the Ministry as aides and advisers.

In addition to dealing with standard matters, Peres gradually extended the scope of the Defence Ministry's activities. In contrast to Dayan, whose concept of security was limited to the army and related subjects, Peres perceived the full meaning of security in much broader terms. For example, it was not enough that the army be strong and well-equipped. In order to defend the borders of the state, it was also necessary to maintain a tight chain of border settlements as an integral part of the defence network. Moreover, reinforcing the viability and staying-power of these settlements meant the ensuring of full employment for their members. To achieve these objectives, Peres charged Moshe Netzer, the head of the Youth and Nahal Divison of the Ministry, with co-ordinating the whole matter of security settlements, and Elhanan Yishai, a good friend from the days of Alumot, with transferring defence industries to the border settlements.

In connection with these defence industries, one of the trends which angered Peres was the decline in resourcefulness and personal initiative. Officers and civilians alike seemed to be seeking out official approval for every move they were about to make.

Peres did not spend all his time behind a desk or engaged in dialogues about tanks. He also maintained secret contacts abroad. A case in point concerned the Kurdish rebels in Iraq, who were supplied with weapons and advisers in the war effort against one of Israel's most implacable enemies. But the leader of the Kurdish resistance, Mustafa Barzani, was not content with aid alone; he had set his sights on a joint campaign in which Israel would capture Syria while he conquered Iraq. When asked how he could talk of overrunning Syria with the Soviets defending it, Barzani replied derisively: 'Stop pulling my leg. You toppled de Gaulle and Nixon, you can do anything.' There was no way to convince him that the power he ascribed to Israel was more fantasy than fact.

The Kurdish connection raised one of the most ticklish problems that Peres had to deal with as Minister of Defence. While it was clearly in Israel's interest to support the Kurds as much as possible, she had to take into consideration the Iranians, who wanted the Kurds to be strong enough to go on harassing the Iraqis but not more than that, for Iran had five million Kurds living within her own borders. Since Israel was interested in maintaining cordial relations with the Shah, she was forced into a delicate balancing-act over this issue.

In one way or another, the United States was almost always tied in with Israel's arms deals, especially since the production of many items stemmed from co-operation between the two countries and their export was dependent upon American consent. Israel's role in this partnership was primarily as an agent. The American administration was interested in helping certain countries, such as Iran, but could not do so overtly or directly because of the prevailing mood in Congress or of American public opinion. In such instances it was very convenient to provide this assistance through Israel or by encouraging Israel to increase her arms exports to these countries – and on this score, at least, there was no difference between the Republican administration and the Democratic one which superseded it in January 1977.

Israel and the United States also maintained a relationship of mutual assistance between their armed forces and, on at least one occasion, an American military request left the chiefs of the Israeli defence establishment perplexed. Chief of Staff Mordechai Gur told Peres that the Americans wished to have their trainees attached to IDF courses. 'Do they have trainees in other countries?' Peres asked in surprise.

'Certainly. It's common between countries that maintain close relations,' Gur assured him.

'How will they manage with the language?'

'You won't believe it, but they're sending Hebrew-speakers!'

The Peres family, 1945. Left to right, standing: Peres's wife, Sonya, brother Gershon and his wife, Carmella; seated: Peres, his mother and father

Peres on a camel during his pre-state trek through the Negev to Umm Rashrash (Eilat)

Shimon and Sonya with two of their children, Zvia and Jonathan, 1957

With Sonya after receiving the *Légion d'Honneur*, 1957

With Ben-Gurion during the Sèvres
Conference, 1956

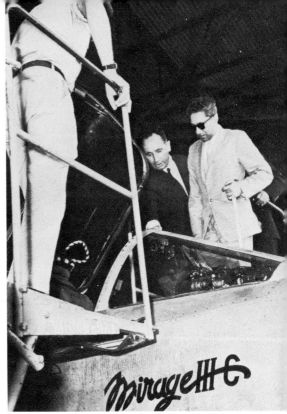

Showing a Mirage jet fighter to the
King of Nepal, 1963

With Prime Minister Levi Eshkol during a visit to Cape Kennedy, Florida, 1964

With two political comrades in Rafi,
1969: Moshe Dayan (left) and
Teddy Kollek

On an Israeli navy missile boat when he was
Minister of Defence, 1976

On the northern border with Rafael Eytan (right), oc Northern Command and later
IDF Chief of Staff, 1976

Peres with Chief of Staff Mordechai Gur (to his left) and other commanders in the Sinai, 1976. On the far left is General Dan Shomron, commander of the Entebbe rescue operation

Welcoming back the rescue unit from Entebbe, July 1976. Prime Minister Yitzhak Rabin is on Peres's left

Surrounded by bodyguards during a visit to London, 1976

Minister of Defence Peres on a tour of army bases, 1977

With President Sadat and former Prime Minister Golda Meir at the Knesset during Sadat's historic visit to Jerusalem, November 1977

With Vice-President Husni Mubarak while on a visit to Egypt, 1979

In the cockpit of an Israeli-made Kfir jet fighter at an Israel Aircraft Industry plant, 1980

With President François Mitterrand at the presidential palace, Paris, 1981

Sitting in his office under a portrait of Ben-Gurion

'Then by all means let them come!' was the Minister's conclusion.

On the broader question of foreign policy, the Americans had made it clear, as far back as President Nixon's visit to Israel in mid-June 1974, that they did not regard the separation of forces agreements with Egypt and Syria as the end of the matter. To bring the process full circle, they wanted Israel to sign a similar agreement with Jordan. It was Kissinger who put aside diplomatic niceties to lay matters on the line: the choice Israel faced was not whether or not to hold negotiations with King Hussein. The sole and undeniable choice was between conducting negotiations now with Hussein or later on with the PLO. But the problem was that from the Israeli standpoint the situations were not quite parallel: a military withdrawal from Judea and Samaria – from the point of view of both security and sentiment – could not be compared to a pull back in Sinai or even on the Golan Heights. Consequently, the Israeli negotiating team – Rabin, Peres and Foreign Minister Allon – tried to come up with solutions that avoided the subject of a withdrawal of any kind, and these proposals were discussed at their first meeting with King Hussein on 29 August 1974.

Late at night the Jordanian military helicopter carrying Hussein and his retinue landed in a Jerusalem suburb, where an IDF helicopter was waiting to transfer them to a government guest-house outside Tel Aviv. The venue was not unfamiliar to Hussein. In fact, most meetings with him had been held and would continue to be held in this building, though a few took place on the border between the Red Sea towns of Eilat and Aqaba. Only a small, close circle of people knew about this arrangement, and, in order to keep the group down to an absolute minimum, the Ministers' senior aides doubled as waiters during the King's stay.

In the spirit of the times, the conversation opened with customary banter about Henry Kissinger. Rabin told Hussein that he was going to visit Washington soon. When Peres added with a smile that Kissinger would be there too, the King – referring to the Secretary's frequent jaunts abroad – added: 'For a change!' Then came an extended exchange of views on the state of the world and the region, after which the Israeli Ministers turned to the question of signing an agreement with Jordan. Rabin spelled out three possibilities:

1. Immediate negotiations towards a comprehensive settlement. Both sides agreed, however, that such negotiations involved formidable complications, making this option unrealistic at present.

2. Reaching an understanding on the principles of a comprehensive settlement and then implementing it in stages.
3. Executing a functional separation of forces or functional arrangements on the West Bank.

As to the separation of forces envisioned by Hussein, Rabin immediately declared that it could not even be classified as an option, for it implied a unilateral withdrawal, and that was out of the question for Israel. Peres took up the baton and began to lead off in a direction he had adopted long before: a federative arrangement on the West Bank. He proposed that Israel and Jordan enter into an agreement that would include security and economic elements, joint positions and something along the lines of joint administration of the West Bank. He didn't care what this creature was called – condominium, federative government, local government. What counted was how it worked. Then he began to enter into details: the flag of the West Bank would be the Jordanian flag or a similar design; passports would be Jordanian; the Arab inhabitants could vote for and be elected to the Jordanian parliament; the Jewish inhabitants could vote for and be elected to the Knesset. Peres admitted that the idea might sound fantastic, 'but fantasy is the only way to resolve the situation'. Hussein treated these high-flown ideas with a certain degree of derision. It was obvious, he said, that much thought had been invested in shaping them. Therefore they must be studied carefully, and he promised to do so, but suggested that they 'talk about the present now'. Israel had entered into agreements with Syria and Egypt (the separation of forces agreements). It was, therefore, imperative that she sign an agreement with Jordan based on the same principles.

One of Hussein's chief aides was more incisive and outspoken than his King, adding another option to the ones enumerated by the Israelis: if there were no separation of forces agreement, Jordan might wash her hands of the whole matter, willingly or by yielding to the pressures of the other Arab states. Although the Israelis listened attentively, they had no change of heart about a separation of forces agreement. After hearing their final word on the subject, Hussein remarked bitterly that the irony was that if Jordan had joined in the Yom Kippur War, she would easily have attained such an agreement.

Then Hussein changed the subject by complaining about Jordan's difficulty in acquiring American arms because of their high price, and Peres said that Israel was all too familiar with that problem. Strange to say, the leaders of the two enemy states were weeping on each other's shoulders about the difficulty of buying arms to use against each other!

Hussein returned to Amman. The murmur of the forthcoming summit of Arab leaders at Rabat, the capital of Morocco, could already be heard from afar. On the conference agenda was the Palestinian problem, and, in anticipation of future contacts with Jordan, the Israeli Government began to take stock of itself politically. As a result, two camps emerged within the Cabinet: the 'Jordanian camp', headed by Yigal Allon, which favoured pursuing political moves with Jordan before any others; and the 'Egyptian camp', headed by Rabin and Peres, which held that the next step must be to sign a further agreement with Egypt.

Since the United States was clearly nudging Israel in Jordan's direction, the question was whether or not to report to Dr Kissinger on the recent meeting with Hussein. Peres was against it. Rabin addressed the problem to the Israeli Ambassador in Washington, Simcha Dinitz, who differed with Peres on this question. He reasoned that even if Hussein said he would not tell the Americans anything about the meeting, there was no guarantee that he really would remain silent. And if the King did get word to the Americans and Kissinger found out that Israel had been withholding information from him, it might cause 'a great deal of damage'. Dinitz therefore suggested that he be authorized to inform Kissinger that a meeting had taken place, add a few general sentences about its content and promise that Foreign Minister Allon would provide further details on his next visit to Washington. Rabin agreed, and that was how Kissinger was advised of the meeting.

A week before the opening of the Rabat summit, on 19 October, another meeting took place with Hussein and his aides, and once again the Jordanians raised the question of a separation of forces agreement. Rabin put forward the idea that if the Rabat summit gave Hussein a mandate to negotiate with Israel, it would be in Jordan's best interests if Israel began its second round of negotiations with Egypt. Then there would be an Egyptian precedent, and Jordan would not be burdened by the stigma of being 'the first'. Hussein's adviser was quick to forgo this concern for Jordan's welfare. Precedents already existed, he pronounced, and there was no need for more. Why set one's sights on a precedent which might not evolve rather than work from an existing one?

'Well, then, how do you envisage the separation of forces agreement?' Peres asked, and the adviser began to spell things out, stipulating a pull back of Israeli forces from the Jordan Valley and restoration of

Jordanian rule there. Rabin replied that the Israeli public would never stand for a military withdrawal from the West Bank. First of all, the people will want to know what was given in return, 'and what can I tell them?' he asked. The Jordanian adviser suggested that he repeat everything they were told with regard to the Egyptian and Syrian agreements. When Rabin countered that these agreements had been negotiated by a different government, the Jordanian asked in feigned innocence: 'What? Isn't there any continuity?' and won a round of laughter from all present.

Now Peres took a turn in sounding out the Jordanians by noting that in exchange for peace, Israel would be willing to make territorial concessions. 'Would she be prepared to withdraw from the Jordan Valley?' Hussein asked. While refusing to commit himself, Peres said that if Jordan were ready to enter into a peace agreement, then he, who was generally considered a hawk, would reassess all his views. On the other hand, a separation of forces agreement wasn't worth a wooden nickel to him, since from Israel's standpoint it represented a reversal rather than an improvement in the situation. Rabin tried to sweeten the pill by promising that no matter what, 'as far as the Palestinian problem in the West Bank is concerned, Israel has one and only one partner: Jordan'.

As to the forthcoming Rabat summit, neither the Jordanians nor the Israelis really believed that any shift would result, for they concluded by affirming that after the summit they would continue to elucidate the options on which future negotiations might be based. But on 26 October, reality came down on them like a deluge of cold water. The resolution adopted at Rabat was ruthlessly unequivocal: King Hussein would no longer represent the West Bank and was not authorized to negotiate on behalf of the Palestinians; his place would be taken by PLO chief Yasser Arafat.

Rabin convened a small group of senior Ministers for consultation about the new state of affairs, and the exchange of views between them illustrated the confusion wrought by the unexpected Arab decision. This time Peres reached new heights with his propensity for unconventional solutions. He proposed dividing Israel and the territories into ten districts – three of them being Judea, Samaria and Gaza – and establishing a parliament in each. Before he could get any further, Rabin cut him off curtly: 'What do you need ten parliaments for? One isn't enough for you?'

'I would announce', Peres continued, ignoring the sarcasm, 'that the Government is considering granting home rule to the Palestinians in the West Bank while maintaining the IDF's control over security and the right of Jewish settlement.'

Yisrael Galili wanted to know what the purpose of that move would be: to have a single state?

'For the meantime, yes,' Peres replied. If there were a war and the PLO were in charge, he reasoned, many Arabs would flee the West Bank and Gaza. If they went and there were a wave of Jewish emigration from Russia, the picture would change radically. Another course, Peres offered, would be to establish four administrations: in Gaza, Judea, Samaria and Jerusalem. If there were more Arabs than Jews in Judea or Samaria, it would be possible to concede one of the two areas. All this would be effected within borders that everyone will have become used to in the meantime, providing they were determined soon.

Rabin asked Peres to refrain from bringing his proposal before the Cabinet, in order to avoid unnecessary arguments. Jokingly, Peres retorted that he would raise the idea 'to confuse the enemy'.

'As long as it's the enemy who gets confused,' Rabin said drily.

The first meeting with Hussein after the Rabat summit did not take place until 28 May 1975. The King was still angry with his Israeli hosts and made no attempt to conceal his feelings. 'If you had consented to a separation of forces agreement, the Rabat resolution could have been averted.' Later on in the meeting, one of the King's aides exploded: 'Everyone makes reference to the Palestinian problem, but no one knows what it is. Why don't you change your policy? Conduct negotiations with the PLO on the West Bank and Gaza and afterwards [the territories] will revert to us.'

From then on, that approach remained the Jordanian line: 'We've been banned from the arena,' the Jordanians claimed. 'Please address yourselves to the PLO and then we'll see.' Consequently there was no longer any doubt that for Israel the next realistic step had to be further negotiations with Egypt. The uncontested hero of this venture was Henry Kissinger, who mediated, conciliated, smiled, shouted – and, at the critical moment, exerted pressure that stopped just short of being brutal. And for that reason, their attitude towards Kissinger went a long way towards determining the Israeli Ministers' approach to the negotiations.

Peres's attitude towards the United States in general – and Kissinger in particular – was 'Respect it and suspect it', often placing the accent on the 'suspect'. This had been clear as far back as a discussion held in Tel

Aviv before his first visit to Washington as Minister of Defence. The question under scrutiny then had been, how many military secrets could and must be revealed in the course of submitting the arms requests which Peres was taking with him to the United States. Since the Yom Kippur War, and especially after the aid agreement for $2.2 billion was signed as a rider to the separation of forces agreements, the Americans demanded that requests for aid be accompanied by as many details as possible of Israel's overall defence posture. Before the war, this stipulation would not particularly have concerned the heads of the defence establishment, for the political alignment in the Middle East was definitive: Egypt and the Soviet Union on the one side, Israel and the United States on the other. But this situation no longer held true. Word reached Israel about the close co-operation between the security services of the United States and Egypt, and Peres was concerned lest the Americans leak vital secrets to the Egyptians – either inadvertently or deliberately.

When the Defence Minister first laid eyes on the shopping-lists prepared by his aides and advisers, he was taken aback. 'We're dropping our entire concept right into their laps and stripping stark naked,' he croaked in astonishment. The Chief of Staff agreed with him, but expressed the fear that the Americans would refuse to honour their commitments 'if they don't know what's going on'. In the end, a number of emendations were made in the list.

Peres went to the United States at the end of June 1974, and his first meeting in Washington, on 24 June, was with Kissinger. He found the American Secretary of State in a sullen mood, for he had just returned from testifying before the Senate subcommittee on SALT and the chairman of the committee, Henry Jackson, had accused Kissinger of lying about a commitment he had made to the Russians. What shocked Kissinger even more was the fact that Jackson had produced a sheaf of secret State Department documents to prove his charges. Kissinger poured out his bitterness to Peres: 'There's no government in Washington right now. Jackson has more secret documents than I do!' For this reason the Secretary hinted to Peres that he refrain from discussing the financial aspects of his mission during this visit because 'all the figures will be leaked'.

After he had calmed down a bit, Kissinger explained that Peres had not come at a good time because he himself would be away (he was about to leave for Moscow), and relations between the State Department and the Pentagon were very poor. He portrayed the

Secretary of Defence, James Schlesinger, in very forbidding tones, adding that 'you have no choice but to turn to him. But if he has political ambitions, he won't be very helpful to you. In which case, you'll have to wait until I return from Moscow, and I'll take care of everything.'

Considering this build-up, Peres was anticipating an unpromising, not to mention unpleasant, meeting with Schlesinger. These expectations were reinforced when he reached the Defence Secretary's office on 26 June. Their meeting was scheduled for eleven o'clock and was supposed to run over into lunch at 12.30. But Schlesinger was not in his office when Peres arrived at the appointed hour. He finally arrived at 12.30, apologized for the delay and invited Peres to join him in his office, where the two sat for three hours with Schlesinger forgetting completely about lunch.

The reason for the bad blood between the Pentagon and the State Department, Peres discovered, was a series of pieces by CBS correspondent Marvin Kalb implying that Schlesinger was the man who had delayed the airlift of arms to Israel during the critical first days of the Yom Kippur War. No one harboured the slightest doubt that the inspiration for these articles came from Kissinger, but they also quoted sources in the Israeli Embassy supporting Kissinger's version of events. The Secretary of Defence was smarting over the affair and told Peres that on the decisive day he had come to his office specially to deal with the problem and had worked until one in the morning to enable the airlift to come off 'in Israel's hour of need'. He even surprised his guest by confessing that while 'Kissinger says he is for Israel but against its conquests, I say that I am for Israel enjoying full military security, without reference to conquests or no conquests.'

This statement melted the ice between the two men, and the rest of their talk was conducted freely and frankly. Schlesinger never hesitated to state his reservations, but Peres found him attendant and open to persuasion. Israel's principal requests were:

1. Lance and Pershing missiles. Peres explained that they were needed as an answer to the Scud and FROG missiles possessed by the Arabs. Schlesinger expressed his agreement to the Lance, but had doubts about the Pershings because of their capability of carrying nuclear warheads.

2. Cobra helicopters. Schlesinger immediately warned that supplying such aircraft to Israel meant that they would have to be supplied to the Arabs, too, and that implied a certain escalation from the point

of view both of the types of weapons involved and of the financial investment. Peres explained that the helicopters were needed primarily for night fighting against terrorists attempting to infiltrate Israeli territory. 'If we can catch the terrorists before they enter our territory, we can prevent the murder of women and children and obviate the need to cross the border to pursue them.' Schlesinger conceded that he had never thought about the Cobra from that standpoint and relented on the spot. A similar exchange took place regarding the next item: laser-guided bombs and rockets.

When Peres had exhausted his list of items, Schlesinger quickly summed up the total and told the Israeli Defence Minister: 'In the United States our outlay on defence is $400 per capita. If we fulfil all your requests, going by the number of people in Israel, we'll be spending $600 per capita on you. Do you want us to spend more per Israeli than we do per American?'

'It depends on how you do the counting,' Peres quickly parried. 'The proper calculation must be made according to the number of Arabs, not Israelis, for the weapons are needed against Arabs, not Israelis.'

Peres came away from this meeting with the impression that 'Schlesinger is a prudent, brilliant man with whom it is a pleasure to talk'. He had the distinct feeling that Kissinger's opinions of the Defence Secretary were a good deal less than ingenuous and that he was involving Israel in his personal rivalry with Schlesinger. From then on Peres was Schlesinger's champion in Jerusalem, perhaps his only one. During a Cabinet meeting, when Rabin sarcastically referred to Schlesinger as 'the saint of the generation', Peres shot back: 'When the time comes to divide the world into saints and villains, I am not at all sure where Schlesinger will fall and where Kissinger will.'

Apart from his rapport with 'Schlesinger, however, Peres had quite a few misgivings about Kissinger's way of operating. On the eve of Yigal Allon's trip to Washington in August 1974, he described to his team of aides what the Foreign Minister could expect there.

I'll tell you how it will go. Yigal will get to America and Kissinger will tell him: 'We have to plan a joint American-Israeli strategy for the next phase' [of negotiations]. Yigal is delighted. Then Egyptian Foreign Minister Fahmy comes to America and Kissinger says the same thing to him about a joint American-Egyptian strategy. Fahmy is delighted. Each one is confident that Kissinger is wedded to his side. Afterwards there is a leak in an Israeli paper damaging to Kissinger. He calls Dinitz in for a talk and tells him, all aggrieved: 'I'm your best friend. . . .' And then we apologize and try to vindicate ourselves.

In a private meeting with Rabin, Peres reduced this thesis to a single sentence: 'With all due respect to Kissinger, he is the most devious man I have ever known.'

In October 1974 Kissinger went to Jerusalem and Cairo to sound out the parties on negotiating an interim agreement, and it soon became clear that there were two main points of disagreement between Egypt and Israel: (1) Egypt's demand that Israel withdraw beyond the Mitla and Gidi passes; and (2) Israel's demand that the agreement include a clause demanding the end of the state of belligerency between the two countries. Preparing for the talks with Kissinger, the Israeli ministerial team adopted a stand against ceding the passes. But in a meeting with Kissinger held in the Prime Minister's Jerusalem home on 11 October, the Secretary of State pronounced that this position would be unacceptable to Sadat and would therefore sabotage any chances of reaching an agreement. The ministerial team wanted to consult privately, so Rabin, Peres and Allon withdrew to Rabin's study adjoining the drawing-room where the meeting with the Americans was being held. As soon as they were seated, Peres was quick to state, 'I am not prepared to go beyond the passes.' To his astonishment, Rabin countered brusquely: 'I am.'

'I suggest that you don't give away the passes immediately,' Peres cautioned.

'I'm for pulling back an average of 50 kilometres [including the passes],' the Prime Minister insisted.

'If so,' Peres rose as he spoke, 'there's no point in my being here. I'm against giving away the passes,' and he began to make his way out when Allon grabbed his arm and urged him to stay. Then Rabin continued, this time *sotto voce*: 'He [Kissinger] will ask about the passes again.'

'You don't have to answer him,' Peres contended.

'All right,' Rabin conceded. 'We agree that we won't talk to him about the passes.'

This incident illustrates the confusion that was so characteristic of the ministerial team at that time. It stemmed primarily from a lack of experience and led to a loss of self-confidence and a sense of pulling in opposite directions. Each member of the team had served in various posts in previous governments, but this was the first time the burden of decision was on their shoulders alone. And during the first months, at least, they had difficulty bearing up under it. The disarray was particularly true of Rabin, who got tangled in a web of contradictory statements which spread confusion both in Israel and beyond. On 3 December 1974, he gave an interview to the daily *Ha'aretz* and stated that Israel's demand to renounce the state of war was not realistic; but some two months later, in an interview for the ABC television network, he essentially said that such a clause was a *sine qua non* of any agreement.

Rabin was not alone, however, in his muddled state. During his visit to the United States, Allon fumbled over the Americans' intention to supply the Egyptians with a nuclear reactor. When Allon's report on his talks in Washington reached Jerusalem, Peres made his way to Rabin's office at top speed. 'What is he doing? From what he's saying to the Americans, the implication is that since we already have a nuclear reactor we don't need another one,' he complained. Rabin read Allon's cable again. 'You're right,' he said. 'I forgot that just before he left we agreed on the position that neither they [the Egyptians] nor we [should get a reactor].'

Peres, for his part, was having difficulties with the subject of non-belligerency. In closed meetings he passionately argued the need to insist on an Egyptian commitment to that effect, though publicly he refrained from promoting this position – which allowed him, a few months later, to contend in a background briefing to *Ha'aretz*: 'I demanded the cessation of belligerency? Can you show me where I said that?'

But he did say it. At one point he even began to doubt the point of continuing the negotiations. 'I wish to say that I am in favour of going to the Geneva Conference,' he announced in a closed meeting in his office on 27 December 1974. 'I think it's a mistake to oppose it. I'd rather spend 1975 in Geneva than on a fortification line of one kind or another in which we'll have to invest a lot of money.'

Yet so long as the negotiations with Egypt continued, Peres took the toughest stand on the Israeli side, while Rabin and Allon ultimately toed his line. As a result, Kissinger began to press on a very sensitive nerve. As a first step he retracted – or suspended – a few of the commitments which Schlesinger had made to Peres and went out of his way to find fault with the Israeli Defence Minister, whom he regarded as the root of the problem. In a talk with Ambassador Dinitz on 6 October 1974, Kissinger complained about the attacks against him in the Israeli press and mentioned Peres as being the man behind them. Some two months later, Rabin telephoned Peres to say: 'There's a problem in that Kissinger has his sights trained on you. Let's cool him off. We should give him a personal massage.'

The suspicions sometimes reached Machiavellian proportions. During that period, Vice-President Nelson Rockefeller telephoned Ambassador Simcha Dinitz with a serious complaint. The subject of his call was American military assistance to a Middle Eastern country. Kissinger was interested in having it continue and even expand, but there was serious resistance to it in the Senate because of a conflict between this country and a European state. The word on the Hill, Rockefeller claimed, was that Israel was working against Kissinger on this issue with the aim of weakening him. Dinitz categorically denied the charge, but Rockefeller did not content himself with protestations of innocence. If Israel was not working against Kissinger, he suggested, there was no reason why she shouldn't work in his favour. He asked that the Embassy use its good auspices with the Jewish lobby in Congress to have the latter try to persuade the senators to back the administration's policy.

All the while political talks with Kissinger were in progress, Israeli ears were attuned to any hint that hostilities might break out. In mid-July 1974 Peres was convinced that he heard a rumour of war coming from Syria. He told Rabin that 'all signs point to a war breaking out', and, when the Prime Minister concurred, Peres proposed calling a meeting of the Cabinet in the War Room within two days. In the end, the scare turned out to be a false alarm. There were other instances of this kind, but after the grim lesson of the Yom Kippur War, the Government wasn't taking any chances.

At the end of October Peres appointed Major-General Yisrael Tal to head a team charged with the preparation of political and propaganda groundwork against the possibility of war breaking out in the near future. He told Tal not to rule out any option. Tal wasted no time in formulating a programme and submitting it to Peres and Rabin.

In mid-March 1975 the negotiations with Egypt reached their moment of truth. Kissinger executed a few more shuttle trips between Cairo and Jerusalem, but failed to bridge the gap in positions between the two sides. In a last-ditch effort, during his final visit to Jerusalem, he demanded that Israel cede the passes and commit herself to a similar withdrawal from the Golan Heights within six months. In a dramatic

Cabinet meeting, the Israeli Government decided to reject these demands, with the Prime Minister, Foreign Minister and Defence Minister presenting a united front. Kissinger warned his Israeli hosts of the dire consequences that they could expect. But although aware of the problem, they were scarcely prepared for what came next. Kissinger initiated his campaign against the Israeli Government in mid-air, from the Boeing 707 which was carrying him from Tel Aviv to Washington. In a background briefing for the journalists accompanying him, he fumed at the members of the Israeli negotiating team, his sharpest thrusts directed against Peres, whom he called an 'insidious hawk, by Dayan's leave and in Dayan's shadow, who casts terror over the rest of the members of the Cabinet'. Even when he spoke reprovingly of Rabin, it was by way of mentioning the Defence Minister: 'A little man [Rabin] whose only concern is what Peres will say about him.'

In Washington, Kissinger did not stop at implied, albeit vitriolic, reproaches. Wherever he went, he blamed Israel outright for the breakdown of the talks. The most painful stab came in the form of a note sent to Rabin by President Ford – at Kissinger's instigation. This stated that 'considering the latest developments', the United States would 'reassess its policy in the Middle East'. Whoever questioned the meaning of that reassessment did not have long to wait for concrete illustrations: various kinds of weapons which had been promised to Israel simply failed to arrive; economic aid was reduced to a scale of millions, instead of the billions of dollars that had been agreed upon; and the Minister of Defence, who was scheduled to visit Washington in April for talks on further arms purchases, was told that for the present he had best stay at home.

As was often true of Peres, the greater the difficulties, the more he was flooded by a sense of almost mystic optimism. At a convention of officers from Southern Command on 10 April, he confessed that Israel was facing 'a difficult crisis with our only friend'. But there was no doubt in his mind that she would overcome it 'because what we have here is an unprecedented phenomenon. A nation which should have vanished from the pages of history long ago has made a come-back and reattained its youth. Great peoples are forged in trying times.' But behind closed doors the first cracks began to show as the heavy pressure left its mark on Yitzhak Rabin. His self-confidence was plummeting at a dizzying rate, and the fact that Peres's popularity within Israel was rising wore his nerves to shreds.

Immediately after the contest between them in the Party's Central Committee, Peres and Rabin agreed and announced that their rivalry would no longer influence the relations between them. Peres made a great effort to keep this promise. Though disappointed by his defeat, he did not feel beaten, for in the final analysis he had won a high proportion of the votes and had become the number two in the Party and the Government. Obviously he would have preferred the Prime Minister's seat, but after years in opposition and in relatively junior cabinet posts, he had ample reason to feel satisfied about occupying the seat formerly held by David Ben-Gurion and Moshe Dayan. He accepted Rabin's pre-eminence without question, and the Prime Minister never had any reason to claim – and never did claim – that his Minister of Defence failed to report to him or request his approval on any matter that required it.

Nevertheless, in contrast to this solicitous attitude, Rabin showed signs of hostility almost from the start. The most classic expression of this overt antagonism was his habit of interrupting Peres whenever he spoke at meetings. It was not just some 'baiting instinct' that motivated Rabin's behaviour, but polar differences in character and mentality between the two men. Rabin is a realist-pessimist, dry and extremely pragmatic. Peres is just the opposite: his thinking is associative; facts are important to him only as general lines, not as instruments to work with, analyse, break down. Most of the time he oscillates somewhere between relative realism and mind-boggling optimism. Which is preferable? 'In the State of Israel,' Knesset Member Micha Harish once commented, 'merely to see the facts without seeing beyond them is the difference between reconciling oneself to a state of affairs and trying to contend with it.'

Precisely this difference could be seen in the two men's approach to the basic problems which the Government faced. Rabin worked towards a solution of the most immediate problems through conventional means; Peres looked farther into the future and preferred long-range, unconventional solutions. In a quiet discussion between the two at Rabin's house on Saturday, 17 May 1975, for example, Peres held forth on the plan that had been nagging his mind for a long while.

We must try to initiate a national renaissance – something like neo-Ben-Gurionism – to settle the region between Rafiah and Beersheba. There are 5,000 second-generation *moshavniks*, the best farmers in the world. We have to desalinate the sea water and irrigate the hundreds of thousands of acres there. And until the water arrives, an aeronautics industry should be established there to manufacture hundreds of millions of dollars of equipment for export. The Government has to break away from developing the country's coastal plain. We should invest and build only in the Galilee, the Negev and Jerusalem.

Rabin looked at his Defence Minister as if the man were talking Greek. Even if he wanted to, he was incapable of thinking on a scope and in terms such as these.

Before the total break occurred between them, they used to meet on Saturday mornings in Rabin's house, far from the bustle of people, reports, cables. The atmosphere of the day of rest spread a mantle of calm, almost intimacy, over their chats. Peres, by nature the more talkative of the two, gave free rein even to his most secret and fantastic ideas in the belief that the talks were confidential and would never be used against him. Thus on another Saturday, 7 December 1975, he proposed that 'we turn to the Russians directly, without America's knowledge, and intimate that in exchange for their renewing emigration on the scale of 100,000 Jews a year, we'll evacuate part of the Golan Heights.' The Prime Minister asked for some time to think it over. In the course of time, however, Peres realized he was dead wrong in assuming that these talks would remain confidential, for Rabin described this episode in his autobiography, citing it as an example of Peres's wild ideas.

Following the crisis with the United States in the spring of 1975, the acrimonious verbal clashes escalated during and between Cabinet meetings. For instance, during one Cabinet discussion on political affairs, the two men locked horns over the following:

Peres: 'Schlesinger told me that he always knew Kissinger never intended to keep his promise to give us a billion and a half dollars for defence.'

Rabin: 'He didn't promise a billion and a half dollars, that's a fact.'

Peres: 'I challenge that fact.'

Rabin: 'You can check the minutes of the meeting with President Nixon. . . .'

Peres: 'I have no objection to that. He did say "support" and not "grant", but these are diplomatic formulas. . . . Schlesinger said in his statement that it should be announced that we will give them additional rifles.'

Rabin: 'He didn't say rifles. He said guns, and guns are not rifles.'

Peres: 'He said rifles, not guns. The Hebrew word *roveh* is rifle.'

Rabin took special pleasure in flaunting his military expertise, which he thought superior to Peres's. For example:

Peres: 'I can tell you that the Arabs are holding exercises according to a plan that will enable them to bomb our emergency stores.'

Rabin: 'That's not new.'

Peres: 'What is new is that it can happen.'

Or:

Peres: 'One result was that Jordan almost lost its armoured corps and air force. . . .'

Rabin: 'Armoured corps, true. Air force, not so.'

In the course of these exchanges, the rest of the Cabinet would sit distraught and embarrassed, their heads bowed, waiting for the storm to blow over. In January 1975 Transport Minister Gad Ya'akobi told Peres that he ought to go to see Rabin and tell him in no uncertain terms that if he persisted in goading him, Peres 'would respond sharply and make his response known publicly'.

'It's too early for that,' was Peres's reply.

Ya'akobi thought that Peres's restraint at this time 'was almost superhuman. Nerves of steel.' In fact, it was Ya'akobi who broke and went to see Rabin. 'Look,' he told the Prime Minister, 'you're insulting Shimon in a way which will ultimately damage the entire Government, yourself included. If I were in his shoes, I would have struck back long ago.'

'You're not in his shoes,' Rabin snapped, 'and you don't resemble him, either.'

It was inevitable that this atmosphere of confrontation would spread to the realm of the army as well. Prior to a discussion on the balance of forces in the Middle East in February 1975, Chief of Staff Gur complained to Peres that he had the feeling 'the army has been dragged into the hassle between the Prime Minister and the Minister of Defence', adding that he didn't understand Rabin's position and would not enter the debate. Gur's plaint tripped a warning light in Peres's mind. He believed it imperative that the army not become involved in his contentious relationship with the Prime Minister. Peres approached Rabin, therefore, and proposed that 'at the General Staff meeting, it's best that we hear them out and not sum up conclusions. We don't want the General Staff to judge between the Prime Minister and the Defence Minister.' Rabin replied that he only intended to present 'the picture' to the members of the General Staff. 'Without summing up conclusions,' Peres requested. 'Last time they sensed a conflict between the Prime Minister and Minister of Defence.'

Rabin did sum up the meeting. What's more, his attitude towards the
IDF and the Chief of Staff began to be influenced by his feelings towards
Peres, who sometimes found himself acting as a mediator and conci-
liator. During one discussion, Rabin abruptly asked the Chief of
Intelligence to present an Intelligence assessment on terrorist actions.
The Chief of Staff said that the subject was not on the agenda, so that the
appropriate material had not been prepared in advance. Rabin insisted.
When Gur held his ground, Rabin demanded that he 'cut out the act'.
Peres remarked that the Chief of Staff meant that if it were supposed to
be a situation assessment, it had to be prepared in an orderly way. 'So
we'll consider it a disorderly situation assessment,' Rabin shouted.

Matters reached the point where the Chief of Staff refused to
participate in a Cabinet meeting to which he was summoned at the end
of March 1976. 'I didn't come to the meeting because I didn't want to
blow up,' he explained to Peres. 'I wouldn't be surprised if one day I
explode in response to the Prime Minister's statements. Prime Minister? He doesn't behave like one.'

The crucial point in Peres's futile but constant war of words with
Rabin came in May 1975, when he realized that the Prime Minister
intended to appoint Major-General (Res.) Ariel ('Arik') Sharon as his
adviser. Rabin's flirtation with Arik Sharon had begun much earlier. A
hero of the Yom Kippur War, Sharon wanted to return to the ranks of
the IDF. The Chief of Staff was not particularly enthusiastic, perhaps for
fear that Sharon would overshadow him, but agreed. Peres also wanted
to allow Sharon to contribute his talents. The interesting point is that it
was Rabin who voiced a dissenting opinion that fell just short of
outright opposition. In a talk between the two Ministers on 27 February
1975, Peres reported that Sharon – who in the meantime had received an
emergency appointment in the IDF – 'is hinting to me that he wants
to return to the army'. Rabin commented that 'Motta Gur spoke
so negatively in the Knesset Foreign Affairs and Defence Committee
that I don't know whether it's a good idea.' Three weeks later Rabin
expressed his opposition more definitely. 'Arik said that he wants
to return to the regular army and that Motta is against it. I'm against
forcing him on the Chief of Staff. It was stupid of us to give an emergency appointment to Arik and not to Talik [Major-General Yisrael
Tal], who's moping around.'

Having established himself clearly on one side of this question, Rabin
fed Peres the bad news in instalments. He first revealed something of his
thoughts on Saturday, 17 May 1975, telling Peres, almost incidentally,

that 'Arik wants to be my adviser. I told him that I don't have any authority in security matters, so that I wouldn't be able to involve him in defence affairs. And as a plain ordinary adviser, he wouldn't have anything to do.' But later on in this talk, Rabin added that he could see the political advantage of bringing Sharon, a *Likud* man, into the establishment. Peres's advice was that 'the appointment may ease things for you politically for a few months, but after that Arik will become frustrated and disappointed'. He parted with Rabin convinced that the appointment of Sharon as an adviser was one of those ideas which one might float but never actually act upon.

His astonishment was therefore all the greater when, a few days later, the papers reported that it had been agreed between Rabin and Sharon that the latter would become the Prime Minister's adviser. And not just any adviser, but his adviser on defence affairs! The move was a stinging, flagrant slap in the face, first and foremost to Peres, but also to the Chief of Staff and senior IDF officers as well. No other Prime Minister ever had an adviser on defence affairs for the simple reason that the Minister of Defence and Chief of Staff were regarded as his advisers in this sphere.

At the Cabinet meeting held on 1 June 1975, Moshe Kol, the Minister of Tourism, asked Rabin whether the press reports were true.

Rabin: 'I decided to appoint Sharon as a general adviser.'

Peres: 'The paper had it that he was being appointed an adviser on defence affairs. I presume that's not what you meant.'

Rabin: 'A general adviser.'

Peres: 'What will he do as a general adviser?'

Rabin: 'The Cabinet does not have to confirm the appointment. Therefore, the subject is not open to discussion.'

What Peres – like all the other members of the Cabinet – did not know was that Rabin had told them only part of the truth. In a conclusive meeting with Sharon two days beforehand, it was agreed that Rabin would announce Sharon's appointment as a general adviser in order to avoid an uproar; but the written document he gave Sharon stipulated that the retired General would 'accompany the Prime Minister to any military or political forum in which he takes part'.

In July Rabin appointed Sharon as his adviser against the will of the Defence Minister and the Chief of Staff. By the beginning of August, the first incident had occurred and proved that the appointment was affecting the performance of the Prime Minister and the Minister of

Defence. An understanding between Rabin and Peres regarding the scope of Sharon's competence predicated that Sharon would do nothing to create the impression that he enjoyed a position superior to that of the Chief of Staff. On 7 August the Prime Minister, Minister of Defence and Chief of Staff were about to embark on a tour of army camps when Peres discovered that Rabin intended to bring Sharon along. He called the Prime Minister and protested that Sharon's presence was in contradiction to their agreement, but Rabin countered that it would not be interpreted as detracting from the Chief of Staff's standing in any way and that 'Motta should stop carrying on'.

Peres: 'But you told me that Sharon would not deal with defence affairs.'

Rabin: 'He's not dealing with army affairs.'

Peres: 'Then why is he coming along?'

Rabin: 'He's coming because I'm going.'

Peres: 'You have to be mindful of the Chief of Staff's prestige.'

Rabin: 'I am being mindful, but I'll bring along whomever I choose.'

Peres: 'If that's the case, and if the person you choose to bring along is Arik, then Arik cannot be subordinate to the Chief of Staff in his other capacity [emergency appointment].'

Rabin: 'I don't see it that way.'

Peres: 'Then I request an opinion from [Minister of Justice] Zadok. That's my right as a member of the Cabinet.'

Rabin: 'If you're appealing the question, then by all means let's cancel the visit tomorrow.'

Peres: 'Fine. We'll cancel the visit.'

And so an important tour by the Prime Minister and Minister of Defence was cancelled because of Rabin's refusal to be parted from Sharon – though in return Rabin never won any token of appreciation from his adviser. Throughout his term, Sharon made one outrageous statement after another, embarrassing the Government as a whole and its head in particular. Finally, in December 1975, he presented Rabin with his letter of resignation. Sharon's main reason for resigning – and the one he gave the press – was: 'I am not prepared to be a partner to security blunders.'

The affair was damaging to Rabin within the Party, as well, for the appointment of a *Likud* man to such a high post stuck in the throats of many Party functionaries, and they would not easily forget this transgression. From a personal standpoint, Rabin was perceived as a man whose judgment was open to serious question. The dominant feeling in the country was that Sharon had made a fool of him and exploited him – which was exactly the opposite of what the Prime Minister had intended. But the greatest damage of all was caused to Rabin's relations with Peres. If the Defence Minister had any illusions left, Sharon's appointment put them to rest once and for all. 'The move was designed to oust me,' Peres confided to Micha Harish, indicating that now he understood he was in a corner and would have to resort to his fists to get out of it. From then on, Gad Ya'akobi could no longer complain that Peres was meeting Rabin's abuse and provocations with silence.

On the eve of Sharon's appointment, however, Peres had suffered a setback that hardly aided his efforts to block the move. The incident also shed additional light on his special attitude towards Moshe Dayan. Since the constitution of the Rabin Government, Dayan had not held any official position – other than his membership in the Knesset – but in Peres's eyes his value could not be measured by his title or lack thereof. In fact, Peres consulted Dayan regularly and, as soon became known, even let him in on detailed and highly secret reports.

At the beginning of July 1975, an Arab employee of the King David Hotel was cleaning up the dining-room when he noticed a sheet of paper on the floor. He was appalled to find that it was an Intelligence document classified 'Top Secret', and gave it to the hotel manager. The document was returned to the Government, and the subsequent investigation produced the following picture: that day Moshe Dayan had been a guest in the hotel. He had eaten breakfast with Shimon Peres, in the course of which the Defence Minister had shown him some classified documents; evidently one of them had fallen on the floor without either of the two men noticing. The incident was known only to officials in the Prime Minister's Office and the Ministry of Defence, so that when details were leaked to the press, Peres naturally turned to Rabin. 'How can that be?' the Prime Minister asked in surprise. 'I only showed it to [Justice Minister Chaim] Zadok. The [military] censorship should have quashed it.'

The disclosure sent shock waves through the defence establishment, and Peres's name was crossed off the list of people to whom Intelligence reports were circulated. This drove the Defence Minister wild. Peres pronounced that he would not stand for a system that excluded him from access to secret material. He returned to this subject in a talk with Rabin, challenging him: 'Do I ask you who you show secret material to?'

'I only *tell* Golda,' Rabin parried.

'Well, what's the difference between your telling her things and showing her material?'

Months later Peres learned that the order to delete Peres's name from the circulation list had come from Rabin, and the Prime Minister had rescinded it after his talk with Peres.

Undoubtedly this incident did nothing to enhance Peres's image. He was subject to harsh criticism, far out of proportion to the importance of the affair. Keeping a former Minister of Defence in the picture was not, in itself, out of the ordinary. Many other Ministers had done so in various Ministries before him. But since the Yom Kippur War, there was a heightened sensitivity to Dayan being involved in security matters in any way. If there were grounds for chastising Peres, they weren't for reporting to his predecessor, but rather for not being sufficiently alert to the justified public sensitivity *vis-à-vis* Dayan.

While the tension between Rabin and Peres continued to mount, there were some bright signs on the political front. Henry Kissinger's bleak forecasts – made when the negotiations broke down in March – were not borne out. The war he had predicted did not come. On the contrary, it soon became evident that both Egypt and Israel were interested in renewing contacts through the auspices of the United States. But Kissinger was in no rush to resume the talks. This time he wanted to be quite sure that if his mediation efforts were renewed, they would end successfully. So he continued to activate his steam-roller, which proved highly effective, and at the same time he strove to reach an understanding with the man he believed held the key to moderating Israel's position: Shimon Peres.

At the beginning of May 1975, when Ambassador Simcha Dinitz celebrated his son's *bar mitzvah* in Washington, among his guests were Dr Kissinger and the Deputy Director of the Israeli Foreign Ministry, Ephraim (Eppi) Evron. Kissinger mentioned to Evron that he was interested in holding a secret meeting with Peres in Europe 'to find a way to break the ice'. Evron duly reported this 'feeler' to Peres, and, after consideration, Peres replied to Kissinger via Yossi Ciechanover, the head of the Defence Ministry's Mission in New York, saying that he preferred an open meeting. In a blunt reference to the cancellation of his visit to Washington, he added that their talk could take place when Schlesinger officially invited him to visit the American capital. But in order not to close off all options, Peres added that he would not rule out a secret meeting when he visited the Paris air show – if he attended the event. When Peres reported the initiative to Rabin, however, the Prime Minister vetoed the idea of a meeting. So the political stalemate continued, and with it grew American pressures – which placed the defence network in an ever more distressing position. Peres began to seek a formula to break the deadlock.

On Sunday, 29 June, he met Rabin and advanced a proposal which contained two elements:

1. Israel would not relent in her opposition to returning the Mitla and Gidi passes to Egypt, but neither would she retain them. The solution: the passes would be turned over to the Americans. If this idea met with opposition, the Americans could be stationed on the eastern (Israeli) side of the passes and the Russians on the western side (at this time, the UN force in Sinai included twelve Russian observers).

2. Either Peres or Arthur Ben-Natan would attend a secret meeting to inform Kissinger of the proposal.

Rabin accepted the first part of the proposal enthusiastically but rejected the second. He preferred that Ambassador Dinitz be the one to meet Kissinger and phoned Dinitz on the spot, passed the proposal to him and asked him to sound Kissinger out. When Dinitz called the Secretary of State, who was on holiday in the Virgin Islands, Kissinger replied that the idea could serve as a basis for discussion and agreed to hold a meeting. Dinitz left Washington immediately.

This was the turning-point in the crisis, for the Egyptians regarded Peres's proposal as viable, and negotiations were renewed. Kissinger came to the Middle East for another round of shuttle diplomacy, and this time his mission was successful. On Tuesday, 2 September 1975, Israel and Egypt initialled an Interim Agreement. As many technical details still remained to be worked out, however, Major-General Herzl Shafir was sent to Geneva as head of a delegation charged with negotiating these points with a parallel Egyptian delegation.

While these contacts were going on in Switzerland, Israeli Intelligence received reliable information about plans to overthrow President Sadat. That the information should be passed to the Egyptians immediately was beyond question. The only problem was how to do it. Peres wanted to pass the Intelligence directly to Egypt so that Israel would get the credit for it and thereby earn the goodwill of the Egyptian President. In the past, however, such moves had always been effected through the United States. Peres, therefore, suggested

the following process: the information would be sent to Herzl Shafir
in Geneva with orders to pass it on to the head of the Egyptian
delegation, General Majdub, within four hours. During that time,
Kissinger would be informed of what was about to transpire.

Rabin wavered and was anxious about Kissinger's response. After
talking it over with Peres, the two agreed that both Kissinger and
Shafir should pass the information to the Egyptians – Kissinger
directly to Cairo, Shafir through Majdub. But Kissinger had other
ideas. As soon as the information reached him, he phoned Dinitz and,
after thanking him for the item, said that he would be willing to pass it
on to Egypt on condition that Israel would not operate through any
other channel, including Geneva. The reason he gave was that Majdub
had no way of getting to Sadat except through the bureaucracy;
Kissinger, on the other hand, could speak to Sadat directly. Peres
believed that the real reason for insisting on this procedure was
Kissinger's desire to take all the credit himself, but at this point he had
no interest in introducing friction into Israel's relations with the
United States – which were tense enough already. So he telephoned
Shafir and ordered him not to pass on the information about the *coup*.

The signing of the Interim Agreement opened the American
sluice-gates, which had been closed for the previous six months. Now
Peres was invited to Washington to discuss details of the US assistance
promised in a rider to the Egyptian-Israeli accord. On Monday, 22
September, the telephone rang in his hotel room in New York, where
he was staying *en route* to Washington. On the line was John Adams,
Kissinger's secretary, who told Peres that the Secretary of State
wished to meet him 'on a personal basis for a private talk which would
reamin confidential'. This time Peres responded affirmatively without
consulting anyone.

The meeting took place at 11 p.m. the next day in Kissinger's
apartment at the Waldorf Astoria, and it was immediately clear to
Peres that the point of the get-together was not a political discussion
but a 'heart-to-heart' talk. After removing his jacket, to set an
informal atmosphere, Kissinger described himself as 'one worried
Jew'. His forte, he said, was knowing how to assess situations
properly, and that was why he was warning of a deep erosion that had
begun to make itself felt in Israel's position in the United States. (Peres
was surprised by this concern, for he was convinced that Kissinger,
more than anyone else, was responsible for this erosion.) Kissinger
wanted to know what Israel would do if she were forced to return to

the 1967 borders. When Peres replied, 'We'll fight,' the Secretary returned to the Jewish theme, asking in an injured tone why the Jews weren't proud of the Jewish Secretary of State – 'and Jewish not just by origin, but by virtue of his historic responsibility', he stressed. Peres replied that 'the Jews don't know how to be proud of their sons until the "after hours" of history – usually when they are no longer alive'. Nevertheless he said, he had come across an abundance of admiration for Kissinger, even pride in his work, in many Jewish quarters.

If Kissinger's aim had been to relax Peres's attitude towards him, this conversation went a long way towards achieving it. Thereafter, the relations between the two men were to grow steadily closer – though they never reached the point of close friendship.

Not long after Israel emerged from the political crisis with the United States – at no mean cost – she stumbled into an internal crisis so grave that it threatened to topple the Government. At the beginning of December 1975, a group of Israeli settlers from the nationalist organization, *Gush Emunim*, ensconced themselves on a plot near the ancient site of Sebastia, in Samaria, and proclaimed the establishment of a settlement called Elon Moreh. This was the seventh attempt to found the settlement. On each of the previous occasions, the settlers had yielded to the Government's demand that they evacuate the site, but this time they were well-organized and determined not to give in.

On 4 December Peres went to see the *Gush Emunim* squatters, who were confident he was bringing them word that they would be allowed to remain on the site. When he arrived at their improvised settlement, hundreds of people crowded around him in song and dance. Then the Defence Minister and the settlement group's secretariat shut themselves in a room in the building that had once been Sebastia's railway station. After ten minutes the door suddenly flew open and out stalked Rabbi Moshe Levinger, one of the leaders of *Gush Emunim*. Flushed with anger, his mouth bleeding from a self-inflicted wound, he cried out: 'Brothers! Rend your clothing! Chant lamentations! They're demanding that we clear the area, that we abandon our home!' Once he had calmed down a bit, Levinger pronounced: 'We have no complaints against Shimon Peres the citizen. Whoever orders Jews to leave Samaria is not a Minister and his Government is not a Government!' On his way back to his helicopter, Peres was no longer surrounded by a crowd of exultant settlers and their supporters; this time he was escorted by an IDF guard to protect him from possible assault.

News of the Government's decision to evacuate the settlers spread like wildfire throughout the country. That same night the roads leading to Sebastia were crowded with thousands of members and supporters of *Gush Emunim*, who were on their way to support the settlers. The Government seemed to be split into two camps: the dovish Ministers, headed by Yigal Allon, demanded the immediate and unflinching evacuation of the settlers on the grounds that any other course would do damage to Israel's image as a state based on the rule of law. Facing them was the Rabin-Peres camp, which called for restraint.

On Saturday, 7 December, Peres and Rabin met for a talk in the Prime Minister's home in Tel Aviv and the first crack in their front appeared. The change of heart was prompted by the Jewish Solidarity Conference, which was being held in protest against the UN resolution defining Zionism as a racist movement. The convention was scheduled to open at about that time, and both Rabin and Peres feared that a 'war of the Jews' in Sebastia would cast a shadow over its proceedings. To avert such a development, Peres suggested promising the settlers that in exchange for their voluntary evacuation the Government would consider the establishment of a permanent military settlement or work camp on the site. Rabin agreed and the proposal was taken to the settlers by Minister Yisrael Galili. They rejected it, reiterating that they would never leave the site willingly.

Now came the second crack, which brought down the dam. After visiting the improvised settlement, the poet Chaim Guri suggested to Galili a compromise whereby the settlers would leave Sebastia in exchange for the Government's agreement to transfer them to the nearby army camp of Kadum until the fate of their settlement was decided. Galili brought the suggestion before Rabin and Peres, who agreed to it. Then, unbeknownst to Peres, Rabin authorized his adviser, Ariel Sharon, to negotiate with the settlers on the basis of Guri's proposal.

The settlers welcomed the Government's retreat as a great victory for their tenacity. On the other hand, the Government's compromise roused the anger of those opposed to the illegal settlement. When Labour's Knesset faction convened to discuss the proposal, Yigal Allon had biting words for Rabin and Peres. Together with the other dovish members of the faction, he demanded that the Government retract the compromise and evacuate the settlers forthwith. 'I will not remain silent any longer,' Allon bristled. Rabin, who was evidently

unprepared for this irate backlash, threatened to resign if his decision on
the Sebastia affair were reversed. But to placate its opponents, he added
that the settlers would be evacuated from the camp at Kadum within a
few weeks. With that, Allon, who had likewise threatened to resign if the
evacuation were not effected immediately, backed down. Weeks passed,
and months and years, but no evacuation took place. The *Gush Emunim*
settlement was a *fait accompli*.

The Elon Moreh affair was a fateful turning-point for the Rabin
Cabinet, for it proved to one and all that the Government was not strong
enough to enforce the law. Henceforward, the Cabinet stumbled from
bad to worse, blunder following blunder, until its ultimate demise. It
seemed that neither Rabin nor Peres grasped the significance of the
retreat from their original, implacable stand. And if they did understand
it, they lacked the courage to follow through on what it implied.

At the end of 1975, the civil war in Lebanon flared up in full strength.
Facing the Christian community were Lebanon's Moslems in league
with the PLO, and this development added a new dimension to Israel's
involvement in Lebanese affairs. Hitherto, Israel's attention had been
focused on the Palestinian terrorists concentrated in southern Lebanon.
In an effort to prevent them from mounting incursions into Israel, the IDF
fostered a relationship of close co-operation with the Christian villagers
in the area, who likewise considered the PLO a dangerous enemy. When
the civil war broke out, this alliance was extended to include the
Christian community throughout Lebanon.

Peres made frequent visits to Israel's border with southern Lebanon,
on one occasion even joining an Israeli force when it struck at a terrorist
concentration inside Lebanon. But usually his trips were devoted to
checking Israeli defences and meeting Christian leaders. On one of these
tours, Peres walked up to the electrified fence which was designed to
detect terrorist incursions. A car appeared on the other side and a woman
emerged carrying an infant in her arms. Seeing the group of Israelis, she
approached the fence and explained to Peres that her child was ill and her
village, which had been under mortar attack for a number of days by the
Palestinian terrorists, lacked any medical services. 'What do you do in a
case like this?' Peres asked the CO of Northern Command, Rafael Eitan,
who was escorting him. 'We provide them with medical aid,' Eitan told
him matter of factly.

Then Peres noticed an opening in the fence through which Lebanese
residents in need of medical assitance could slip into Israel. 'Why not do
this in an organized way?' Peres wondered aloud, and that was the

genesis of the renowned 'Good Fence'. Within a short time, an infirmary had been built and a doctor and nurse were on duty there. At first only a few people took advantage of the new arrangement, but word spread through the Lebanese countryside and within a few weeks the trickle of visitors had turned into a flood. And the Lebanese did not come solely for medical assistance. Labourers arrived at the fence in search of work, farmers came seeking a market for their produce. The 'Good Fence' became an instrument that brought down the barriers between the residents living on its two sides.

While the opening of the 'Good Fence' was a security and public-relations *coup* for Peres and the Defence Ministry, those achievements were threatened by the shadow of growing disarray in the ranks of the Cabinet. Close to midnight on Thursday, 29 January 1976, for example, Peres received a telephone call from Yossi Ciechanover in the United States. As he listened to Ciechanover's tale, a look of astonishment spread over his face. A few minutes later he hung up and sat down mumbling, 'What's he doing? What's got into him?'

'He' was the Prime Minister, Yitzhak Rabin, who was then on an official visit to Washington; and what Ciechanover told Peres over the phone was published the following day in all the media – and in even more lurid detail. According to the reports, on Thursday evening, after meeting leading figures in the American administration, Rabin invited the Israeli journalists stationed in Washington to a background briefing at Blair House. When the newsmen arrived, they had the impression that the Prime Minister was in a state of exhaustion. He spoke of his meetings in a rambling, muddled manner. When he came to the subject of the arms lists he had brought to America, Rabin startled the journalists by launching into a strident and unprecedented attack, whose target was unmistakable: 'The arms lists we presented to the Americans were no credit to the State of Israel,' he began. 'They were disorganized. . . . They included accessories that are not vital in wartime. . . . Fortunately I corrected that. . . . Experience shows that whoever in the defence establishment thinks he knows what he'll be thinking in another year is wrong!'

When reports of the briefing reached Jerusalem, the reaction in government circles was close to mortification. These arms lists had been discussed at a number of Cabinet meetings and in more limited forums chaired by Rabin. Never once had he expressed the least qualm about them. It was within his power and authority, had he deemed it appropriate, to delete any item from the list; but never once had he exercised this prerogative. But the most astonishing thing of all was the time and place the Prime Minister had chosen to air his criticism. It was absolutely unprecedented for a senior Minister, let alone a Prime Minister, to vent such biting criticism of a Cabinet colleague outside the borders of the state.

What was he complaining about? One of the items on the list was the Pershing missile. Rabin came up against an American refusal to supply it for the two reasons already mentioned: its ability to carry a nuclear warhead and its exceptionally long range. Peres addressed himself to both these objections in a meeting with military correspondents:

> Up until a few weeks ago, the whole country was in an uproar because the Arabs had Scud missiles and we had no answer to them. Now all at once it's being said that we don't need an answer. I want to say first of all that the Pershing is a first-class deterrent weapon. Suddenly it's being said that the Pershing can carry a nuclear warhead! Well, so can the Scud! So can the FROG! So can the Lance! As to its range, the problem is very complicated. The Arabs can hit Israel from short ranges, but we don't have a single target, as they do. We have a series of targets and a variety of ranges.

When the next hubbub broke out, it was over a far more crucial issue, and once again it was painfully evident that the rivalry between the Government's two top Ministers was affecting their ability to deal in a businesslike manner with issues vital to the welfare of the state.

Since the conquest of the West Bank in the Six Day War, Israeli policy had been predicated on the belief that granting the maximum rights and freedom to the inhabitants of the territories would make it possible to maintain the occupation with a minimum of difficulties. The primary ingredient of this policy was freedom of movement – within Israel proper and from the territories to Jordan over the Open Bridges. However, Peres had long believed that another element must be added to these principles. The chairmen of the local councils in Judea and Samaria were appointees who had been installed by the Jordanian authorities before the 1967 war. Peres held that allowing the inhabitants of the territories a first-hand experience of the values of democracy would give them a greater sense of self-rule and in turn mitigate the less appealing effects of the occupation. He therefore proposed – and the Cabinet agreed – to hold elections for the municipal authorities in Judea and Samaria. The balloting was set for 12 April 1976.

But the closer these elections came, the more it appeared that going through with them could prove a mistake. Reports coming in from the field indicated that many of the mayors considered to be moderates might lose their seats to more radical candidates associated with the PLO. It was also becoming evident that Israel would have difficulty ensuring the democratic nature of the elections. PLO henchmen were active in fomenting riots with the clear purpose of terrorizing the local population into voting for the PLO-backed candidates. In Israel there was talk that it might be best to postpone, if not cancel the elections altogether. But Peres was against this idea for two reasons. First, postponing the elections – once the decision had been made to hold them – would undermine Israel's position in the territories and in world public opinion. His second reason was based on faulty information or on a misreading of the information available to him. At the Cabinet meeting on 4 April 1976, Peres admitted that he could not 'guarantee the results of the elections', but added that he 'read with regret articles in the Israeli press which make it sound as if the left and the PLO have already won. If you look at it from the standpoint of the lists [of candidates], there's a new element here that is still unknown.'

Peres would have done well to read the Israeli press reports with care, rather than regret, for the results of the elections left no doubt that the papers had been right. The radical elements won a landslide victory, and their representatives swept up key posts in most of the local councils.

Rabin reacted as if he were the head of the opposition, charging, in an interview in *Ha'aretz* on 12 May, that 'the Minister of Defence erred in his assessment, and his error led the Government of Israel to take steps that did nothing to enhance its prestige'. The charge itself may have been valid, but it certainly was a jab below the belt, for all the information about the likely outcome of the elections was at Rabin's disposal also. If he had arrived at a different assessment, he had the authority to postpone or cancel the elections. Peres even gave the Government an opportunity to do so at a Cabinet meeting on 4 April, a week before the balloting, when he stated explicitly: 'If anyone has second thoughts about holding these elections, now is the time and place to air them.' None of the Ministers, Rabin included, let out so much as a peep.

Rabin's interview in *Ha'aretz* infuriated Peres, who took the opportunity at a session of the Labour Party's Executive on 13 May to demand that, if Rabin was not satisfied with the way his Minister of

Defence was functioning, he should resign and form a new Government without him. The consequent atmosphere of crisis threatened the stability of the entire Government, which spurred the tried-and-true Party bureaucrats into action. They managed to bring Rabin and Peres together for a reconciliation meeting at which it was agreed that 'the conflict has been put to rest and from now on they will refrain from public clashes and criticism'. But this was merely another cease-fire which would last only until the next tiff shattered it with a bang. It was a welcome truce, nevertheless, for waiting in the wings was a trial which would demand the maximum of co-operation between the Prime Minister and his Minister of Defence.

On Sunday, 27 June 1976, Peres's military secretary, Brigadier Aryeh Baron, reported that an Air France plane carrying passengers from Tel Aviv to Paris had been hijacked after a stop in Athens. Its present destination was unknown. A few hours later it was learned that the plane had landed in Casablanca, where it was to spend the night. The next morning it took off for Khartoum, but the authorities there refused it permission to land. As it was possible that the plane would try to reach Amman or even land in Israel, a state of emergency was declared at Ben-Gurion Airport. Peres called Rabin and the two agreed to allow the plane to land, if requested. Then he ordered an IDF force to station itself near the airport and be ready to take the plane by force if it landed.

Peres visited the unit near the airport where, while waiting for further information, he mingled with the soldiers and stopped alongside the unit's commander, Yonatan ('Yoni') Netanyahu, exchanging ideas as to the best course of action. While they were talking, the aircraft was reported to have changed course and to be moving southwards. As the tension dissolved, Peres and Yoni began to talk about poetry and discovered that they were both enamoured of the works of Natan Alterman. The two parted without either of them suspecting that it was the last time they would see each other.

Late on Tuesday morning word arrived that the hijacked plane had landed at Entebbe Airport near Kampala, the capital of Uganda. In return for freeing the hostages, the hijackers were demanding the release of forty PLO terrorists imprisoned in Israel, another six prisoners from Kenya, five terrorists from Germany, one from France and a few others from Switzerland. All of them were to be flown to Uganda by Thursday; otherwise the plane would be blown up.

At a consultation that morning in Peres's office, the possibility of a rescue operation was discussed. The Chief of Staff outlined a plan calling for Israeli soldiers to enter Kenya, rent a boat and cross Lake Victoria towards Entebbe, infiltrate the airport, kill the terrorists, withdraw to the boat and return to Nairobi. But Peres could not drum up much enthusiasm for the plan because it made no provision for extricating the hostages. Then the Chief of Operations Branch, Major-General Yekutiel Adam, floated an idea for hoodwinking the hijackers, but it required the co-operation of a European state. Peres was not very happy with the plan because of the European connection, but in the absence of any other he did not reject it outright.

To deal with the crisis, the Cabinet appointed a team of Ministers composed of Rabin, Peres, Allon, Galili, Transport Minister Gad Ya'akobi and Interior Minister Yosef Burg. Their consultations revealed a clear inclination to give in to the hijackers' demands. The chief proponent of this line was Rabin, who noted that there were precedents for yielding to the terrorists. Peres countered that Israel had never yet released a terrorist convicted of murder. Rabin asked the General Security Services to prepare a list of all the terrorists ever released by Israel; there turned out to be murderers among them.

On Wednesday morning Peres summoned three Israeli officers who had served in Uganda at various times and who were acquainted with Idi Amin. Lieutenant-Colonel Baruch Bar-Lev had been head of the Defence Ministry delegation in Uganda and had helped Amin execute the *coup* which brought him to power; Moshe Bedichi had served as Amin's pilot; and Lieutenant-Colonel Yosef Soen had been chief of the air force delegation in Uganada. Peres grilled all three of them on Amin's personality, habits and how he arrived at decisions. From their replies he concluded that Amin was likely to co-operate with the hijackers and would try to drag out the affair in order to keep international attention focused on himself for as long as possible. Peres's last question to the three men was: 'Let's assume that we decide to use force. Will the Ugandans fight?' 'The Ugandan army isn't an army,' Soen replied. 'It's a pushover to capture the airport,' was Bar-Lev's assessment.

From all he had heard about Amin, Peres also deemed it worthwhile to try to keep in direct contact with the Ugandan leader. He asked Bar-Lev to do this, using the telephone in his private office. This move subsequently proved to be of the greatest importance. Bar-Lev held three conversations with Amin, and they gave Peres a feel for what was going on in Entebbe and how the negotiations with the terrorists were proceeding. After the recordings of these conversations were studied, Peres and his senior advisers were convinced that Amin was co-operating with the hijackers. Their last doubts on this score were put to rest by a slip of the tongue when Amin related that the chief PLO man had arrived in Entebbe forty minutes earlier and he used the expression 'he told me to tell you'.

On that day, Wednesday, Rabin grew even more inclined to yield to the terrorists' demands. 'I don't see any military option,' he said at a meeting of the ministerial team. 'Tomorrow the whole thing may blow up or a few people may be murdered.' Nevertheless, the final decision on how to handle the matter was put off till the next day.

On Thursday the tension reached its peak, for the deadline on the ultimatum was 11 a.m. Uganda time – meaning 1 p.m. Israeli time. At 7.45 that morning Peres summoned to his office the Chief of Staff, the Chief of Operations Branch and the Chief of Intelligence Branch, Major-General Shlomo Gazit. Motta Gur was forthright in his declaration that, 'As Chief of Staff, I cannot recommend any military operation to free the hostages as long as we lack sufficient Intelligence. So my final word will be to recommend releasing the terrorists.'

At 10 a.m., when the full Cabinet met to decide how to proceed, Yisrael Galili proposed a draft statement announcing that the Cabinet had authorized the ministerial team to continue in its efforts to liberate the hostages, including the exchange of men imprisoned in Israel. Rabin demanded a vote, and Peres realized that he was in a weak position. He lacked a military plan to recommend to the Government and found himself in a state of less than splendid isolation as a civilian who supported the principle of military intervention against the considered opinions of a former Chief of Staff (Rabin) and the present one. He therefore had no choice but to declare that he would vote for the proposed wording of the announcement, 'but only as a ploy – and I want that fact recorded'.

With the publication of the Cabinet decision, all settled down to an anxious wait for the hijackers' reply, and when it arrived a sigh of relief was almost audible in Jerusalem. The hijackers postponed the deadline of their ultimatum to Sunday in order to allow for the exchange of prisoners.

That same day, for the first time since the crisis began, a viable military plan was put forward by the chief paratroop and infantry officer, Brigadier Dan Shomron, a down-to-earth young man, who had wasted no time in pulling his thoughts together. From the outset of the affair, he later explained, he had the feeling that sooner or later the military option would be considered, so he took the initiative and formulated a plan. In a nutshell, it called for flying out a small, select military force accompanied by a second plane. The two aircraft would land at Entebbe, and the force, exploiting the element of surprise, would take over the airport by using a series of diversionary tactics. The liberated hostages would then embark on the second plane, and the two aircraft would return.

Peres ordered the plan to be advanced to the operative stage even though it was not problem-free. The main stumbling-block was the matter of refuelling, for the Hercules transport plane which was to fly the soldiers to Uganda could not reach Entebbe without refuelling *en route*. This problem was solved when Kenya agreed to help.

As the plan evolved in greater detail, Peres felt the burden of responsibility weighing down on him. Sending dozens of soldiers so far away into essentially unknown circumstances – was not this a rash decision? He felt the need to consult a man whose judgment he valued and respected. He picked up the telephone and dialled Moshe Dayan's home. Told that Dayan and his wife had gone out to dinner in Tel Aviv, Peres went to the restaurant, accompanied by his military secretary, Aryeh Baron. He found Dayan in the middle of the soup course and, asking Mrs Dayan to excuse them, took the ex-Defence Minister to a secluded table to outline the plan to him. Dayan was instantly enthusiastic, assuring his successor that 'It's a beauty of a plan!' Peres left Dayan to his soup and departed, feeling encouraged and convinced that they finally had something to go on.

One man not yet convinced of the plan's feasibility, however, was the Chief of Staff. At 12.30 a.m. Peres summoned him for a personal talk.

> I don't intend to propose a plan to the Cabinet without the Chief of Staff's backing, and it will be even more difficult to propose a plan over the Chief of Staff's objections. But this time the fate of the nation, of the state, of Judaism and Zionism are in the balance. I know I can't demand any guarantees of success. And I haven't deluded myself that if the action fails, I won't have to draw the appropriate personal conclusions. I admire your responsible approach. But now is a time for boldness. If we yield, there won't be anything left of us.

Gur listened intently and didn't say much. Afterwards he said that this talk convinced him that it was imperative to work towards a military solution, whatever the cost.

At the Friday meeting of the ministerial team, Peres did everything possible to talk his colleagues into accepting the plan. 'If this [affair] ends in Israel's total surrender, it will be a terrible blow,' he warned. 'We must pursue the military option.' But Rabin remained sceptical. His position was undoubtedly the most difficult, as he bore ultimate responsibility for the outcome of the crisis. 'While I am in favour of having all the preparations for a military action continue,' he hedged, 'I suggest that we regard it as secondary to the main effort of negotiating on the means of exchanging terrorists for hostages.' All this time the force chosen to execute the mission continued its exercises on a hastily built model of Entebbe Airport. It was decided that if the Cabinet voted in favour of the operation, the force would embark on Saturday afternoon.

At dinner on Friday night, Peres and his wife were host to the editor of *Ha'aretz*, Gershom Schocken, Mrs Schocken and Professor Zbigniew Brzezinski, top aide to presidential candidate Jimmy Carter. At one point during dinner, Brzezinski turned to Peres and asked, 'Why don't you try to liberate the plane at Entebbe with a military force?' The conversation missed a beat as Peres just barely managed to cover up his awkwardness and began to cite a whole list of difficulties. After Brzezinski left, however, Peres asked Schocken for his opinion, and the editor replied that he was against negotating with the hijackers and would welcome a military operation. Not a muscle moved in Shimon Peres's face.

At 2 p.m. on Saturday, the full Cabinet met to hear, for the first time, of the plan it would have to approve or reject within a matter of hours, since the second deadline would run out the next morning. If there was to be a military operation, the planes had to leave no later than 3 p.m. that day – or not at all. The discussion in the Cabinet room dragged on and on, but the Government could not make up its mind. At 3 p.m. one of Peres's aides, Chaim Yisraeli, passed him a note: 'They must take off. Afterwards the planes can be recalled, but it's best that they leave on time.' When he failed to receive a reply, Yisraeli sent another note: 'It's 3.30 now. Should they take off?' On the same piece of paper, Peres scrawled: 'Let them take off.'

Yisraeli pounced on the nearest telephone, and when his call was over he passed a third and last note to Peres: 'Shimon, they're taking off now.' Silently, Peres sent the note on to Rabin, who studied it briefly and looked up. For a split second their glances met, and the two sworn rivals saw eye to eye as they never had before and probably never would again. More than any other member of the Cabinet, these two men felt the weight of the crushing responsibility they had taken upon themselves and were now placing upon others. Each of them had a critical role in this drama: Peres as the prime mover, Rabin as the one who had the courage to make the final decision.

A few moments later, the Cabinet ruled (in Decision 819) that:

> Henceforth the matter of releasing the hostages of the Air France plane in Uganda will be handled by means of a rescue mission. [The Government] has decided to approve the execution of an operation to have the hostages in Uganda rescued by the Israel Defence Forces following the plan submitted by the Minister of Defence and the Chief of Staff.

Afterwards Peres left for his office to listen to the reports coming in over the operational telephone. Then, so as not to arouse any suspicions, he attended the *bar mitzvah* reception for the grandson of Herzl Rosenbloom, the editor of *Yediot Ahronot*. Rosenbloom happened to comment that some of his readers were asking what would become of the hostages at Entebbe. When Peres offered that 'They'll be home in another twenty-four hours,' everyone within earshot laughed. In another part of the hall, Arik Sharon approached Hannah Zemer, the editor of the *Histadrut* daily, *Davar*, and filled her ear with blistering criticism of the Government's footdragging: 'If it were up to me, I'd have given the terrorists to the hijackers four days ago and brought all the hostages home.'

Back in his office, Peres could hear Dan Shomron's voice over the communications network reporting that 'Everything is fine.' He proceeded to the Chief of Staff's office, where he found Minister of Commerce and Industry Chaim Bar-Lev (whose son, Omer, was with the force attacking Entebbe) and Major-General Rafael Vardi. Vardi's elder son had been killed in the Yom Kippur War and his second and only surviving boy went out to Entebbe. The Chief of Staff was openly angry about that. 'An only child should not have been sent on this mission,' he grumbled. But Vardi remained perfectly composed. 'If the boy is serving in the paratroops, he should do what all his friends are doing. That's what he wants. I told his mother that he's on leave. But she knows him. She knows.'

Finally word came through that all the planes had taken off from Entebbe and were on their way to Kenya.

Mission accomplished.

Peres summoned Baruch Bar-Lev to his office and asked him to telephone Idi Amin one last time to deliver a brief message: 'Thanks for the co-operation.' As Bar-Lev spoke, however, it became clear – to the astonishment of all present – that Amin did not know what had happened. The transcript of the conversation reads:

Amin: 'President Amin speaking.'

Bar-Lev: 'Sir, I want to thank you for the co-operation and thank you very much, sir.'

Amin: 'You know that you didn't succeed.'

Bar-Lev: 'What? The co-operation didn't work out? Why not?'

Amin: 'Have you done anything at all?'

Bar-Lev: 'I did exactly what you wanted.'

Amin: 'What happened? Can you tell me?'

Bar-Lev: 'No. I don't know. I may call you again tomorrow morning.'

When Peres rang the Prime Minister and told him about this conversation, Rabin burst out laughing – the laughter of release. He invited Peres to come to his office, where the leaders of the opposition, Menachem Begin and Elimelech Rimalt, were already present, sharing jokes and more serious exchanges with Rabin and the others. When Peres ventured that the operation would change Israel's status in the world, Begin added that it would 'heal the nation of the trauma of the Yom Kippur War'. At 2 a.m. on Sunday, 4 July, as the planes made their way back to Israel, the official communiqué on the rescue operation was released for publication. Then someone brought Peres the news that Yoni Netanyahu had been wounded. He was startled by the report, but pleased that at least the soldier who shared his love for Alterman's poetry was alive.

Peres returned to his office at 3 a.m. and lay down on the narrow military cot that had served as his bed for the past week. He closed his eyes, but a rush of thoughts came instead of sleep. Suddenly the lights went on and, as Peres opened his eyes slowly, he saw the erect figure of Mordechai Gur, his face twisted in a grimace.

'What happened?' Peres asked in alarm.

'It's Yoni. A bullet got him in the back. Sliced into his heart. He's gone.'

For the first time during that entire mad week, Peres was unable to control his emotions. He turned his back to Gur and allowed his tears to flow freely onto the rough army blanket.

On Friday evening, 9 September, a Westwind executive jet was placed at Peres's disposal for a 'secret' journey to Teheran. During the reign of the Shah, the relations between Israel and Iran were based on intense co-operation deriving from common interests. The secrecy in which these ties were shrouded was essentially of the 'official' kind; everyone seemed to know about the relations between the two countries, but preferred to pretend that they did not exist. In this way, the Shah did not anger the Arab states too much while enjoying the benefits that stemmed from his relations with Israel. The Shah's interest in Israel was limited primarily to arms and co-operation in various fields. Israel, for her part, was certainly interested in exporting weapons, but her chief motivation was oil.

As the Defence Minister's Westwind entered Iranian air space, Peres peered out at the landscape below. 'What you see from the outside', he later recorded, 'are the oriental-style walls that enclose the gardens, and further within are the homes. Most of the houses, like the women, are hidden from view.' From Teheran Airport the Israeli delegation was taken to a guest-house, 'a small palace built of marble and secluded in an exquisite garden at whose centre was a large pool and an iridescent fountain. Fairly nice, a bit Levantine.'

On Saturday morning the Israelis were escorted to the imperial palace 'like a bride to the wedding canopy and led into the Shah's office. He looked very thin, stately, but athletic. His face seemed relatively small, and through his glasses his eyes appeared large and intelligent.' In the subsequent free flow of conversation, the Shah proceeded to inaugurate what he characterized as 'a new page in relations between us'. He expressed his resentment that the Jewish lobby in Washington was adverse, as he put it, to Iran's interests in Congress and her standing in American public opinion, and he asked Peres to lend a hand on this score.

Peres returned to Israel with a sense of accomplishment – and with good reason: he had a number of achievements behind him in Iran and various other countries, not to mention the Entebbe affair. But this feeling was soon dampened when it became clear that the truce in his relations with Rabin, engendered by the Entebbe episode, was only a short-lived reprieve. They were again locked in battle a few days after the hostages had returned to Israel, this time over credit for the rescue operation. Rabin began to voice the claim – reiterated in his autobiography – that Peres's role in the affair was marginal, at best, and actually of no more than nuisance value. At this stage Peres conceded to Gad Ya'akobi that his relations with the Prime Minister had finally reached the point of no return. 'Either I am going to be Prime Minister or, if I am not Prime Minister, I cannot be a member of a government headed by Rabin.'

Galvanized at last, Peres did not stop at words. He began to size up his own standing in the Party, while the media were not oblivious to his moves. Information began to filter out to the press that he intended to put forward his candidacy for the premiership at the Labour Party Central Committee meeting scheduled to take place before the November 1977 elections. Word of this challenge again led Rabin to *Ha'aretz*, which published an article on 8 October under a headline quoting the Prime Minister as saying: 'If Peres wants to contend for the premiership, he must resign as a Minister first.' At the same time, Rabin vented sharp criticism of Peres's policy in the administered territories. This latest barrage led Peres to consult Ya'akobi again, this time because he felt that he ought to resign. 'How can I go on after the things he's said about me?' he mused aloud. Ya'akobi made a bee-line from Peres's office to Rabin's and marched in to see the Prime Minister without an appointment. Now he told Rabin, 'If Peres resigns, it means a Government crisis, and that is bad for the country, for the Party and for you yourself.' Moreover, Ya'akobi left no doubt about the fact that if Peres resigned, he would follow suit. Rabin asked what action he thought was in order, and Ya'akobi suggested that he invite Peres in for a talk and issue a 'clarifying' statement.

In his subsequent talk with Peres, Rabin claimed that the headline in *Ha'aretz* did not reflect what he had really said; and indeed, when the full interview was published, it emerged that Rabin had not actually mentioned Peres by name. What he had said was, 'If a Minister decides he wants to contend for the premiership, he must resign from the Government' – but the implication was clear. Now, however, to avert a crisis, Rabin issued a statement reaffirming that he 'did not ask for the resignation of any Government Minister'.

The constant friction within the Cabinet merged with the deteriorating economic situation and the seemingly incessant strikes to create a general sense of malaise in the country and widespread discontent with the Labour Government. Gradually a thirst for change emerged among a growing portion of the Israeli electorate, and it focused primarily on the person of Professor Yigael Yadin. This charismatic professor of archaeology had been the IDF's Chief of Staff during the early 1950s, but had shied away from political life to pursue his academic career, in which he had earned an international reputation. Throughout the years, despite repeated requests and attempts to lure him, he adamantly refused to have anything to do with politics. But now he was prepared to found a new Party, and all the signs indicated that it would make an excellent showing at the polls.

Curiously enough, the declining fortunes of the Rabin Government and the Labour Party did not detract from Peres's own image. Public-opinion polls showed that only 35 per cent of those questioned were satisfied with Rabin's performance as Prime Minister while 51 per cent preferred Peres. Rabin's condition, politically speaking, appeared to be fatal. So it was almost natural that when the opportunity arose he made a desperate move – and one which ultimately toppled his Government and pushed the Labour Party out of power.

The opportunity presented itself when the National Religious Party, the second largest partner in the Labour coalition, abstained in a no-confidence vote called over the issue of violating the Sabbath during a ceremony marking the arrival of the first F-15 fighter-bombers purchased in the United States. Everyone expected Rabin to content himself with rebuking the delinquent Ministers. Instead, he went to the President and submitted his resignation – which, by law, carries with it the resignation of the Cabinet as a whole. From then on, the forum continued to function as a caretaker Government until the next general elections – which were brought forward to 17 May 1977.

Rabin's political ratings did indeed rise during this period. The move he effected won him kudos for political *savoir-faire* and was described as a 'brilliant maneuvre'. Not until the votes were counted in the general elections was it seen for what it really was: a brainstorm which played right into the hands of the *Likud*.

Nevertheless, the NRP – and especially the *Likud* – did not wish to wait until May to be rid of Yitzhak Rabin. On 20 December the leaders of the *Likud*, Menachem Begin and Simcha Ehrlich, approached Peres and proposed that he form a Government composed of the *Likud*, the NRP and sections of the Labour Party opposed to Rabin. Peres spurned these advances, telling the opposition leaders that he had no intention of operating outside or against his Party. He even reported it to Rabin, who claimed that 'he already knew about it and appreciated Peres's stance'. Advancing the date of the elections naturally brought forward the contest for the top post in the Labour Party as well. Formally speaking, Peres refrained from announcing his candidacy, but he declared publicly that he would not waive his right to do so in the future.

Once again he adopted a tactic in which Abba Eban played a central role. When the race for the Party's leadership began. Peres asked Eban to throw his hat in the ring. The reason, as he explained it, was that 'It isn't easy for me, as Minister of Defence, to declare my candidacy so early on, but your candidacy will establish the principle of a contest.' Eban agreed to make his bid, though it was perfectly obvious on whose behalf he was acting. But with one man ostensibly in the race already, the veteran leadership of the Labour Party, headed by Golda Meir, began to exhort Peres not to forward his own candidacy. 'It's just not acceptable to turn out a Prime Minister,' Yehoshua Rabinowitz chided. 'If it's dumping people we're talking about,' Peres shot back, 'then it was Rabin, after all, who booted Abba Eban out of the Government.' In addition, he claimed that with Rabin at the head of the list, the Labour Party had practically no chance of winning the election.

It was in a television interview on 11 January 1977 that Peres formally announced, 'I shall run for the premiership.' A little less than a month later, Abba Eban convened his 'supporters' at his Herzliya home and amid applause announced that he was withdrawing his name from the race and transferring his support to Peres.

Once again Peres found himself up against the Party establishment, but this time the veteran leadership, like its candidate, was far weaker than it had been in 1974. The closer they drew to the hour of decision, the better Peres's chances became – which only heightened the friction in the already tense atmosphere. Never before had the Labour Party deposed an incumbent Prime Minister, but there was a feeling that this time it was about to happen.

The Labour Party Convention met on 23 February 1977, and, after Rabin and Peres had addressed the plenum, the polling-booths were opened. Before long the Peres camp realized that something was amiss. One of the Druze delegates approached Aharon Harel, head of the Peres headquarters, and asked to speak to him privately. Earlier, a number of Druze and other Arab delegates had promised their votes to Peres. But just as the polling-booths were about to open, they were called in to see one of Rabin's men, who (completely without Rabin's knowledge) explained that because of a quirk in the balloting procedure, it would be possible to figure out how the Arab delegates had voted. This revelation was clearly understood as a threat of political retaliation against those who voted for Peres.

The polls closed at 11 p.m. For hours the two candidates had been sitting in separate rooms surrounded by their closest supporters as they waited tensely for the results. They began to trickle in now – first a slight advantage to Rabin, then a slight advantage to Peres; neck and neck all the way. Peres's face set in a frown of dejection when the final tally became known: 1,445 votes for Rabin; 1,404 for Peres – just forty-one votes difference. For all intents and purposes, a mere twenty-one people had come between him and victory.

Peres made his way to the stage of the convention hall. At the edge of the platform, he hesitated. From behind the curtain he could hear the roar of the audience, which already knew the result. He felt that he just could not face them. Micha Harish touched his arm gently and whispered: 'Shimon, you've got to go out there.' When he walked on to the stage, the delegates received him with a standing ovation.

It was obvious to everyone that the Druze and Arab votes had decided the election (80 per cent of them had gone to Rabin). On his own initiative, Aharon Harel had requested and received a sworn statement from the Druze that pressure had been exerted on them by Rabin's people. But when he approached Peres with the document, confident that 'On the basis of this, we can disqualify the election', the Defence Minister's reaction was a crisp 'Out of the question!'

'Why?' Harel pressed. 'We have an open-and-shut case.'

A sad smile informed Peres's face. 'Let's say there's another vote and I win. The other side won't accept it, and there'll be a split in the Party. If I lose, then I'll be beaten a second time. So it's not worth it in either case. Let's just swallow it and keep quiet.'

From then on Peres and Rabin devoted most of their energies to the struggle against the *Likud* and Professor Yadin's Democratic Movement for Change (DMC). It was undoubtedly the calmest period in their relations for many a year, but as time went on it became painfully clear that the shift had come too late. The Labour Party's election campaign limped along while the *Likud* and the DMC were coasting on a wave of mounting popularity. And every time it appeared that the Labour campaign was finally getting off the ground, something came along to shoot it down again with a resounding thump. The party was especially hard hit by a spate of corruption scandals, two of which rocked the entire country. The first made the headlines in the autumn of 1976, when Moshe Sanbar's term of office as Governor of the Bank of Israel was drawing to a close. Various candidates were proposed to replace him, but Rabin chose the Director-General of the *Histadrut*'s Sick Fund (*Kupat Holim*), Asher Yadlin, who was also one of the leading functionaries in the Labour Party. Shortly after Rabin announced his choice, however, a press report charged that Yadlin had taken bribes for work apportioned to various parties on behalf of the Sick Fund. Brought to trial, at the close of a highly publicized police investigation which provided endless grist to the newspapers, he confessed to almost all the charges and was sentenced to five years' imprisonment.

The second scandal broke at the close of 1976, when rumours of personal and bureaucratic corruption were voiced against Housing Minister Avraham Ofer, a front-line member of the Labour Party leadership. Ofer vigorously denied the rumours published in the press. Then, on the morning of 4 January 1977, the citizens of Israel awoke to tragic and depressing news. A passer-by had found Ofer in his car on the beach north of Tel Aviv, a bullet imbedded in his brain. His revolver was lying on the seat next to the note in which Ofer gave the reason for his suicide.

All this added to the overt friction within the Labour Party and resulted in a general sense of bewilderment. The Party could only hope that the public would forget these scandals before the elections in May. But now a third scandal provided the proverbial last straw, breaking both Rabin's back and that of the Labour Party.

The item published by Dan Margalit in *Ha'aretz* on 15 March 1977 held no hint of the cataclysmic events to come. It merely disclosed that the Prime Minister's wife, Leah Rabin, had a bank account in Washington, DC, though Israeli currency laws strictly forbade the maintenance of a bank account abroad. Before long the plot thickened when it emerged that the Prime Minister was himself a joint signatory to the account. Rabin confirmed the veracity of the press item, but quickly added that the account contained a mere $2,000. The gravity of this kind of offence was usually measured by the sum involved, and it was customary for the Government to content itself with imposing a fine if the sum did not exceed $5,000; criminal charges were pressed only in cases where the amount was greater than that figure. On the basis of Rabin's statement, therefore, the Attorney-General, Professor Aharon Barak, told the Prime Minister that he had nothing to fear, and slowly the echoes of the affair began to die down. Barak, however, acting as he would *vis-à-vis* any other citizen of the state, demanded that Rabin present his bank statement as proof. And when he did so, it turned out that he had lied: not one bank account existed in Washington, but two. And not $2,000 were deposited in these accounts, but about $23,000. Barak informed Rabin that he had no choice but to place his wife on trial; Rabin himself would get the benefit of the doubt that he had been ignorant about the amount.

On the night of 7 April 1977, the citizens of Israel were glued to their television sets watching the European Basketball Championship match between the Israeli champions, Maccabi Tel Aviv, and Mobilgirgi Varese. Peres was dining at the Ebans' home, together with Sir Isaac Wolfson and the British Ambassador. At one point Eban brought a portable television to the table and turned it on without the sound. The other guests found it difficult to understand why Eban and Peres were so interested in a basketball game.

Peres did not wait for the game to end. Fairly early in the evening, he asked to be excused and went home.

When they entered their apartment, Sonya turned on the television. The basketball game was still on. Peres said that he was tired and went to bed.

Just as he was dozing off, the bedroom light went on and Peres saw Sonya standing in the doorway. 'Come watch television, quickly,' she said.

'Who won?' Peres asked.

'No, no,' Sonya said excitedly. 'It's Rabin.'

Peres followed her into the living-room and saw the screen filled by Rabin's face set in a grim expression. In a trembling voice he announced his resignation from the premiership and chairmanship of the Labour Party. 'It's a sad ending,' he uttered feebly.

Sonya turned off the set and stared at her husband, who sat there without saying a word, his face frozen as if he were suffering from shock. Then he stood up and went silently back to bed.

The *Likud* was also having difficulties at this juncture, for its own candidate for Prime Minister, Menachem Begin, was in hospital recovering from a serious heart attack. The people manning the *Likud*'s election headquarters, especially Ezer Weizman, began to fear that they might have to run a campaign with their chief candidate confined to bed.

One day during this period, Brigadier Aryeh Baron, Peres's military secretary, was eating lunch in a Tel Aviv restaurant. Ezer Weizman and his close friend, the public-relations magnate Eliezer Zurrabin, were sitting at a remote table. Suddenly Zurrabin came up to Baron and asked him to join them. As soon as Baron was seated, Zurrabin launched into his bid: 'Tell Peres to leave Rabin and all that corruption and come with us. I'll write him a cheque for the premiership.' Baron addressed himself to Weizman as he replied, 'It's not logical that he should join you. He's about to take over the leadership of the Labour Party. It makes more sense for him to establish an independent list and for you to join him.'

Zurrabin glanced at Weizman, who nodded almost imperceptibly. 'We're prepared to go into that, as well,' he said.

When Baron reported the conversation to Peres, both ideas were rejected instantly. Word of Peres's refusal was passed to Zurrabin, who was unwilling to accept it as final. 'I want to meet Peres,' he said. 'I want it to be recorded in your log that I offered him the premiership and he turned it down.' Baron set up the meeting and, upon hearing Peres's implacable refusal for himself, all Zurrabin could say was: 'You're making a big mistake and you'll yet regret it.'

As there was no precedent for a Prime Minister resigning as a result of personal dishonesty, a number of legal problems cropped up. As head of a caretaker government, Rabin was unable to resign. Thus the only solution was for him to go on leave. The first question was, who would take over from him? Party functionaries began to scurry around in search of a candidate. Some of them suggested Justice Minister Chaim Zakok. Others said the post should go to Yigal Allon by virtue of his being Deputy Prime Minister. Rabin rejected both suggestions, essentially before they were made. On the morning after his televised announcement, he phoned Peres and, after expressing his regret that he was not able to give him prior notice of his intent to resign, said that he had decided to turn the position over to him. 'It will be a long time before I return to political life,' he said.

On 17 April Rabin sat at the head of the Cabinet for the last time and declared that, 'It is my intention to take leave from Friday, 22 April, until after the elections. I have asked Minister Shimon Peres to chair the Cabinet meetings during my leave of absence.' Nevertheless, the *de jure* and *de facto* situation remained a strange one. Peres's official title was not Prime Minister or even Prime Minister *pro tem*, but rather 'Chairman of the Cabinet meetings'. Rabin was the 'Prime Minister-on-leave' and the work arrangements called for the Prime Minister's bureau chief and the Cabinet secretary to 'update the Prime Minister on all matters raised for discussion'. This state of affairs led to a fair share of confusion, and the following exchange at one of Peres's weekly meetings with his aides (on 15 April) was typical:

Peres (to the Chief of Staff): 'I want you to know that I didn't ask Rabin to go on leave. He suggested it.'

Maj.-Gen. Yisrael Tal: 'He's on leave? You're not his replacement?'

Peres: 'No. He remains Prime Minister, formally and in every other way.'

Tal: What will you do if you get a telegram from Washington, for example? Will you reply on your own cognizance or go and ask him?'

Peres: 'I'll ask him and do whatever he says.'

Thus a month before the general elections, the Labour Party was left with a Prime Minister-on-leave, a stand-in who wasn't a replacement and a candidate for premiership who had withdrawn his name from the race. The Party was about to correct at least the last of these flaws by calling a special meeting of the Central Committee to chose a new candidate for the premiership.

On 21 April, the Central Committee met to confirm Peres's candidacy for the premiership. No one bothered to count the hundreds of hands raised in his favour. Only eight people voted against him and eighteen abstained. After two contests and an incessant, exhausting wrangle with Rabin, Peres advanced another step on his way to the top. But the legacy he bore weighed so heavily on him that conquering the peak would take almost a miracle.

An American figure who occupied Peres's attention during these days – and unexpectedly, at that – was Henry Kissinger. After Jimmy Carter's victory in the American presidential elections, Kissinger had returned to private life, but he evidently found it hard to surrender his role as a catalyst in international affairs. On 11 April 1977, the Kissingers hosted Ambassador and Mrs Dinitz at their home, and at one point the former Secretary of State led Dinitz into his den, explaining that he wanted to talk privately. He began by warning that if the subject of their conversation were to get out, he would deny it ever took place, but 'as a Jew he could not go on if he did not share the information he had'. After this dramatic build-up, Kissinger revealed that in a meeting between President Sadat and President Carter in Washington, the Egyptian had said that 'he would be willing to join Israel on a course of normalization above and beyond the abrogation of the state of belligerency'. He mentioned commerce, tourism via a third country, and so on. But the really important revelation was that

Carter had told Sadat, 'The United States will lead Israel to withdraw to the 1967 borders and reach an agreement about the establishment of a Palestinian state. In the event that security problems crop up, they will be solved by means of demilitarized areas.' Dinitz asked Kissinger what he thought Israel should do. 'Organize forces in the United States and Israel,' Kissinger replied. 'Don't appear hawkish but be determined. The trick is to fight Carter's plans in a resolute manner.' Kissinger wanted to know who Dinitz intended to pass the information on to, and Dinitz naturally said Rabin. Kissinger objected. When Dinitz suggested Peres, Kissinger agreed. 'But only to Shimon,' he stressed.

After 'not sleeping a wink all night', as he put it, Dinitz telephoned Peres, who immediately shared the information with Yigal Allon. The two were naturally very concerned about what Carter had in store, but decided not to take up the matter until after the elections. So a day later Peres was surprised when his secretary announced a call from Washington. On the line was none other than Henry Kissinger, saying that he had heard about Rabin's resignation and decided to call 'to tell you that your friends wish you the best. You're taking over during a very difficult time.' Peres thanked him for the good wishes and asked whether Kissinger had any plans to visit the area in the near future. If it would help, Kissinger said, he would find a way to get there. It was just a matter of 'finding a pretext so that the visit will not be directly related to the elections'. And speaking of elections, 'How are they coming along?' he asked.

'No one knows,' Peres replied. 'Actually, I'm optimistic. I hope that I can be as optimistic about the post-election period as I am about the elections themselves.' As matters turned out, both his optimism and his pessimism proved to be well wide of the mark.

'If I understand anything about elections, we've lost this time.' These were the words of Knesset Member Yossi Sarid a few days before 17 May. His audience, the leaders of the Labour Party's election headquarters, were not in the least surprised. They lived among the people and wherever they went encountered hostility that sometimes slipped over the line into enmity. Sarid did not propose to give up. He said that they must consider what could be done 'to salvage something' from the elections, and his first suggestion was 'to announce the makeup of the next Government and include a lot of new faces – a revolutionary line-up that carries a new message.'

Peres was enthusiastic at the idea. Perhaps from despair and exhaustion, or perhaps because he recalled the telephone conversation of a few days earlier, he began to slip into the world of the absurd, contemplating a Government made up of the best Jewish minds. After all, hadn't Ben-Gurion asked Professor Albert Einstein to be the first president of the state? Soaring on an updraught of his own rhetoric, Peres began to list his candidates. He would offer a senior political portfolio to Dr Henry Kissinger. Another possible figure would be Arthur Goldberg, for whom he would create a new post: Minister of Jewish Affairs. His listeners were almost in a state of shock. The first to recover was Yossi Sarid, who explained that he had meant an original Government, but not quite *that* original!

As the election drew closer, it seemed that only a televised debate with Begin could reverse the state of affairs. When this idea was first proposed, the Labour Party ruled it out. Its leaders still believed they were leading in the race. 'We're in Government now. Why should we give Begin a platform?' was how they looked at it. But their outlook changed once it was clearly beyond doubt that the Labour Party had sunk to the position of underdog. Now there was nothing to lose. Sarid, who was in charge of public relations, told Peres just how bad the situation was. 'The campaign just isn't taking off. The motors are revved up, but it's not taking off. The only thing that can save us is a debate with Begin.'

Sarid's assessment was based on the fact that Peres was then regarded as a 'television star'. Another consideration – perhaps the most important one – was that Begin had just been discharged from hospital and looked thin and wan. Sarid's thinking was, 'the public will see the face of a healthy man contrasted with a combination of a corpse and a clown'.

Peres prepared for the debate in the most thorough manner possible. A communications expert, Natan Yannai, drew up a memo instructing him to 'speak to the interviewer, talk to the viewers and relate least of all to Begin. You're speaking as a Prime Minister, so you must not create an illusion of equality by unnecessarily glancing at Begin.' It also included dozens of other points about what to say, what not to say and how to do both simultaneously. Since the questions were agreed upon in advance, Peres sat for two full days working with teams of prompters until he knew every answer by heart – down to the last detail.

On the day of the debate, Sarid accompanied Peres to the TV studio in Jerusalem convinced that he was ushering a sure winner. But the closer they came to air time, the more nervous and stiff Peres became. Sarid's last hope was that Peres would recover during the broadcast. But 'it was a lost cause. He wasn't himself. That man on screen was someone else.'

As the debate drew to a close, an advertising firm hired by Sarid began taking a telephone poll about the outcome. Sarid intended to release the results to the press in order to make one last stab at projecting Peres as a winner. But the results obtained by the poll indicated a tie: 40-40 (the remaining 20 per cent replied that both contestants had lost the debate). 'That meant we lost, so nothing was released for publication.'

The miracle that the the Labour Party needed so desperately was not about to happen. On the morning of 17 May, the Israeli electorate began to make its way to the polling-booths to wreak the greatest political upset the State of Israel had known since its establishment.

5
Opposition and Renewal

The Labour Party headquarters in Tel Aviv's Hayarkon Street, facing the sea, was so silent that through the open window of Shimon Peres's room one could hear the murmur of the waves. Of the dozens of people who had crowded into the room earlier in the evening, only a few remained now. Peres sat at the head of the table, his face pale, reddened eyes glued to the television screen where the anchorman and his team of reporters provided a steady stream of data bearing out the startling forecast announced at the beginning of the broadcast: for the first time in the twenty-nine years of the state's existence, the *Likud*, headed by Menachem Begin, would be the leading Party in the Knesset.

Silence reigned in the Spartan room so typical of the Labour Party's institutional décor. It was as if those present – and Peres most of all – still could not believe what was happening. A thought flitted through his mind: 'It's just as well that Ben-Gurion is not alive to see Menachem Begin in the flush of victory.'

The more the situation sorted itself out, the more the grim silence was broken by cars stopping in front of the building, their horns sounding in provocation. Occasionally a booming shout penetrated from the street: 'You're washed up!' or 'Crooks! We've finally got you!' But if the taunts penetrated Peres's consciousness, one certainly wouldn't have known it from his expression. He just went on staring blankly at the screen as if hypnotized by it. Not until close to three in the morning did he finally place both hands on the table – as if using it for support – and stand up slowly. 'That's it,' he said and turned to leave. Peres descended the narrow stairs with a heavy tread to find the entrance deserted. The security guards who had stood there at the start of the evening were gone now, reassigned to the building housing the

Likud's headquarters, where they were guarding the man destined to be the next Prime Minister of the State of Israel.

Peres left the building as a chill wind blowing in from the sea sent a shudder through him. He was about to cross the street when a taxi drew up opposite him and its driver, recognizing Peres, opened the window, thrust his head out and spat at the exhausted figure. Peres hurried into his car and it immediately moved out, taking him home. 'Everything has collapsed,' he thought, 'we have to start all over again.' And at that moment he wasn't at all sure that he had the inner strength to do so.

Waiting for him at the door, Sonya placed her hand on his arm without uttering a word. A few minutes later, Peres's friends Arthur Ben-Natan and Mira Avrech arrived. The television was still broadcasting, and they sat down to watch. At close to four in the morning, Peres turned to his wife and murmured: 'I should call and congratulate Begin, shouldn't I?' Without waiting for an answer, he stood up and began to walk towards the telephone in the kitchen. But just at that moment, the anchorman announced that Begin was about to speak. Peres stopped in his tracks. 'If he's talking now, I can't very well phone him,' he reasoned. 'I'll wait till he's through.' Then Begin's figure appeared on the screen, a microphone was thrust towards him, and he delivered a victory speech of greeting and gratitude, adding at the end: 'And now I am waiting for a congratulatory telegram from Shimon Peres tomorrow morning.' The hint of a bitter smile appeared on Peres's face as he sat down again. 'Well, if that's what he's waiting for, I guess there's no point in calling him.'

The following morning Peres rose at 6.30, his usual hour, and went to his office in the Defence Ministry. For the first few hours, he busied himself with Ministry affairs, but towards the middle of the morning some of his close aides began to gather around him. 'What now?' was the question hovering in the air. It was at times like these that Peres's faculty for bouncing back, nourished by seemingly inexhaustible reserves of optimism, came to the fore. As long as there's a shadow of a hope – even if only an illusory one – he will try to use it to reverse what others perceive as a *fait accompli*. 'All is not lost,' he soothed his aides, explaining that there was still a chance that the Labour Party could form the next government. His calculations ran as follows: the Labour Party plus *Mapam* (the Alignment) had thirty-two seats, Yadin's DMC fifteen and the National Religious Party eleven. Together that made fifty-eight. If a few of the smaller parties joined the coalition, they would complete the majority.

Peres did not content himself with speculation. He met representatives of the DMC – drunk with victory over winning fifteen seats – but they told him that as far as they were concerned, the people had had their say and it was a clear-cut demand for a government led by the *Likud*. Dr Yosef Burg of the NRP had a similar message for Peres and, at the end of their meeting, allowed himself a personal reflection: 'You're starting out a new race on a two-hump camel,' he told Peres in a colourful reference to *Mapam* and the *Ahdut Ha'avodah* faction. 'They won't let you be. I feel sorry for you.'

Menachem Begin had an entirely different idea about the composition of the next government. He came to Peres's office at the Defence Ministry to propose that the Labour Party join his Government in a wall-to-wall coalition of national unity. Asked what his policy would be on Judea and Samaria, Begin proclaimed that he would not yield an inch of land. When Peres asked how he intended to rule a million Arabs, Begin replied: 'By the sword and faith.' On those terms, it was evident to Peres that he and Begin had no basis whatsoever for collaboration.

Before long, however, it turned out that Begin had found a common language with another senior member of the Labour Party. One Saturday night towards the end of May, Peres was at home reading when the telephone rang and Sonya announced, 'It's for you. Moshe.' For a fraction of a second, Peres's heart seemed to skip a beat. The rumours had already reached his ears; taking the receiver, he now heard Moshe Dayan confirm them. 'Begin offered me the foreign affairs portfolio. I've decided to accept it,' he said.

'I'm sorry to hear that,' was all Peres could summon up in reply.

'I've decided that that's the best way I can serve the state. I can't see myself sitting in opposition for four years.'

In the ensuing silence, Dayan felt the need to answer the unasked question. 'I didn't speak to you earlier to avoid creating the impression that there's any kind of collusion between us or that you're responsible for my deed.'

'I see,' Peres allowed, though his tone left even this as a moot point.

Peres hung up and returned to his book, but the words seemed to be dancing before his eyes, so he laid it aside and sat musing about the period following the Yom Kippur War. At that time, when the public was calling for Dayan's head, he, Peres, had not taken any account of personal interests or even how best to serve the country. Even though no one asked it of him, he had stuck by Moshe Dayan – as he had done all his life. But now, in his most difficult hour, Dayan had simply dropped him like a disposable tool which had served its purpose and wasn't needed any more. He felt bitter, though hatred was something he was incapable of feeling for Dayan even now, when the knife stuck deep in his back was causing him such anguish. In a conversation with Samuel Lewis on 26 May, the newly appointed American Ambassador asked whether Dayan's move 'would strengthen the Cabinet on the road to peace'. 'Yes,' Peres replied. 'He's a very original and flexible thinker. I just hope he won't be neutralized.' In fact, that assessment was borne out soon afterwards, but his own alliance with Moshe Dayan came to an end. No other partnership in the history of Israel had left such a deep and controversial mark on the political map.

Dayan's desertion was not the only surprise awaiting Peres during the post-election period. Five days after the balloting, on 22 May, he telephoned Rabin about a routine matter and was astounded by Rabin's announcement that he had decided to resume the premiership. That same day, Peres and Rabin met and came to an understanding that Rabin would return 'to sum up the work of the Cabinet and ensure a smooth transfer of power' while Peres would continue to be responsible for 'all Party affairs and the coalition negotiations'.

The political upset became an established fact when a proud and pompous Menachem Begin presented his Government to the Knesset on 20 June. Two days later Ezer Weizman turned up at the Defence Ministry to assume command. In a heavily attended ceremony, Peres presented him with three thick tomes, which contained a summary of the Ministry's activities during his years of office and a breakdown of the subjects still on the agenda. As he shook hands with the people who had worked with him for much of his adult life, Peres was afraid to speak lest the tears he was choking back flooded out into the open.

Now came grey days of oblivion – without the Defence Ministry to go to every morning or Cabinet meetings to attend. Peres's emotional barometer swerved wildly from dark despair to cautious optimism. One day a close friend asked him how he felt. 'I don't know,' he answered listlessly, almost numb. 'I wake up every morning and don't know what for.' He had more than enough time – too much, in fact – for thinking and taking stock of himself. In private conversations he blamed the fiasco on the scandals which had come to light during the previous year and which had reached their peak with the Prime Minister's bank account. At other times he looked for scapegoats where none were to be found.

When he had time to think about it, Peres realized that in addition to losing his government post, he lacked an official position in the Party. Being in opposition was a new state of affairs for which Labour was unprepared. Hitherto the Prime Minister – who had always come from the ranks of one or another incarnation of the Labour Party – had been head of the Party as well, while the organization's day-to-day affairs were handled by the Secretary-General. In order to deal with the new situation, the Executive decided to change the Party's constitution and create the position of Party Chairman, who would inherit the authority of the Secretary-General. Shimon Peres was unanimously chosen to assume this post. However, the decision had to be ratified by the Party's Central Committee, which convened for that purpose on 30 June 1977. This time there were no other candidates for the office, for the objective was not the premiership or a senior Cabinet post. Everyone knew that the lot of the Party Chairman would be the mundane, tedious work of rehabilitating the Party after its stunning defeat, and no one objected to letting Peres bear that burden. But there was one man who could not bring himself to support Peres even for this thankless task.

Ensconced in the first row of the audience, a few feet from the stage on which Peres sat, was ex-Prime Minister Yitzhak Rabin. When the vote was taken, he remained in a demonstrative slouch, hands hooked into his belt in a characteristic pose. Neither one of those hands budged, and the glance he shot at the stage from time to time bristled with hostility, as if to say: 'This is not the end of the matter.'

Peres became Chairman of the Labour Party but still not its universally acknowledged leader. For Golda Meir was not a woman to forgive or forget. In a meeting of *Mapai* veterans at her Ramat Aviv home, she voiced the suspicion that Peres would try to bring the Labour Party, or parts of it, into Begin's Government. 'I've known this Shimon for a long time. He comes to me once a week to report,' she said contemptuously.

And what Golda was doing behind closed doors, Rabin was doing openly. 'I don't regard Peres as my leader,' he proclaimed in August 1977, because, he elaborated, Peres 'tried in every way possible to oust me as Prime Minister.' Henceforward, Rabin's strategy would be to lead up to another contest with Peres. He would treat the new Government and its Prime Minister with kid gloves; but when it came to Peres, his fists were bared, his blows direct and punishing.

Jabs of this kind almost destroyed Peres at the time. 'I'm not going to contend for the candidacy for Prime Minister any more,' he told one of his aides, Yossi Bailen, in a moment of emotional and physical exhaustion. 'If someone else wants the job, let him have it.' But that was a fleeting mood. By the time the Central Committee met on 8 September 1977, he had changed his tune. 'If anyone wants to contest the position,' Peres snapped in a clear reference to Rabin, 'let him get up here on stage and do so.'

Naturally, no one did. In fact, the consensus seemed to be that there was nothing to fight over. The top echelon believed that the Party had been sent into the political wilderness for a long time to come, though assessments varied as to just how long: the optimists spoke of eight years, the pessimists of twenty! The only ray of hope during these days came from the *Histadrut*, for in their elections held on 21 June 1977, the Labour Party not only held its own, but even increased its strength substantially. The response within the Party was comparable to a terminally ill patient suddenly discovering that there is hope of recovery.

But preserving hegemony within the *Histadrut* could not make up for losing control of the ship of state. The Labour Party headquarters reverted to its dull greyness. Party bureaucrats who had lost their influence along with their positions continued to desert the fold. And when Peres declared that the Party 'must be prepared for new elections within two years', many shook their heads in disbelief, almost in pity. But while others were shaking their heads, Peres turned his thoughts to the task of rehabilitating the Party. Within a few months, working together with former Finance Minister Yehoshua Rabinowitz, he had wiped out all its debts and placed the Party on a strong economic footing. His major achievement, however, was rebuilding the Party's branches, which he looked upon as the roots from which the broader organization would draw its strength.

The drive which Peres demonstrated in the realm of organization ground to a halt when it came to the subject of appointing the members of the Party's central bodies. Here he walked on tiptoe; for quite a while, in fact, he stood marking time. Despite pressures and other forms of lobbying from various quarters, he refused to be rushed into putting these bodies together. As a result, Peres was often accused of pussyfooting and no less often left himself open to the charge of indecisiveness. And there were other kinds of accusations raised against him. 'This is not going to be a one-man show!' Rabin railed. Actually, there is probably nothing more alien to Shimon Peres's character than one-man, autocratic rule. He is a 'team man' by nature and he needed the Party bodies just as much as the Party itself did.

Then why the procrastination? Primarily because he was well aware of the character and sensitivities of his colleagues. A cardinal law of politics is that when you appoint a man to a position, you make one friend and dozens of enemies. This sensitivity becomes all the more prominent when the personal side of the issue is also a factional one. Everyone seemed jumpy. The *Rafi* people worried that Peres might show undue favour to the *Mapai* and *Ahdut Ha'avodah* factions in a bid to win their reciprocal favour, and the members of *Mapai* and *Ahdut Ha'avodah* were expecting him to appoint his *Rafi* friends to central positions at their expense.

Peres was aware of the criticism against him. 'It's not that I made compromises for the sake of unity,' he later explained. 'I just decided that without unity there would be no Party, so I subordinated everything to this theory.' To achieve that elusive concord under his leadership, he steadily and patiently extended his base within the Party by drawing traditional opponents into his camp and sometimes by drawing away from his traditional friends.

The upshot of these manoeuvres was a rash of fissures in the solid core of Peres's friends and supporters. But they did remain behind him – albeit less enthusiastically – for lack of any real alternative. On the other hand, Peres's own political margins extended outwards and, in the course of time, would transform him from the leader of a faction into the leader of the Party. Not until this process was consummated, however, would he be ready to begin constituting the Party's committees in the confidence that his authority would carry him over the pitfalls of individual sensitivities. And indeed, when the Party's Executive was finally chosen, the operation went off without a hitch.

Peres took a similar tack regarding the election of the Party's Secretary, who was supposed to free him of the administrative burden. To prevent the matter from turning into an inter-faction confrontation, he offered the post to Chaim Bar-Lev, both because of his talents and because he was not overtly identified with any one faction or another. Thus in August 1978 Bar-Lev was chosen Secretary of the Labour Party and, in 1981, Peres was able to say, 'To this day we sit door facing door without ever having had a single scrap.'

In daily affairs Peres was unwilling, perhaps unable, to place himself in the hands of a single man. Throughout his career, someone was always favoured at any given moment and then neglected in favour of someone else. Little wonder that uncertainty and even bitterness have been known to dog those people who were close to Peres once, but who were subsequently 'banished from court'. Nevertheless, he is always surrounded by people who have been connected with him during various phases of his career, and he feels a certain obligation towards them. They continue to meet him, report to him, make requests of him. Without doubt they have an influence over him. One man who has worked close to Peres defined the situation as follows: 'Everyone has friends from twenty or thirty years ago. It costs you half an hour from time to time, but it has no operative meaning. With Peres, that isn't true.'

In addition to aides and long-standing friends, Peres is surrounded by a third circle of people who can be classified as 'friends from abroad', such as Karl Kahane of Austria and, especially, Jean Friedman of France. These men make no demands of Peres. They help him – by giving of their time and providing funds – because they believe that it is in the best interests of the State of Israel. Peres knows that he can trust them implicitly at all times and regardless of the matter in question. But his very association with them has created a good deal of resentment among his Israeli associates.

It is characteristic of Peres that when he must make an operative decision, he has no problem doing so, but in human relations he has a very hard time saying no. Sometimes this weakness creates problems that have a way of inflating to crisis proportions. If that is a flaw of character, then it is a conscious one. For as Peres himself admits: 'I am no Ben-Gurion. I know how to strive towards an objective, but I can't copy someone else's style.' What may have been interpreted as a shortcoming, then, was essentially a deliberate approach that testified to an awareness of his own strengths and weaknesses. Most important, it enables him to provide leadership when it is truly needed – as he has proven repeatedly in regard to Franco-Israeli relations, the atomic reactor, the arms industry and the Entebbe operation.

Peres would offset the monotony of Party work by using what little free time he had to do the things he enjoyed. Even if he returned home at midnight, he would take a book to bed with him and read for an hour or two. His aides knew that Friday afternoons must be left free, for that was when he took great pleasure in watching the Arab films, with English subtitles, broadcast from Egypt. He once explained that he finds simplicity and touching human sensitivity in them. Undoubtedly they remind him of his youth and his visits to the Alhambrah theatre in Jaffa.

If there is a gap in his day's schedule and it is sunny, Peres likes to walk down to the beach and sit in an easy chair under the warming rays of the Mediterranean sun, though he never goes so far as to take off his shirt. The lifeguard is known to bring him a glass of water, and sometimes people come over and ask for his autograph. More important than the few minutes of relaxation is the fact that his face be tanned. Even when travelling by car, he makes a point of sitting on whichever side catches the sun.

Lunches are part and parcel of the working day, and Peres uses them for business meetings. He loves good food and is *au fait* with the full culinary lexicon – a legacy of the days when he visited Paris often. But he is very careful – sometimes fanatically so – not to overeat. He firmly believes that the people do not like fat leaders, and his slender figure proves that his appetite for leadership is far greater than his gastronomic cravings.

On Friday, 18 November 1977, Peres and his wife took a plane from Miami to Los Angeles on the next lap of a lecture tour for the United Jewish Appeal. When they reached Los Angeles, he was tired from the long flight and his only desire was to get to his hotel and rest. He couldn't possibly have guessed that the next time he lay down on a bed would be in his own home in Tel Aviv a few days later. For as soon as they disembarked from the plane, Peres and his wife were approached by Israel's Consul-General in Los Angeles, who informed him that President Sadat was scheduled to arrive in Israel on Saturday night and recommended that he return home immediately.

Despite the startling content of this announcement, Peres was not surprised, because the possibility of a visit by the Egyptian President had received wide coverage in the media. Peres never got out of the airport. An hour or so later, he was on a plane to New York, hoping to catch an Air France flight to Israel. But an accident on one of the runways at Kennedy meant that Peres's plane was forced to spend three hours circling in a holding pattern. During this time another venerable passenger eager to return to Israel was aboard the Air France plane. Golda Meir knew that Peres's plane had been delayed and asked the Air France pilot to wait for him. The pilot delayed departure for more than an hour, but finally had to leave without the Pereses.

When the Los Angeles plane finally landed, there were no more flights to Israel or Europe that day, and Peres was sure that he would miss Sadat's historic visit. Members of the Israeli military delegation in New York discovered that an El Al cargo plane, loaded with industrial piping, was leaving for Amsterdam at 3 a.m. Peres and Sonya boarded the cargo plane only to find that it hadn't a single seat, so they spread blankets on the floor of the fuselage and lay down. They reached Amsterdam on Saturday morning and caught an El Al flight to Israel.

Peres arrived home on Saturday afternoon having spent thirty-six hours *en route*. Only then was he informed that he was scheduled to make a speech in the Knesset in honour of the visiting President. Originally there had been opposition in the Cabinet to having Peres speak – in addition to Prime Minister Begin and President Sadat. But Dayan demanded that the head of the opposition be allowed to share the platform, and Begin backed him on this point. Now Peres had to prepare his speech. He asked Yitzhak Navon to come over and give him a hand, and sat down to write. When Navon arrived and asked how he could help, Peres said, 'Find me an apt quotation from the Koran.' Navon began his literary search while Peres finished writing the speech. Then he gave it to Navon to read, and the future President of Israel said: 'You don't need any verse from the Koran. This is an excellent speech.'

At about 6.30 that evening, Peres quickly changed his clothes and left for Ben-Gurion Airport, which was flood-lit and cordoned off by hundreds of policemen and security guards. The strip was already crowded with thousands of invited guests as Peres was led to his place in the middle of the reception line-up. (Abba Eban was placed at the end of the line and was obviously in a frustrated mood that night. Pointing to Yitzhak Rabin, who was standing not very far ahead of him, Eban grumbled to his neighbour, Gad Ya'akobi: 'If it weren't for him, we would be standing at the front of the line and Begin would be here at the end.') Finally, Sadat's plane could be seen on the horizon. At 7.58 p.m. the Egyptian President stepped out of the aircraft and the dream of an entire generation came true.

Peres returned home late that night and fell on his bed in exhaustion. But despite the fact that he hadn't slept a wink for two days, he had trouble nodding off now. The sight of Anwar Sadat embracing Menachem Begin lingered before his eyes, giving him no peace. He felt like a man mocked by history. Once again he had the feeling that while he had been doing the work of ensuring Israel's security, someone else had come along and walked off with the laurels.

Herein lay the tragedy of Sadat's visit from Peres's vantage-point. From a national point of view, he shared the feeling of overwhelming satisfaction, but from a personal and Party point of view, the Sadat-Begin 'peace festival' was a disaster. All the hard-won achievements – the elections to the *Histadrut*, the strides made in the rehabilitation of the Party – had been dwarfed by this historic event. The *Likud* Government would be the one to sign the first peace treaty – and with the largest of the Arab states, at that. Now Peres, too, began to think that the *Likud* would be invincible for many years to come. Irrationally, he began to believe that 'Things just aren't going our way. The whole world is against us. Even Sadat!'

As leader of the Labour Party, Peres was about to become acquainted with an institution through which he would derive both personal satisfaction and an international standing: the Socialist International. The occasion for doing so came at the beginning of February 1978, when the International's Executive was about to meet, and the West German Social-Democratic Party invited Peres to be its guest before the International's leaders convened. The second invitation he received was for a seminar on the Middle East organized by the Austrian Chancellor Bruno Kreisky, to take place after the Executive sessions.

Peres's first stop was Bonn on 6 February 1978, and his entire day was taken up by meetings. When he returned to his hotel just before midnight, a tense Micha Harish was awaiting him. 'President Sadat wants to meet you,' he told Peres. 'He's going to be stopping over at Salzburg on his way back from the United States.' Peres's immediate reaction was, 'We have to talk to Begin.' The Prime Minister was located in Geneva and told Peres that he had no objection to the meeting.

Two days later Kreisky returned from a visit to the Soviet Union and served as a go-between for additional clarifications with the Egyptian delegation in Salzburg. The outcome was to schedule a meeting between Peres and Sadat in Salzburg on Saturday, 10 February. But during the evening of the 8th, a mini-crisis developed. Kreisky phoned Micha Harish in Hamburg and told him in a tone of unconcealed rage that he no longer believed Peres had any intention of meeting Sadat because Ehud Avriel, a senior official in the Israeli Foreign Ministry and a man known to be closely associated with Peres, had told a reporter that 'Sadat invited Shimon, but Shimon will be smart and not show.' Harish assured the Austrian Chancellor that Avriel's statement was just prattle and bore no relation to the truth.

On Friday evening, 9 February, Peres left Hamburg for Salzburg. At the airport he heard that Kreisky had issued a statement about the meeting, although Peres had asked him that it be kept secret. Peres spent the night in Munich and the next morning was on his way again, accompanied now by the Deputy Mayor of Salzburg, with a German police escort to clear the way for them. The convoy stopped at the entrance to Kleisheim Castle near Salzburg. When Peres entered the castle, which was replete with all the grandeur of Baroque architecture and furnishings, Kreisky was already waiting for him and welcomed him cordially.

The conversation between Peres and Sadat began, as scheduled, at 12.30 and lasted more than two hours. From the outset, Peres made it clear that he was not an envoy on anyone's behalf, that he had no authority to conduct negotiations and that in Israel there was only one address for anything related to foreign affairs – the Cabinet. Sadat said he appreciated all that, but suggested that their conversation be candid and 'remain between us'. Peres would not comply and turned down the suggestion politely but firmly. 'I am obliged to report on the content of this conversation to the Prime Minister,' he said, Sadat agreed to these terms.

The President was in a gloomy mood that day. Earlier he had told the German Chancellor Helmut Schmidt that his visit to the United States had not been successful. He regarded President Carter's behaviour as insufferable: his statements were riddled with contradictions, he proved to be unfamiliar with his material and he had a very poor grasp of strategy. Now Sadat complained to Peres about the difficulties he faced with the Israelis, stressing that he had been misled on the matter of the settlements in Sinai. (At the time Israel was still opposed to dismantling these settlements.) During his talks in Jerusalem, he claimed, no one mentioned the subject at all. He was sure everyone understood that the settlements must be evacuated. Then Begin suddenly raised the issue at the meeting in Ismailiya a few weeks later – which was why the negotiations reached a deadlock. His main problem, however, was the Palestinian question, and on this score Israel had not issued a single statement to make things easier for him. 'I wanted Arafat to join the talks,' he continued excitedly. ' "This is a great opportunity," I told him. But Arafat refused to come to Cairo. Now he has sent a special envoy to see me, but I told him that he had already missed the boat." '

Peres asked to clear up a number of points 'even if they are somewhat unpleasant'. 'That's all right,' Sadat assured him. 'I don't like formality, Shimon. We'll talk as friends. After all, I am a country boy.'

'As far as the settlements go, Begin represents a national consensus,' Peres explained. 'You said you would agree to border changes. Why not apply this agreement to the Rafiah salient?'

Sadat confirmed that he supported the notion of border changes, but not in Sinai, only on the West Bank, 'because Israel has security problems there, and I can appreciate that. Neither do I have any objection to Israel having security footholds on the West Bank. I have no intention of conducting negotiations on behalf of the Palestinians and Jordan. I know that Hussein wants me to do the dirty work for him so he can come out of it looking like a hero.'

As the talk went on, Sadat remarked that he would have preferred to conduct the negotiations with Golda Meir rather than Begin. 'She is a brilliant woman, and I admire her enormously.' He spoke of Moshe Dayan as a 'showman' and expressed disappointment about his attitude. At this point the Egyptian President asked Peres to tell him a little about Ben-Gurion. When Peres had finished his thumb-nail sketch, Sadat mused: 'I could wrap everything up with him. He was a man of great decisions.'

As the talk ran on, Kreisky came to remind them that lunch and a press conference were awaiting them. Sadat ended by telling Peres that he had heard good things about him from Schmidt and Kreisky, and their talk had confirmed it all. He expressed his confidence that they would be able to maintain a relationship of mutual trust. Finally, as they started to walk out, he moaned: 'You know, all of Egypt is free except for me. I feel like a life-term prisoner. Wherever I go I am surrounded by people. Schmidt came to visit me and I wanted to talk to him, but people came at us from all sides to express their good wishes and deprive me of my privacy.' Whether in jest or otherwise, Sadat also made a number of references to his age. At the beginning of their talk, he commented that he was already old and the rigours of travel were difficult for him, which was why he had rested in the mountains for two days before their meeting. And as they left to meet the reporters outside, Sadat was dressed in a warm winter coat and noticed that Peres was only wearing his suit. 'Well, you are young,' he remarked. 'You can get away with it.'

Immediately after his talk with Sadat, Peres telephoned Begin, and upon his return to Israel he reported to the Prime Minister's office in the Knesset building, where Begin received him warmly. As Peres leaned forward in a gesture suggesting that he was about to begin his report, the Prime Minister said: 'Careful, now. There are microphones here. We don't want to let the same thing that happened to President Carter in India happen to us!' Catching on to the Prime Minister's needling humour, Peres broke into a grin. These were to be the last smiles between the two men in meetings of this sort. From then on, Peres's international travels and talks with national leaders would be the subject of bitter outbursts and mutual recrimination.

Peres did not stay in Israel for very long. About a month after his return from Salzburg, he went to Bucharest at the head of the first Labour Party delegation ever to be invited by the Romanian Communist Party. On 11 March 1978, he met the Romanian President, Nicolai Ceauşescu. The President had become deeply involved in the Israeli-Arab dispute as a consequence of serving as go-between prior to President Sadat's visit. Yet despite this first-hand involvement, their talk opened with a philosophical exchange on the nature of incumbent regimes. Peres led into that subject by commenting that Europe was gradually turning into a socialist continent divided between democratic socialism and communistic socialism. 'Even though I am not a disciple of the communist system, I can see a place for pluralism and co-operation,' he added, 'for the socialist culture strives for peace, the elimination of poverty, disarmament, and scientific and cultural co-operation.'

'There is room for pluralistic co-operation and even the dismantling of the blocs,' Ceauşescu agreed. 'But I am not as optimistic as you are about the state of the social democrats in Europe. They have not managed to cope with their economic problems. The system we call "democratic" does not allow for involving the masses in the development and management of the country.'

On that note, the talk shifted to the deadlock in the negotiations between Egypt and Israel, as disagreement continued to mark the rest of the conversation. Peres explained that Israel was a democratic country, which sometimes made decision-making a relatively slow process. Ceauşescu retorted that he did not believe Begin displayed the degree of responsiveness called for by President Sadat's visit to Jerusalem. He pointed out that attention must be paid to the shift in the position of the Great Powers. The USSR had begun to intervene in areas where its presence had not been felt before, so there was no point in trying to keep the Russians out of the picture. If the USSR were given a constructive role to play, it would help, not harm, the negotiations.

As to the inescapable subject of the PLO, Peres argued that the organization represented the Palestinian diaspora, a disgruntled minority, rather than the Palestinians *per se*. 'Therefore a solution reached through the auspices of Jordan is preferable.' Ceauşescu protested that the PLO should also be included in the negotiations, 'not the PLO alone, but the PLO as well. It also has moderate elements within the organization.'

At this point Ceauşescu proposed taking a break and holding another meeting at a later time. Peres and the members of his delegation spent the next few days touring throughout Romania on an itinerary that included industrial enterprises, agricultural projects and museums. The second meeting with Ceauşescu took place towards the end of his visit, on 19 March, when the Romanian President returned to the Palestinian problem and noted that he wished to speak frankly and dispense with diplomatic euphemisms. 'Frankness', however, is also a diplomatic euphemism – usually for harsh, biting words.

The talk was held in the shadow of the brutal murder of twenty-eight Israeli civilians, including women and children, by Palestinian terrorists on the country's main coastal road, just north of Tel Aviv. 'This action again proves that the PLO is a negative factor,' Peres asserted. But Ceauşescu claimed that it illustrated the gravity of the Palestinian problem and the critical need to find a solution. 'I am opposed to terror,' he avowed, 'but you must remember that anarchistic elements exist in every nationalist movement. Arafat is not responsible for the action on your coastal road. He was abroad at the time, and the PLO spokesman denied that his organization plans actions of that sort.'

'Evidently word hasn't reached you yet,' Peres prefaced his announcement: 'Today the PLO spokesman confirmed his organization's responsibility for this action. He even boasted of it!'

It was evident that Ceauşescu had not heard about this, and an embarrassed silence fell over the room. Finally, Ceauşescu picked up the thread of conversation by choosing to ignore the PLO's latest announcement and again insisting on the Palestinians' right to self-determination. To manifest that right, he proposed that a plebiscite be held in the West Bank. But Peres was extremely wary of this course. 'A plebiscite cannot solve anything when it is held under the threat of the gun' – by which he meant the PLO terrorizing the population of the West Bank into backing its candidates. 'It reminds me of a story by Damon Runyon, who tells about a crap game in which the dice aren't marked. When the banker is asked how the players will know who wins, he says: "I'll tell 'em." '

Ceauşescu managed to squeeze out a polite but not very enthusiastic smile.

When Peres asked him to urge Sadat to be patient and not to press for a quick conclusion to the negotiations, the Romanian replied: 'You want me to ask Sadat not to rush. I want you to tell Begin to put on some speed!' Ceauşescu's parting message was: 'On what we have agreed upon, we shall act together. As to the rest, time is the best teacher.'

After a short rest in Israel, Peres went abroad again at the beginning of April – this time on a US lecture tour on behalf of the United Jewish Appeal. As usual, however, these jaunts were not limited to fund-raising alone. In Washington he was seen by Vice-President Walter Mondale, Secretary of State Cyrus Vance, and President Carter's national security adviser, Zbigniew Brzezinski. Their talks centred on issues that were being contested by Israel and Egypt and delayed the resumption of the negotiations. It is interesting to note the differences between Peres's various colloquists on these issues. Mondale and Vance were willing to see both sides of the question and showed understanding of Israel's difficulties regarding Judea and Samaria. They advanced various suggestions in an effort to find a middle road between Egypt's demands and Israel's attitude. Brzezinski's stand was far more trenchant. He seemed to place all his eggs in the Palestinian basket and placed responsibility for the deadlock squarely on Israel's shoulders. The main problem, he said, was Israel's refusal to concede the principle of a withdrawal from the West Bank. This, in turn, prevented Sadat from endorsing a declaration of principles on the West Bank – a framework that could justify his independent initiative in the eyes of the Arab world.

Peres's visit to the United States might well have been just a routine, even tiresome, affair had it not been for a telephone call he received while in New York. 'Shim. Can you come to dinner?' Peres immediately identified the warm, hoarse voice of Harry Belafonte, as the singer quickly added that he meant an intimate dinner-party, 'so that we can talk freely'. When the two men had met in Canada some two months before, Belafonte had told Peres that he was part Jewish, for his grandfather was a German Jew, an adventurer who roamed the world generously spreading his blood and his seed. 'I, Harry, am a mere token of remembrance of his visit to Jamaica.'

Belafonte's apartment on Manhattan's West End Avenue was permeated by an atmosphere that testified to its inhabitants' principal interest: Africa. In addition to large, stark-coloured drawings on the struggle for liberation, the shelves were filled with attractive African figurines. There was an Asian element to the furniture – iron and wooden chairs fashioned with impeccable taste – and the single exception to this décor were the figurines of a donkey and rider and the three pioneers which Belafonte had brought back from Israel. Only the bar and the butler dressed in white jacket and gloves were all-American.

As Peres walked in, he saw that all the other guests were Black: the United States Ambassador to the UN, Andrew Young, and his wife; Belafonte's sister and brother-in-law; and, of course, the hosts, Belafonte and his wife, Julie, a Jewess and ex-ballerina. All six, Peres noted, belonged to the New York Black aristocracy – a fashion-conscious, weight-conscious, well-travelled, articulate crowd. Young said that when he and his wife visited Israel, they met the 'great man on the kibbutz' (meaning Ben-Gurion at Kibbutz Sdeh Boker), adding with a smile that the old man had asked him whether his wife was of Yemenite origin, whether he had found her in Israel and by what right he was about to steal her away from the country!

As the banter continued over drinks, Belafonte suggested that Peres and Young retire to a corner so that they could talk privately. It wasn't long before the two men got to the most important topic: the Palestinians. 'We see it as a Jewish issue, not just a Palestinian one,' said Peres. 'We don't want to rule over a million Palestinians, for we have no desire to be a nation of overlords.'

'I don't support the Palestinians,' Young qualified his position carefully. 'There are moderate men among them, but they aren't the ones who decide policy. It's difficult to understand Saudi Arabia and Jordan. Why are they opposed to Sadat's initiative? At tomorrow's Cabinet meeting, I am going to express surprise and annoyance at Saudi Arabia's opposition. Do you think I should raise the idea that the United States can and must pressure Saudi Arabia and Jordan?'

Peres naturally replied in the affirmative.

When they joined the others at the dining-table, someone asked why Israel was supplying arms to Somoza. Peres explained that when the War of Independence broke out the Somoza family had helped Israel acquire weapons for its defence and 'we haven't forgotten it'. The conversation wandered on to various other subjects, but every time it touched upon African affairs the temperature in the room shot up. All the people around the table displayed an uncommon familiarity with Africa's leaders, factions, struggles. Peres felt that for them, Africa meant what Israel meant to the Jews. He was also surprised to hear Young speak in a tone of warmth about the attitude of the American South towards the Blacks while criticizing the attitude in the North. 'Northern liberalism is nothing more than an intellectual put-on,' he pronounced. 'The fact is that the people in the South treated the Blacks with more tolerance and understanding than the Northerners do.'

Dinner lasted for more than five hours and, at its end, Young offered to take Peres back to his hotel. On the way there the subject of conversation shifted to Jimmy Carter, with Young denying that he was an intimate friend of the President. 'Carter is a bright man. He picks things up quickly and he has a knack for assimilating amazing amounts of material. But he's no saviour.' Young added that he didn't think that he had got such a wonderful deal by being appointed Ambassador to the UN. 'All in all, I am the representative of twenty-five million Blacks who discovered they carried more weight by exercising their electoral power than by rioting and holding demonstrations.'

Peres returned home to a political development that afforded him great pleasure. The fourth President of Israel, Professor Ephraim Katzir, had completed his term of office and had decided to retire. As his successor, Begin proposed a totally obscure personality, Professor Yitzhak Shaveh, and within days it was obvious that his candidacy was doomed. The name of Elimelech Rimalt – Begin's original partner in establishing the *Likud* on behalf of the Liberals – also came up, but it was scotched because of the Prime Minister's outright antagonism towards his old colleague. So it was that a Labour candidate, Yitzhak Navon, found himself seriously in the running. Peres's initial reaction was not very enthusiastic. 'You're going to leave me?' he asked Navon. 'Who are you leaving me *with*?' Navon could well understand Peres's predicament. There were few men in whom the Party's Chairman had complete trust, and Navon was one of them – perhaps foremost among them.

Still, Peres knew that Navon wanted the office, so he backed him all the way. A few days before the Knesset vote, Navon turned up at his home to suggest that they drop the whole idea. 'I haven't got a chance,' he insisted dejectedly. 'It will just be an embarrassment.' But Peres urged him on. 'Yitzhak, at this stage it's better to lose than to drop out of the race,' he counselled his old friend, 'and I'm telling you that you *won't* lose!' And he didn't. On 19 April 1978, the Knesset chose Yitzhak Navon as the fifth President of the State of Israel. In one of those ironic twists of Israeli politics, Begin's inexplicable gambit brought one of 'Ben-Gurion's Boys' to the lofty, albeit figurehead post of President of the state. But the climb of another of 'Ben-Gurion's Boys' to the highest executive post in the land would be much longer and more arduous – both within the framework of his own Party and beyond it.

In May 1978 Peres met one of the leaders of the continent with which Harry Belafonte and his friends felt such a strong link. The background to this event was a meeting of the Socialist International in Dakar, the capital of Senegal. Peres's plane landed at Dakar Airport at 4 a.m., but despite the ungodly hour, President Leopold Senghor was there to greet his Israeli guest – though they almost missed each other. Senghor and his entourage waited for Peres by the stairs drawn up to the door of the first-class cabin, but Peres, as usual, was flying tourist class. When he descended the steps and noticed the to-do at the front of the plane, he assumed that Senghor had come to welcome another figure. As soon as he realized his mistake, the Senegalese leader marvelled to his aides: 'See what a PR man that Peres is. He flies tourist class!'

All the delegates to that meeting – including Germany's Willy Brandt and Mario Soares of Portugal – were housed at a local hotel; Peres, however, was invited to stay at the presidential palace. Despite the fact that diplomatic relations between Israel and Senegal had been broken after the Yom Kippur War, Senghor had the Israeli flag flown over the presidential palace throughout Peres's stay there. Peres even took all his meals in the palace in the company of the President and his wife.

While still in the airport, after a short speech of welcome, Senghor drew Peres aside and told him in a whisper that Yasser Arafat was in the area and was prepared to meet him. Worn out from the flight, Peres pleaded for a breather: 'Mr President, give me a chance to freshen up, please. I'll talk to you about it in detail later on.' Peres took his brief rest and then explained to Senghor why he was neither able nor willing to meet Arafat so long as the latter headed an organization dedicated to the destruction of the State of Israel. Senghor tried to persuade him to reconsider, though it was clearly out of the question. But the African did not give up easily. If not Arafat, he jockeyed, then at least meet Hassan, King of Morocco. This was an idea to which Peres found himself thoroughly amenable, and the meeting did take place, on Moroccan soil, some two months later in July 1978 – and, incidentally, led to a sharp political confrontation and further deterioration in the relations between Peres and Menachem Begin.

In June 1978 Begin and the members of his Government were, at any rate, in a skittish mood. The negotiations with Egypt had run aground over the issue of linking the proposed peace treaty between the two countries to a declaration of principles regarding the West Bank. Sadat demanded it, Begin categorically rejected the idea, and, as a result, the Egyptian President announced the suspension of negotiations and his refusal to meet Begin or anyone representing him. At the same time, there was a steady decline in the Government's performance – and that of the Prime Minister, in particular. Secrets were leaked from Cabinet meetings while the sessions were still in progress. The inflation rate soared. Obstinate rumours were circulating that the Prime Minister's heart condition required him to take drugs that induced radical mood swings and affected his self-control. To top it all off, a year after the Begin Cabinet had been installed there was already talk about a change of government, together with reports that Peres was holding contacts with the National Religious Party to investigate the feasibility of forming a new government under his own leadership. (Such contacts did indeed take place, but none of them got very far. For although the leaders of the NRP contemplated the prospect of the Government falling, they clearly were not inclined to be the ones to bring it down.)

It was against this background that Peres received a telephone call from Bruno Kreisky, who was troubled about the stalemate in the peace negotiations and felt that something should be done about it. Kreisky believed that a meeting between Peres and Sadat might help and asked whether Peres was prepared to have him look into the idea. Yes, Peres was interested, but he qualified his assent by explaining that the final decision must be subject to the Prime Minister's approval. On Friday, 30 June, Peres received word that Sadat was prepared to join in a four-way parley (with Peres, Kreisky and Willy Brandt) to be held in Vienna. He immediately telephoned the Prime Minister's bureau and asked for an urgent meeting with Begin. The talk was scheduled for Saturday afternoon.

When Peres arrived at the Prime Minister's residence in Jerusalem, he found Begin about to depart for a reception in honour of Vice-President Walter Mondale, who was on an official visit to Israel. Consequently his talk with Begin was brief. He told the Prime Minister of Kreisky's initiative, and Begin consented to the meeting, but suggested that Peres first meet Foreign Minister, Moshe Dayan, to run through the positions he would present to Sadat.

Peres did as he was asked, arranging to meet Dayan in the Knesset on Tuesday. That day Peres also ran into Yigael Yadin in the Knesset building. The Deputy Prime Minister said that Begin had told him about the proposed meeting with Sadat. He wanted to wish Peres well, adding that it would be wonderful if he could persuade Sadat to meet Begin too. It seems that the Prime Minister was deeply offended by Sadat's personal boycott of him. (In the meantime, word had got out about the meeting between Peres and Sadat, and there was good reason to believe that the leak had come from Sadat's side with the aim of embarrassing Begin.) Peres said he believed Sadat was cold-shouldering the Prime Minister because Begin had not answered the question posed by the United States about the future of the nego-tiations – to which Yadin replied that the answers were not forthcom-ing because Begin didn't know who to fear more, Ezer (Weizman) or Dayan.

On that same Tuesday morning Dayan was presenting a briefing to the Knesset Foreign Affairs and Defence Committee and, practically as soon as he began speaking, he launched into a sharp attack on Peres's intended meeting with Sadat. Dayan conceded that the Prime Minister had agreed to the meeting, but immediately countered that he was categorically against it because he believed it would devalue the consultation between the Israeli and Egyptian Foreign Ministers scheduled to take place in London at the end of July. Without warning, Peres found himself in a position to which he was unaccustomed: a head-on clash with Moshe Dayan. Ever since Dayan had bolted from the Party, Peres had gone far out of his way to avoid a show-down with the new Foreign Minister; but this time he was left with no choice. Chafing at the vehemence of Dayan's attack, he snapped that Israel was a free country and he would meet whomever he pleased.

Two days later, on Thursday, 6 July 1978, the situation took a reverse turn when Peres met Begin again and found him wavering and distraught. Now the Prime Minister asserted that there was something to be said for Dayan's criticism of the proposed meeting with Sadat. Actually, he said – to Peres's amazement – he hadn't given his consent to the meeting because he did not believe it was necessary. And considering the criticism in the press, he continued in embarrassment, he might state publicly that he had not given his blessing to Peres's trip – without saying anything about consent. The stunned Peres explained that if Begin had so much as hinted at his reservations on the previous Saturday, he would have cancelled the trip without another word. But now, after he had agreed to meet Sadat – on the basis of receiving the Prime Minister's approval to do so – to cancel the meeting would be a grave step. Yet the most Begin would offer in an attempt to conciliate the peeved opposition leader was to refrain from mentioning the affair publicly.

From the Prime Minister's office Peres flew north on a visit to one of the Druze villages in the Galilee. Afterwards, during lunch at the guest-house of Kibbutz Gesher Haziv, a call came from Begin asking whether Peres would not, after all, reconsider the trip yet again, because he, Begin, had to say *something* about it publicly. Peres sensed that Begin was under heavy pressure from Dayan. He replied that cancelling the trip did not seem feasible to him, but that the Labour Party's Political Committee was scheduled to meet that evening and he would consult his colleagues and give Begin his final answer afterwards.

The members of the Political Committee were placed in a difficult position, but all of them – including Golda Meir – supported Peres. At the end of the consultation, Yigal Allon called Begin, informed him of the committee's decision and asked him to refrain from making any public declaration against the meeting because any such statement would seriously damage Israel's standing in Europe. Begin agreed.

At the same time, close to midnight, Peres was on his way to Dayan's home to tell him that he would be going to Vienna and to co-ordinate positions with him. He was perplexed, therefore, when Dayan told him that Begin had just called to relay Yigal Allon's news that the Political Committee had decided against the trip. When Peres expressed his surprise at the misunderstanding, Dayan made a gesture of impatience with his hand, as if to say that he wasn't willing to waste any more time over the incident. Upon reaching home, Peres called Allon, who also was taken aback by Begin's statement to Dayan, and he agreed to call the Prime Minister in the morning and clear up the misapprehension.

After a mere three hours' sleep, Peres left for Ben-Gurion Airport to fly directly to Vienna. *En route* he remarked to Micha Harish that they had not made arrangements for transport in Vienna and would have to hire a car. But when the plane landed, it turned out that his concern had been unnecessary. Peres received a welcome worthy of a head of state: a convoy of motorcycles, dozens of bodyguards and two helicopters accompanied him wherever he went.

At 11.30 a.m. on Sunday, 9 July 1978, Sadat, Kreisky, Brandt and Peres met in the Austrian Chancellor's office. The four settled into soft leather arm-chairs and exchanged small talk, beneath a large Venetian chandelier in the hall that once had held the famed Congress of Vienna, while correspondents and photographers buzzed around them. After the press had left, the conversation began, and it was divided into two parts: first, subjects related to the Socialist International; then, matters related to the Middle East. Kreisky said that after the affairs of the International had been discussed, he and Brandt would leave Sadat and Peres on their own. But it appears that curiosity got the better of the two European leaders, for they stayed for the later-part of the discussion as well.

Sadat said that he had had a letter from President Carter asking him to receive Dayan. 'I refused because I don't believe Dayan. Neither do I see any point in meeting Begin. He's a man of the old generation, and it's difficult to make progress with him.' Peres reminded the Egyptian President that Dayan was the architect of the Open Bridges policy on the West Bank and that Begin had made far-reaching concessions in Sinai and with the autonomy plan for the Palestinians. But Sadat did not seem to be very impressed by this.

At two o'clock the four men emerged to attend a press conference and lunch. Then Peres and Sadat continued their talk in the Hotel Imperial, where the Egyptian President was staying. Sadat opened this round of their discussion with words of praise: 'I believe you without reservation. You have proved that you conduct yourself as a statesman and a responsible man. I am sure that with you, Shimon, I would reach agreement on everything. When you said at the press conference that the government and the opposition are a parliamentary matter, but you are one people, I almost shouted: "Marvellous, Shimon. Marvellous. That's the way to talk." ' Afterwards Sadat spoke at length about his thoughts before deciding to go to Jerusalem and on the difficulties he had faced since then with Begin and Dayan. 'Since no solution seems to be in sight,' he said, 'I am thinking about resigning in September. My deputy, Husni Mubarak, will replace me.'

Thoughts of retirement aroused nostalgic memories in Sadat, and he began to speak of his predecessor, President Nasser, 'who found it difficult to make decisions'.

'How do you make decisions?' Peres asked.

'I must think alone. A habit from prison, from the solitary confinement the British subjected me to. Even if my wife is present, it is difficult for me to think – though I am a family man. Did you know that my wife is half-Christian? It's true. Her mother, a Christian, lived with us. Every time I travelled abroad, I brought her back a crucifix. I didn't hide it. Why should I? Members of all religions can live in peace.'

Towards the end of their talk, Peres showed Sadat the draft of a declaration he had prepared for the Socialist International, explaining that Brandt and Kreisky had already approved it. Sadat clapped his hands and his personal aide entered bringing his reading-glasses. As Sadat read the document, Peres could see that he was having some difficulty with the first clause, which called for the renewal of the negotiations that had been suspended in January. The draft read 'to renew contact without interference' and Peres suggested amending it to read 'to renew the Sadat initiative without interference'. Sadat's face lit up, and he approved the clause.

(It is interesting to compare the Vienna document with the Camp David accords. Regarding the borders to be drawn in the peace treaty, in Vienna Sadat signed on 'secure borders in accordance with Security Council Resolutions 242 and 338'. At Camp David he got Begin's agreement to a full withdrawal from Sinai to the international border. On the Palestinian issue, the Vienna statement determined that to reach a solution to their problem, the sides must recognize the Palestinians' right to participate in the determination of their future by means of negotiating with their chosen representatives. At Camp David, Begin signed an agreement including explicit recognition of 'the legitimate rights of the Palestinians'.)

From Vienna Peres went to London, where meetings with Prime Minister James Callaghan and Foreign Secretary David Owen had been arranged. But it turned out that Peres was not the only guest to meet them at this time. Jordan's King Hussein also happened to be visiting London.

The idea of getting Peres and Hussein together was raised by Callaghan, prompted by a message from Constantine, the exiled King of Greece, who was living in London. According to Constantine's letter, Hussein was prepared to hold a meeting in order to renew the dialogue that had begun when Peres was Defence Minister. Peres asked Callaghan first to check whether Hussein was willing to talk about a territorial compromise or joint administration of the West Bank. A few hours later, Callaghan telephoned to say that Hussein was prepared to discuss joint administration for a transition period.

On this basis, Peres telephoned the secretary of the Labour Party, Chaim Bar-Lev, and asked him to contact Begin, report on this latest development and ask his opinion about going forward with the meeting, while emphasizing the need to keep the matter strictly secret. Bar-Lev promptly complied and called Peres back to tell him that Begin was opposed to the meeting for reasons that the Prime Minister would explain upon Peres's return to Israel. Thus Peres regretfully informed Callaghan that under the circumstances he would not be able to meet Hussein. On the other hand, a meeting with another Arab king did come off during this trip.

From London Peres went to Paris and promptly vanished without trace for forty-eight hours. Journalists who expressed interest in his whereabouts were told that he was taking a holiday in a secret place. In fact, he spent those two days, 17/18 July 1978, at the palace of Hassan, King of Morocco, in Rabat, where the two men held long talks about the crisis in the Israeli-Egyptian negotiations, Sadat's standing in the Arab world, the attitude of the Great Powers and various other subjects.

On Wednesday, 19 July 1978, the day after Peres returned to Israel, all hell broke loose. Immediately after his plane landed, Peres telephoned Begin at home and set up a meeting to report on his trip. It was scheduled to take place the next day at the Knesset. But before their meeting, Begin was to make a speech to the plenum opening a foreign-policy debate. When he came to the subject of Judea and Samaria, the Prime Minister suddenly flew into a frenzy. He picked up a piece of paper, ripped it demonstratively in two and shouted: 'There! That is the territorial compromise!' Then, at the same pitch and volume, he charged that during the Vienna meeting, Peres hadn't asked Sadat whether he was amenable to a territorial compromise. Peres protested from his seat that the Prime Minister had yet to hear his report on the meeting and, as a matter of fact, he had put the question to Sadat and the Egyptian had given him an answer (notably that the subject was open to discussion). But Begin ignored the interjection and continued to lash into Peres.

At the end of his address, Begin stepped down from the rostrum, walked over to Peres and smiled at him as if nothing had happened. 'Shall we have lunch together?' he asked. Peres agreed and they walked to the Knesset dining-room, crowded with people, and sat down at a central table. After giving the waiter their order, Peres asked Begin for assurances that he could share secret information with him on the understanding that it would remain classified. Begin, with a broad sweep of the hand, replied: 'Certainly. I won't tell a soul. Not even my wife.' It was on this understanding that Peres began to report on his conversations with Sadat and King Hassan. In the course of the briefing, Begin stood up from time to time to shake hands with acquaintances who approached their table. Each time he sat down again, he apologized: 'You understand, I must do it. You did the same when you were in power.'

Finally, Peres asked the Prime Minister why he had been forbidden to meet Hussein. Begin explained that the Jordanian monarch had refused to meet Government representatives. Instead, he proposed a meeting between Crown Prince Hassan and Deputy Prime Minister Yigael Yadin and then torpedoed this idea as well. 'How come he refuses to meet us but is prepared to meet you?' he asked rhetorically. 'Ben-Gurion wouldn't have allowed it either.'

The luncheon ended, but the debate continued in the plenum and went on through the evening, as Begin sat in the Knesset restaurant with a group of Deputies from his Party. He was in a jovial mood, talking and joking to the delight and boisterous laughter of his followers. There is general agreement about what took place at this merry gathering with the exception of one outburst. Eye- and ear-witnesses later offered the following version of events: Begin began to talk about Peres's trip and, to the amazement of his audience, revealed that Peres had visited Morocco, adding, 'While I'm in charge, he won't see so much as the earlobe of Morocco-Shmorocco again. Just as I didn't let him see Hussein.' And here, according to these same witnesses, the courtly Prime Minister spat out the Russian word *khoi* (the equivalent of the Yiddish *schmuck*).

During that period rumours about the effects of the drugs prescribed for Begin grew increasingly insistent. When word of this incident reached Peres, he was therefore reluctant to make an issue of it. But Knesset Member Yossi Sarid took up the cudgels by telling some of the Prime Minister's close associates exactly what he thought of Begin's behaviour.

Well past midnight there were still some Deputies in the hall waiting for the foreign-policy debate to wind up. Peres was sitting in the Knesset dining-room when Begin entered in a lather, strode up to him and abruptly asked him whether he had heard him use the expression '*khoi*'. Peres replied that he himself had not heard it, but others said that they had. Begin insisted that he had not said anything of the sort. Peres then asked Begin why he had broken his promise and spoken openly about the visit to Morocco and his refusal to let Peres meet Hussein. The Prime Minister was patently embarrassed. He didn't deny a thing and was reduced to blurting out, wearily, 'I'm sorry.' But the damage had already been done.

The deadlock in the negotiations between Israel and Egypt continued. In the hope of breaking it, Secretary of State Cyrus Vance planned a mediation mission to Cairo and Jerusalem in August 1978. Before leaving Washington, however, he heard that Peres was in the United States on a lecture tour and asked to meet him. Vance was interested in details of Peres's talk with Sadat in Vienna, and especially about the declaration of principles on the West Bank. Did Peres think that Sadat wanted the United States to pressure him into having the declaration mention the possibility of border changes? Peres replied that so far as he could see, Sadat was prepared to make this gesture to President Carter in response to American 'pressure'. (Vance took note of this point and used it later on. Neither of the two men had the least doubt that Sadat was using Peres to get this message to the Americans.) Vance was also interested in Peres's talk with King Hassan of Morocco, and Peres explained that the purpose of such meetings was to try and transform supporters of the PLO into backers of the peace process. The Secretary commented that Hassan had wanted to convene an all-Arab summit conference to express its support for Egypt, but the Americans had cautioned him against 'overdoing' it. (Peres was rather perplexed by this disclosure.)

In August Vance carried out his mission, but it did not yield the hoped-for results and the negotiations between Israel and Egypt continued to limp along. At this point President Carter decided to place the full weight of his prestige in the balance by inviting the leaders of Israel and Egypt to a conference at his Camp David retreat at the beginning of September 1978. Just before leaving for the United States, Begin invited Peres for a talk to discuss and co-ordinate their positions as far as possible. They reached agreement on seven points, and, although their talk was not meant for publication, that evening

Begin appeared on television and reported on it to the citizens of Israel. Among other things agreed upon in that discussion, the two men came to an understanding that if there were any shift in his position, Begin would phone Peres from Camp David. As matters turned out, there were many such changes, but never once did the Prime Minister call Peres.

Presidents Carter and Sadat and Prime Minister Begin dug themselves in at Camp David, together with their senior advisers, at the beginning of September 1978. The talks were gruelling, but in the end they produced agreement. On 19 September the three leaders appeared before a select audience and television cameras to sign the Camp David accords, which were to serve as the basis and framework for a peace agreement between Israel and Egypt to be signed within three months.

In Israel the initial reaction to the agreements was one of unrestrained joy, but in a few days feelings cooled considerably once the price began to sink in. Especially painful was the need to forfeit the settlements in Sinai, which many Israelis considered the betrayal of a cardinal Zionist principle. There was also a general sense of betrayal towards the settlers. For both of these reasons, some people in the Labour Party urged Peres to make political capital out of the issue of the Sinai settlements. It was indeed tempting, for nothing could have been easier than to wield the settlements as a weapon with which to batter the Government and pick up points with the public. But Peres was against exploiting such a painful issue for partisan gain.

When the Labour Party's Central Committee met prior to the Knesset debate on the Camp David accords, the atmosphere was particularly tense. Yigal Allon, leading those who were opposed to the abandonment of the settlements, wanted the Central Committee to pass a resolution demanding that the Knesset distinguish between the vote on the agreements and the vote on the clause regarding the settlements. But Peres regarded this proposal, and others like it, as futile parliamentary exercises. Like Allon and many others, he felt that Begin had paid too high a price for the agreement – and subjected him to scathing criticism for it. But his basic stance was that the Camp David accords had to be approached as a single unit, and the Party would have to decide for or against them as a whole. 'The choice is not between a good agreement and a bad one,' he explained. 'The choice is between a chance for peace or reverting to the risk of war. We can't support the positive side of the agreement and oppose the negative one.' It was a fateful hour, Peres said, and 'the Party cannot waver. We must utter a forceful and sustained "Aye".' After a stormy debate, Peres's view was accepted by a large majority. The Labour Party would endorse the Camp David agreement.

Although the agreement's time-scale of three months for working out a peace treaty was not sufficient and four more months were needed to overcome the obstacles encountered during the negotiations, in March 1978 all the sides involved in the peace process could justly feel satisfied. The date for signing the treaty was set for 27 March 1978; the place was to be Washington.

Peres came to the US capital as a member of the parliamentary delegation accompanying the Prime Minister to the signing ceremony. The Israeli air force plane which brought the delegation to Washington stopped in New York to pick up the Prime Minister, who had preceded the rest of the Israeli party to the United States. It was then that Yechiel Kaddishai, the Prime Minister's political aide, told Peres that Sadat wanted to meet him in Washington for a private talk.

Peres found the Egyptian President trimmer than ever, sun-tanned and in excellent spirits. After returning compliments on the progress of his diet, Sadat embarked upon what had become his customary line with Peres: complaints about Begin.

> I met him yesterday for a private talk, and he asked me why I refuse to come to Jerusalem to sign the treaty there and why I am not inviting him to Cairo. He said that I promised Carter I would. I didn't deny it. I was prepared to go to Jerusalem. But on the morning I promised to go, Begin appeared on television and said that Sadat would come to Jerusalem, the indivisible capital of Israel, the eternal capital of Israel. Doesn't he have any understanding of psychology? Couldn't he just say Sadat will come to Jerusalem, period?

As to inviting Begin to Cairo, the Egyptian leader noted: 'I told Begin that he had created a negative image for himself in the eyes of the Arabs. He asked what he should do to improve it, and I told him, "Don't talk so much." ' Afterwards, Sadat related, Begin complained about his forthcoming meeting with Peres. 'I told him, "Every time Shimon and I are together in the same place and time, we shall meet!" '

Begin, however, was not the only target of Sadat's barbs that day; he called Yasser Arafat 'that self-aggrandizing liar'. 'Let him run amok to his heart's content. You don't have to pay any attention to him.

Even if there is a Palestinian state, he won't be heading it.' Then he turned to the subject of Dayan, asking, 'Did you see him on television this morning? A strange man. What is he so pessimistic about? Do you think he'll try to return to the Labour Party? Will you take him back? That man is capable of ruining a lot of things.'

'And now, Shimon, you must come visit Cairo,' he said expansively. Peres thanked Sadat for the invitation, but demurred that although he was Chairman of his Party, he worked with a team that had laboured together with him in the cause of peace and he would like them to come along. 'For sure, for sure,' Sadat said graciously. 'We'll set the visit for a few months from now.'

On the day of the signing ceremony, Peres had lunch with Dr Henry Kissinger. 'Sadat has a special admiration for you,' the ex-Secretary of State remarked. Later in their conversation, Kissinger had harsh words about Begin's autonomy plan for the Arab inhabitants of Judea and Samaria. 'What do you need it for?' he groused. 'Autonomy means returning to the 1967 borders, sooner or later.' Kissinger also thought that Begin had conducted the negotiations with Egypt poorly. 'Why did he come forward with his own proposals? Sadat was forced to reject them for the simple reason that they were Israeli suggestions. Begin should have come to Sadat and said: "You made a daring step in coming to Jerusalem. Good for you! Now, what have you got to offer?" ' Kissinger also judged Begin's strategy towards the United States a peculiar and misguided one. For example, Begin had failed to say a single good word to the Republicans. Senator Howard Baker, the Senate minority leader and a very influential man, approached Kissinger and grumbled that he had spoken in Israel's favour 'three times over the past two weeks. The Israelis turn to me on every issue that comes up in the Senate. But now I see that only the President is worthy of praise and recognition, no one else. I'll remember that when the Israelis turn to me next time.' Finally, Kissinger predicted that Israel could expect heavy pressure from Carter. When Peres asked what the President could use as a lever, Kissinger replied: 'Mobilizing public opinion against you. Every time Begin appears on television here, the number of supporters of Israel decreases.'

Despite the achievement of the peace treaty, the skies above the *Likud* Government remained overcast, growing darker day by day. Galloping inflation, the constant bickering between the Ministers, the eroding image of the Prime Minister's authority and a new spate of rumours about his inability to function all contributed to the gloom. No longer did the Labourites talk of remaining in opposition for years to come. Public-opinion polls began to give the Party a growing lead, making it seem that the road was clear for Labour to return to power after one term in opposition. At the same time, Peres's frequent meetings with world leaders boosted his own standing as a statesman. His appearance in the Knesset, which assumed a classic polemic style, made him into the unchallenged leader of the opposition. In the course of 1978, all the central bodies of the Labour Party were elected without personal or inter-factional turmoil. Peres began to believe that after many years of struggle and sheer hard work, the time had finally come to reap the fruits – the only struggle left being that over the premiership.

It was an understandable mistake on his part, but a bad one, none the less. For, paradoxically, it was precisely Peres's success and the Party's rising fortunes that threatened to be his downfall. Finally there was something worth fighting over. The grand prize was no longer leadership of the opposition, but the premiership itself. Now that he had gone through the drudgery of rehabilitating the Party, there were people who wanted to see Peres go. Yet the direct challenge to his leadership came from the least likely – or, to be more precise, the least expected – quarter, namely, the former Foreign Minister and head of the *Ahdut Ha'avodah* faction, Yigal Allon.

It is difficult to point to the exact date or event that marked the beginning of Allon's race against Peres. First came the rumours that emerged after a meeting of the *Ahdut Ha'avodah* faction with Allon. At the beginning of 1979, Allon began to toy with the idea of pitting his strength against Peres for the leading post in the Party. The reaction of the *Ahdut Ha'avodah* leadership was mixed. They still had trouble swallowing Peres, but were dogged by the double fear that while Allon might fail to mobilize a majority for his candidacy he could create an atmosphere of divisiveness that would leave the delicate fabric of the Labour Party in tatters. Nevertheless, the people closest to Allon, including Yitzhak Rabin, continued to egg him on by reminding him that this was his last chance to capture the leadership. The nation needed a leader of his calibre, they said – a kibbutznik, an ideologue, a man of principles.

Their entreaties fell on fertile ground, for Allon had had his eye on the top post for many years. A number of times, in fact, it had seemed within reach, only to be snatched from his hands at the last moment.

What's more, he did not especially admire Peres. 'He's no Ben-Gurion, Golda or even an Eshkol,' Allon was known to have said, 'so why not me?'

Peres's initial reaction was confident: if there was to be a contest, it should take place immediately. He knew that Allon wasn't ready for a full-scale confrontation yet and wanted to nip the affair in the bud by initiating preparations for an emergency meeting of the Central Committee. Allon began to look for a way to prevent the contest from taking place so early, and Peres's advisers were divided: some called for making a gesture to Allon, others wanted an immediate decision.

Peres hesitated at first and then made a bad mistake: he backed down. Instead of doing everything in his power to catch Allon unprepared and drum him out of the race, he set up a meeting with his rival at which the two worked out a resolution to be brought before the Party Executive on 12 July. It placed responsibility for the competitive atmosphere on the media – even though they were merely quoting Allon and Rabin directly – and determined that the Executive would continue to view Peres as the Party's Chairman and candidate for the premiership while conceding the right to compete for these positions.

The resolution was accepted unanimously by the Executive, and Peres was sure he had won a victory. But in essence he had played right into the hands of Allon and Rabin. 'Shimon agreed to a compromise to the effect that his name is Shimon Peres and he lives in Ramat Aviv,' one of his leading supporters, Eliyahu Speizer, summed up derisively. What he meant was that Peres really hadn't achieved anything. Allon, on the other hand, emerged from the flap with time to organize his camp while managing to keep up the profile of a 'non-contestant'. His motto was: 'The only competition going on today within the Labour Party is over the legitimate right to compete.' But throughout that period he made the rounds of the Party's branches, met activists and conducted a campaign worthy of an election contest. Essentially it was a war of nerves in which Peres was obviously at a disadvantage, for he was the only one who had anything to lose.

During these months, Peres did not get much backing or derive much pleasure from events abroad either. At the beginning of July 1979, his friends Willy Brandt and Bruno Kreisky met the leader of the PLO, Yasser Arafat, and the event turned into a show of solidarity which caused Peres great personal embarrassment. Still, he calculated his response carefully, never forgetting Kreisky's unique standing in the International and Europe as a whole. The extent of the Austrian Chancellor's sympathy for the PLO and its leader was a constant headache for the State of Israel, for the Labour Party and for Peres. The problem was how to deal with this fact of life without creating a situation in which Kreisky's power in the European community would wreak damage on Israel. Peres's solution was to maintain a network of correct-to-warm relations with Kreisky alongside a low-profile ideological debate, meaning that he was careful to stop well short of personal attacks that would anger the Chancellor's colleagues.

Peres planned to attend the Executive of the Socialist International, scheduled to meet in Sweden on 21 July, but before departing he sent Micha Harish to be briefed by Kreisky and Brandt and to prepare him for his meeting with them. In the end Brandt did not turn up, and when Peres arrived in Sweden, he met Kreisky alone for a private talk. They argued for two hours over the Kreisky-Brandt meeting with Arafat and continued their debate for another five hours afterwards, before the members of twenty delegations who attended the convention. Peres surprised his listeners by opening his address with words of praise for Kreisky and for his support of the peace process with Egypt. When he sounded his criticism of the PLO, therefore, it was received with understanding, and Kreisky did not take offence.

This approach to diplomacy earned Peres a solid standing among the International's members, even if he did not achieve the dominant position that Golda Meir enjoyed in this forum. Then again, Bruno Kreisky once said of Mrs Meir: 'I admire her. She's a biblical figure. But when a biblical figure like that walks around your room, you feel a certain uneasiness.'

Peres returned to Israel on the night of Saturday, 21 July, but while still in Sweden he received word that Begin had suffered a stroke, affecting one of the blood vessels that nourish the brain. On the day after his return, he visited the Prime Minister in the Hadassah Medical Centre in Jerusalem and found Begin looking pale and thin, but trying to keep his spirits up. The Prime Minister ordered tea for his guest while giving Peres a detailed briefing about his malady. 'A blood clot has "sneaked into" the blood vessel that feeds the brain cells controlling the field of vision,' he explained. 'I see you very well now, but I cannot read a newspaper all the way through. My vision becomes blurred. And what is our life if not reading?' At the end of his description, Begin tacked on the comment: 'Ben-Gurion also suffered from something similar.'

Peres took this opportunity to inform Begin that he would be going to Egypt in a few days, as President Sadat's guest, and wanted to propose the establishment of an informal union of labour movements from the United States, Europe, Israel and Egypt to support the advancement of peace. The Prime Minister did not take to the idea. 'Don't forget that Sadat is not a democrat,' he cautioned. 'You should avoid praising his regime. Who knows where it will lead?' He closed with the sentence that had become all but a permanent feature of his talks with Peres: 'Perhaps you'll talk with Dayan?' Peres had the impression that Begin's dependence on his Foreign Minister was growing stronger every day.

On Tuesday, 24 July, Peres flew to Egypt at the head of a Labour Party delegation. As the plane crossed the Israeli border, the region of the Nile Delta spread out before him, dotted with villages, textile enterprises, industrial structures and the classic signs of poverty. At Cairo Airport the President's private helicopter was awaiting Peres. (Sadat's pilot assured his guest that the helicopter was British-made and 'among the safest'.) An hour later the aircraft landed in Alexandria, where President Sadat was staying at his summer villa, close to the sea, open to the sea breeze and set in a garden of trees and flowers. Sadat stood waiting for his guests at the entrance to the house and appeared relaxed and full of life. He welcomed Peres with a pronounced display of warmth, showed him round the garden and boasted with special pride that he also had a vegetable garden which satisfied the household's needs.

After drinking mango juice, Sadat took Peres's arm and led him to the house with a 'Come, let's go talk.' They settled into a room whose French windows overlooked the garden and the sea. Sadat asked after Begin's health and said that he had wanted to call the Prime Minister immediately upon hearing that he was in hospital, but since it was Saturday he waited another day. Then Sadat went on to speak of Jerusalem. 'I don't have a plan, but I have a dream,' he began.

'And that is?' Peres asked.

'The city will remain united, but there must be Arab sovereignty over the places holy to Islam. There must be a flag, passports, uniforms. The Western Wall can remain in Israeli hands. That is a place holy to the Jews.'

'What about the West Bank?' Peres pressed.

'I understand Israel's security problems in that area. So if a Palestinian entity comes into being in the West Bank, the area will have to be demilitarized,' Sadat pronounced.

'Israel cannot trust the Palestinians to honour the demilitarization. I don't believe Arafat,' Peres countered.

'Rightly so,' Sadat agreed. 'You can't believe a word he says. He is a man who flees from decisions. Always wavering and manoeuvring. Meanwhile he and his cohorts live like kings. They have money at their disposal and usually don't have to account to anyone for how they spend it.'

They continued talking for quite a while on various subjects and, towards the end of the meeting, Peres presented Sadat with the gift he had brought for him: three figures from the Bible, all of them great but no longer young women, 'so as not to arouse Jihan's anger'. Sadat laughed: 'Even if they were young, Jihan would forgive you.'

The visit came to a close on Friday, 27 July, and, as Peres was about to board his plane, a special car from the President's office drew up to the aircraft and two officials presented Peres with a personal gift of Egyptian *objets d'art*. Peres was very moved and sent Sadat a cable expressing his gratitude. Meanwhile, however, a 'gift' of an entirely different kind was waiting for Peres in Israel – and would make his life miserable for years to come.

It had been an open secret for quite a while that Yitzhak Rabin was writing his memoirs, and few believed that Peres would derive much pleasure from reading them. But what actually ensued was infinitely worse than even the grimmest prognostications. On 8 August 1979, the Israeli television broadcast selections from Rabin's book on its prime-time newscast. The words showered down on Peres like artillery shells, for the former Prime Minister was accusing him of every sin imaginable and ascribed to him every possible negative trait known to mankind. Rabin alleged that Peres had undermined his position throughout the period of his Government, that he had leaked state secrets, was a liar and unworthy of public trust, was not fit to be Defence Minister and certainly not fit to become Prime Minister, and finally that he, Rabin, would never serve in any government headed by Peres. The most amazing thing about these allegations was that not a single one of them was backed by a shred of proof, or even an attempt at proof. A typical example was the charge that Peres had leaked to the press the fact that a Soviet delegation was on a secret mission to Israel. The 'proof': when Rabin suggested that all the Ministers in his Government undergo lie-detector tests, Peres refused 'and turned pale'.

The Party was no less shocked than its Chairman, especially because Rabin seemed to have opened a Pandora's box just as the *Likud* Government was going inexorably to pieces. Many of Peres's close supporters begged him to drum Rabin out of the Party – or at least out of its leadership echelon. But after giving the matter long and serious thought, Peres decided to disregard their advice and react with moderation. There were three reasons for his choosing prudence: attempting to oust Rabin from the Party's leadership might lead to a split; it might also engender a bitter debate that would drag him down to the level of the charges in Rabin's book; and lastly, as matters stood the book was more likely to backfire on its author. Thus in all his media interviews, Peres denied Rabin's accusations, but refrained from mounting a frontal attack against him.

On 12 July 1979, the Party's Executive convened to discuss the publication of Rabin's book. The atmosphere was highly charged as, one by one, former Ministers in Rabin's Government stood up to speak their minds. Each denounced the book as giving a subjective version of events. They asked Rabin many questions that he was unable to answer: if Peres was so bad, why did he choose him as the Prime Minister's stand-in when he went on leave after the bank-account affair? Why did he agree to run on a list headed by Peres? Typical of the general feeling was a comment made by ex-Justice Minister Chaim Zadok: 'This book detracts from Yitzhak Rabin's credibility and casts aspersions on his judgment. Personal enmity has got the better of the author's discretion.' The original idea was to sum up the discussion with a resolution denouncing Rabin and his book, but Peres decided against it. 'I have no summary resolution,' he declared. 'The conclusion is in the essence of what has been said here and the expression of confidence [in me] on the part of all the comrades who have spoken.'

Peres's friends and supporters were baffled. His moderation had the look of timidity about it, and they grumbled that he was incapable of making a decision, was too compromising, too irresolute. Whether or not they judged him fairly, on one point – that the book would backfire on its author – he was right, though, even here, only partially so. The assessment held true so far as the Party was concerned. Even as Prime Minister, Rabin failed to understand the Party's system or the mentality of its loyalists. They might squabble among themselves or support different men, but the one thing they could not forgive was a public assault on the Party. Dirty linen was to be laundered behind closed doors only.

On the other hand, Peres misjudged the effect of the book on public opinion as a whole, and this error was to prove a costly one. Because of his weak reaction, the book emerged as having the dominant say. The charges against him struck root as Rabin acquired the image of a victim and Peres the reputation of a schemer. In fact, Peres would suffer for quite a while as a result of this phenomenon, but in the end his calculations proved valid. He may have lost stature in the public's estimation, but he was a veteran political animal and knew what his short-sighted friends evidently did not: the public does not choose the Labour Party's Chairman and candidate for the premiership; the Party's functionaries and rank and file do.

Meanwhile, Yigal Allon continued to pursue his 'non-candidacy' with vigour, especially since the blow to Peres's popularity had given him a hearty head start. A strange thing had happened: despite the fact that Allon had been in politics for more than thirty years, he was becoming a symbol of freshness, ideology and integrity.

During this period Peres sank into a deep depression and seemed to hit bottom one Friday night when an astrologer appeared on television and forecast that the next Prime Minister of Israel would be Yigal Allon. Normally Peres would not ascribe the least importance to an astrologer's predictions, but these were not normal times; so when it was suggested that he see an astrologer himself, he agreed. The choice was Ilan Pecker, who came to Peres's Tel Aviv office late one night. The two shut themselves in for an hour and a half, and at the end of the session Peres was reported to be feeling a little better.

Soon afterwards, his patience began to give out. At a meeting of the Party Executive early in January 1980, he complained resentfully: 'There is a whispering campaign going on against me within my own Party. I have been involved in politics since the age of sixteen, and never have I heard anyone say that I am untrustworthy. That is a charge which has come out of this building!' Once again he pressed to have the Party reach an early decision on its candidate for the premiership and convened the Central Committee for just that purpose. But Allon appealed to the Party's Constitutional Committee, arguing that only the Central Committee elected by the next Party convention would be authorized to choose the candidate, and the Constitutional Committee accepted his reasoning. Peres was in no mood to buckle, however, and appealed the Constitutional Committee's decision back to the Central Committee on 13 January 1980. By a large majority, with Allon's loyalists abstaining from the vote, the Central Committee determined that it was indeed authorized to choose the candidate for the premiership. Moreover, it scheduled another meeting for the following week to do just that.

This decision finally forced Allon into the open. On 15 January he wrote to Peres that he was setting forth his candidacy for the premiership and chairmanship of the Party and thereby made it obvious that any decision made now would be meaningless. When the Central Committee met again on 20 January, Allon did not submit his candidacy. The Committee was therefore asked to vote for or against Peres, with the result being 457 in favour, 220 against and 41 abstentions.

Peres finally had the decision he had wanted so badly, but Allon made a point of announcing that it was 'just for the time being'. As matters turned out, he was right about that, insofar as Peres was concerned, but tragically wrong about himself. For on Thursday, 2 February 1980, Allon suffered a severe heart attack. By the next day, Allon was no longer alive. On the seventh day after his death, which ends the traditional week of mourning, Peres eulogized his former rival as 'one of the great men of our nation, a commander in the War of Independence, a statesman, an original and sensitive writer, a leader admired by his movement, and one of the prime movers behind the unification of the kibbutz movement'.

Thus the contest between Allon and Peres ended in tragedy. It had been a tense and emotional affair, but it never sullied the attitude of mutual respect that obtained between the two men. With Allon's death, the style of a fair fight departed the arena of competition, for the man who replaced him – Yitzhak Rabin – came armed with the full complement of hatred and bile that were eating away at him.

'Take up the banner that Yigal raised!' Allon's widow cried out to Yitzhak Rabin. It was a curious summons, for it is difficult to imagine anyone less suited to carry Allon's standard. Allon had been a member of the kibbutz movement, a man of values and a gentleman in the fullest sense of the word; Rabin proved to be a pleasure-seeking materialist who had trouble keeping his financial affairs in line, a man estranged from the kibbutz movement and possessed of a brusque, arrogant demeanour. But a number of factors coalesced to make him into the candidate who almost defeated Peres. With Allon's death, *Hakibbutz Hameuchad* was bereft of a leader. The rank and file called for all members of the faction to rally around Peres, but the faction's leadership was on a different wavelength. They feared that without a leader and without a contest they would lose their power and be slowly but steadily overwhelmed by the *Mapai* and *Rafi* factions. The thought of Rabin as the standard-bearer left many members of *Hakibbutz Hameuchad* feeling uneasy, for he was essentially an outsider, an interloper. Then again, he was available and more than ready to serve as the staff on which *Hakibbutz Hameuchad* could raise its banner.

There was another consideration about Rabin. Public-opinion polls taken in January 1980, when Allon was still alive, registered the following readings as to popularity: Peres, 16 per cent; Allon, 8 per cent; Rabin, 5 per cent. But immediately after Allon's death, a dramatic change occurred. Peres's popularity remained static, but Rabin's soared to 18 per cent in March, 22 per cent in April, and as high as 27 per cent in June and still rising! The most common explanation for this phenomenon was twofold: all the affection that Allon had accumulated over the years and which had reached its peak at his death was transferred to Rabin. In addition, he acquired some popularity of his own by his frequent television appearances, coming across as a shy, unassuming character and creating the impression of a down-to-earth, ingenuous type – in contrast to Peres's polished, professional performances. And while Peres always seemed to be harping at the Government for its sins, Rabin's criticism sounded like the commentary of a seasoned, objective observer. One way or another, Peres was confronted with an unpalatable but undeniable fact: Rabin was back and very popular. More popular, in fact, than the leader of the Labour Party.

The Party winced at the prospect of a contest between Rabin and Peres, and attempts at mediation began to pop up sporadically. The first of the mediators was Yeruham Meshel, the Secretary-General of the *Histadrut*, who proposed that Peres invite Rabin to serve as Minister of Defence in the Government he would presumably form after the elections. Meshel was so buoyed by his meeting with Rabin that, on 6 March 1980, he wrote to Peres: 'I had a very constructive talk with Yitzhak. Next week we will continue. I may be able to wrap this up affirmatively.'

What Meshel did not grasp was that he was talking about wrapping up an empty package. The relations between Peres and Rabin had reached a point of mutual distrust which barred any form of co-operation. Peres took the attitude that before he could even contemplate talking to Rabin, the latter would have to publicly recant what he had written in his book. Rabin backed down somewhat by announcing that he no longer ruled out the possibility of serving in a Peres Government, or vice versa; but every time he was asked about his book, he avowed that he would not retract a single word of it.

A number of Party activists began to talk about the possibility of an alternative candidate. Names were even mentioned, including President Yitzhak Navon, who was enormously popular among all sections of the Israeli public. Navon was even approached on the subject, but he adamantly refused to consider the idea. 'If another man were involved, perhaps I would contemplate the possibility of resigning to head the Party,' he confided. 'But I have a problem over Peres. I honestly believe he will make a fine Prime Minister.'

Peres was clearly at a disadvantage here because he was leading in the race and had the most to lose. Rabin knew that his chances of winning were slim, but more than wanting to win he was out for Peres's head. Just as he was glad when Begin won the national election, he was now prepared to turn his support and that of his camp over to anyone in the Party willing to challenge Peres. The chances of Rabin's strategy succeeding depended upon his ability to drag Peres down to the level of debate that would force the Party to disown them both. That is why Peres was always so cautious in word and deed.

Inevitably the Party turned into a breeding-ground of rumour and mutual recriminations, and soon the climate of distrust gave rise to a flurry of anonymous letters addressed to Peres. One of them read: 'Take note: Rabin and a certain activist in the *Likud* are working together against you! You will soon be very surprised by a certain publication!' Signed: 'An employee in the Prime Minister's Office'. Or: 'Sir, I wish to inform you that it has just now come to my attention that a former ambassador is clandestinely and intensively collaborating with Rabin against you! Please beware of that slick cozener.' Signed: 'A Supporter'.

As in the case of Allon, once again Peres tried to avoid a contest. He could brandish the Central Committee's latest decision that he was the Party's candidate for the premiership, but its validity would expire as soon as the Party Convention opened (due to Allon's death, the convention was postponed to December 1980). The only thing that could thwart this scenario would be the fall of the Government, which would bring the elections forward.

Peres's desire to topple the Government found expression in a series of meetings with the leaders of the National Religious Party, a partner to Begin's coalition. Actually, these sessions dated back to early 1978, when Peres dissociated himself from Rabin's 'brilliant manoeuvre' (the sacking of the NRP Ministers, which brought down his Government) and stressed that there was no reason why the historic alliance between Labour and the NRP should not be revived. Later, when a split rent Yigael Yadin's Democratic Movement for Change and the Government lost six votes in the Knesset, NRP leader Yosef Burg put forward an interesting possibility. It was uncertain whether the Government would be able to hold out, Burg told Peres, and he understood that the Labour Party was not interested in joining a coalition headed by Menachem Begin. But, he asked, would Peres be prepared to consider joining a government headed by Yosef Burg?

There were other meetings in which the two sides agreed that Begin's Government was coming apart at the seams, but stopped short of making any operative decisions. Yet, the NRP people did not come merely to gossip about Mr Begin and his Ministers. They wanted to discuss concrete issues, such as postponing the elections to the Chief Rabbinate so as to extend the terms of Chief Rabbis Shlomo Goren and Ovadiah Yosef. The subject came up at a number of meetings, and the members of the NRP intimated that if Labour backed a postponement of the rabbinical elections, it would not be long before the NRP walked out of the Government, bringing it down in its wake. Peres gave the NRP what it wanted – having to overcome no dearth of opposition with his own Party to do so. But after achieving their objective, the NRP negotiators turned around and mocked Peres. They never intended to leave the Government, they now said. They had merely tossed a bone in Peres's direction and, in his burning desire to topple the Government, he snapped at it.

In April 1980 Peres was scheduled to go to the United States on another lecture tour. On previous occasions of this kind, he had met Cabinet-level officials of the administration in Washington. But this time, a few weeks before Peres left Israel, special Ambassador Sol Linowitz raised the idea of a meeting with President Carter. This was the first time an American President had agreed – actually asked – to meet the head of the opposition in Israel, a point which kindled the anger of the Prime Minister and his Cabinet colleagues.

It was impossible to alter the fact of a meeting between Peres and Carter – which was set for 24 April 1980 – but it was possible for the Prime Minister to express his pique. A day prior to the meeting, therefore, Israeli Ambassador Ephraim Evron received instructions from the Foreign Ministry that not he, but the number two in the Embassy, Minister Ya'akov Nechustan (a *Likud* appointee), should accompany Peres to the meeting. The object of this move was twofold: to reduce the value of the meeting and to get a reliable report from a man the Government could fully trust. Peres's immediate reaction was to waive the escort. Evron informed Jerusalem and was told that 'if that's the way he wants it, let Peres go to see the President by himself'. But at 5 a.m. next morning, Foreign Minister Yitzhak Shamir personally woke Evron up to tell him that he would be allowed to accompany Peres. As things turned out, Shamir could have let Evron sleep; the President requested that his talk with Peres be a private one, and Evron waited in Vice-President Mondale's office as the two leaders parleyed.

During the discusssion, very little was said about advancing the talks with Egypt. Most of the meeting was devoted to Jordan, with the President taking an interest in Peres's views on the chances that Hussein would join in the peace process. Carter also displayed an interest in Israeli internal affairs and spoke in terms of the Labour Party's certain return to power. 'Are you thinking of establishing a coalition that will include Yosef Burg, Ezer Weizman and Moshe Dayan?' the President asked.

'I don't think I can or would establish any coalition before the elections,' was Peres's politic reply.

'Will Dayan run on his own ticket?'

'I don't think so,' Peres guessed – incorrectly, as it turned out. 'Dayan doesn't want to be Prime Minister. He doesn't have the patience to deal with all the little things a Prime Minister has to deal with.'

'You're telling me!' was Carter's emphatic response.

The President made an oblique reference to the forthcoming elections in the United States, but the implication was clear enough when he said, 'I don't determine who will be in the next Israeli Government, and I presume that Israel does not want to be involved in the elections to the American administration.' Vice-President Mondale, whom Peres saw immediately after his meeting with Carter, was far more blunt on this issue:

> You know the record of this administration on Israel. . . . Considering that, the White House is disappointed about the results of the New York primary [in which Teddy Kennedy defeated Jimmy Carter]. Carter will be chosen for another term, so what's the point of the Jews voting against him? I'm not asking Israel to do anything specific. I'm just trying to illustrate the President's feeling. The man is only human, and you mustn't forget that.

To a degree, Peres could empathize with Carter's plight, as the political map was changing in Israel, too – particularly with the advent of a new body called the 'Urim Circle' put together by a group of Rabin supporters. The fact that this body existed outside the framework of the Labour Party exempted it from the limitations imposed on a Party institution – which soon expressed itself in the unprecedented venom of its attacks on Peres. The appearance of Rabin's Urim Circle, therefore, left Peres in a quandary. Rabin now had an extra-Party body to conduct his struggle, while Peres relied solely on the Party. But the fact that the Party was not of one mind placed serious limitations on him. Peres's supporters, therefore, decided to establish a framework that would be free to conduct his campaign as it saw fit. At the same time, the Secretary of the Labour Party was seeking a channel to help solicit funds for Peres. The two ideas found a common ground when Bar-Lev asked Michael Piron to head a group which called itself Alef, an acronym for the Hebrew words 'Citizens for Peres'.

First on the list of Alef's priorities was the problem of Peres's image, especially since he continued to lag behind Rabin in the polls. There seemed to be no reasonable explanation for this curious phenomenon. Not a shred of evidence existed to place Peres's personal integrity in doubt. Rabin, in contrast, had been forced to resign because he committed a felony and lied to the public, but he still enjoyed the image of an honest and trustworthy man, while Peres was regarded as an incorrigible schemer.

In order to overcome this distortion, the people in Alef brought in an American expert on election strategy, David Sawyer. In essence, he told Peres what his own people had been saying all along: his TV appearances were too 'professional', not casual enough. Together with a number of Israeli aides, Sawyer worked with Peres in a television studio and tried to teach him how to answer questions in a way that wins hearts. The image-builders could not overcome one thing, though. They never managed to teach Peres to say 'I don't know'. He argued that he couldn't say it because it wasn't true; he knew the answers, if only because he had contemplated the questions for most of his adult life. 'But the television viewer doesn't know that!' the experts whined in exasperation. Peres just smiled bitterly. 'You mean if I'm not honest, then I'm trustworthy. To be credible I have to lie.'

Gradually, albeit slowly, Alef began to make its mark – not so much on the public at large as yet, but definitely on the members of the Party. The Rabin camp's incessant carping about internal Party decisions irritated a growing portion of the rank and file. More than perceiving these complaints as attacks on Peres, they saw them as ruining the Party's chances of winning the forthcoming elections. Peres knew how to play this gambit to the hilt. At every opportunity he made a point of stressing that while he was preoccupied with the struggle against the Begin Government, Rabin and his followers were actively engaged in a war against their own Party and its leader. And it wasn't long before this charge began to sink in.

In July 1980 it became clear that the ramifications of the Rabin-Peres struggle were not confined to the Labour Party alone, but had a direct effect on political decisions of national and even international import. At about that time, Geula Cohen of the right-wing nationalist *Tehiya* Party tabled a draft law establishing that United Jerusalem is the capital of Israel. From a legal standpoint, there was nothing new in the proposed law: Israeli sovereignty had been extended to all parts of Jerusalem shortly after the city was captured in the Six Day War. The significance of the law was purely political, for during that period President Sadat had raised the question of Jerusalem's future, and the purpose of the law was to reinforce an existing fact.

As the date for the Knesset vote on the law drew closer, the Israeli Government found itself under heavy pressure. The United States warned that passage of the bill would disrupt the peace process, while other countries announced that if the bill became law they would transfer their Embassies from Jerusalem to Tel Aviv. Israel's friends and enemies were united against the initiative. For all that, Begin announced that he personally would support the law, but because it was such a fundamental issue, he proclaimed that the coalition would vote for it only if there were a broad consensus in favour of the bill. That meant he was passing the ball to Labour's court.

It was an admirable tactic on Begin's part, for the law posed a very knotty problem. On the one hand, the diplomatic consequences of passing it were obvious. On the other, how could an Israeli honestly vote against the established fact that United Jerusalem was the capital of Israel? It might have been possible to vote down the law – not necessarily on grounds of principle, but because of extenuating factors – had the Labour Party been graced with strong leadership. But Peres did not have his Party entirely under control then, and his leadership was further eroded every hour of every day by Rabin and his followers. Under the circumstances, he could not allow himself – or at any rate thought that he could not allow himself – the luxury of a controversial step such as voting against the Jerusalem law.

So the Labour Party cast its vote in favour of the bill, and it was passed by a large majority. The consequences were even graver than the grimmest forecasts: every one of the eleven Embassies in Jerusalem moved out of the city. When the extent of the damage became clear, a chorus of 'I told you so' echoed through the Labour Party, and the Rabin camp instigated a campaign charging that Peres had mishandled the affair. Finally, the issue came up before the Executive at its meeting on 4 September 1980. It was a pathetic outpouring by people who knew they had made a mistake and were looking for some external factor on which to pin it. Peres reminded the committee that 'no one objected to the essence of the law. The only debate was about the timing. People say they were caught in a trap, and it's true.' And not just the Labour Party was snagged in that trap. The *Likud* had also been outwitted by Geula Cohen. All in all, it was a brilliant parliamentary manoeuvre by a single, fervently nationalist Deputy, and neither the coalition nor the opposition had a leader strong enough to foil it.

On 10 October 1980, Yitzhak Rabin formally declared his candidacy in a letter to Peres which read: 'I wish to inform you that I have decided to forward my candidacy at the Third Conference of the Labour Party for the posts of Party Chairman and the Party's candidate to head the Government to be formed after the elections to the Tenth Knesset.' The letter rambled on and was laden with the usual Party slogans. Peres's answer was one-sentence long: 'This is to confirm receipt of your letter.'

That evening, Knesset Member Adi Amora'i telephoned Peres and quipped in French: '*La guerre comme la guerre*'. And war it was. For in no way did the present struggle resemble the contest with Allon. Peres had to defeat Allon to retain his leadership of the Party; his margin of victory was not important, since it was clear in any case that Allon would remain the Party's number-two man. The same, however, was not true with Rabin. Here Peres could not content himself with victory alone. A sizeable vote for Rabin would make him into a force to be reckoned with, and he would use that position as a cover from which to continue sniping at Peres.

The traditional balance of forces in the Party was 65 per cent to 35 per cent. If Rabin managed to get 35 per cent of the vote, he would be the number-two man; but if Peres culled at least 70 per cent of the vote, he would be able to dictate his own terms. The real struggle, therefore, was over 5 per cent of the ballots.

At the beginning of November 1980, Peres took a breather by leading a delegation from the Labour Party on a visit to Egypt. Even there, however, he decided to use the visit as an opportunity to establish who the Party's leading team would be by taking his candidates along. His retinue was limited to Abba Eban, earmarked to be Minister of Foreign Affairs, and Chaim Bar-Lev, who would get the defence portfolio. Various interest groups within the Party began to press for representatives of their factions to be included in the delegation, and at first Peres was able to resist these demands, but gradually he seemed to be weakening. Two days before the trip, he telephoned Eban to say that he was under heavy pressure to include three other people in the delegation. Eban replied that he personally had no objection to their coming along, but expanding the delegation would destroy its significance *vis-à-vis* Rabin. If three men go, Rabin will be conspicuous by his absence; if a whole group goes, there would be no 'message' in the move.

Peres accepted this reasoning, and in the end only the *troika* made the visit. As Eban foresaw, the delegation was received as the lead team of the Labour Party and of the next Israeli Government. The Egyptian reception was a stately one. Sadat proved to be a warm and gracious host. The only thing that clouded the skies of that visit was the Egyptian position on the 'Jordanian option', which Peres advocated. Peres discovered that in contrast to his outlook at their earlier meetings, Sadat had begun to take a tougher stand regarding Jordan and King Hussein. He refused to be a part of any move that would lead to the immediate inclusion of the King in the contacts related to the West Bank. 'Hussein is a liar and mustn't be trusted,' he pronounced.

Towards the end of that month, on the afternoon of Saturday, 22 November, Peres's aide, Yossi Bailen, got wind of the fact that Rabin was going to hold a news conference that evening and that it had something to do with a libel action. He immediately reported this to Peres, who asked for additional details. By late afternoon Bailen had pieced the whole picture together. That day the French news magazine *L'Express* had published an item linking Rabin to one Bezalel Mizrachi, a Tel Aviv building contractor whose name was often mentioned in relation to the local underworld. According to the story, Mizrachi had lent Rabin money to pay the fine imposed on his wife after her 1977 trial for maintaining a foreign bank account. The *L'Express* story also asserted that Peres had a photocopy of the cheque which Mizrachi was alleged to have given Rabin.

Peres and his advisers were startled and genuinely alarmed. The item appeared in the French magazine just three days before the elections for delegates to the Party convention, and the logical conclusion might well be that Peres and his people had planted the item to smear Rabin's name just before the elections. But there was something very fishy about the story appearing just then and in a French publication at that. For the simple fact is that literally hundreds of people in Israel had known about the story for months. A number of newspapers had considered publishing it at various times, but all had decided against it for lack of evidence. So the question of who 'leaked' the story was actually irrelevant. There was nothing to leak: the item had been in the public domain, as it were, for months, but no one in Israel was interested in it.

Yet Rabin, by a number of shrewd moves, turned the question into a very relevant one and tried to make the maximum political capital out of the story. The first thing he did was call a press conference for eight o'clock that evening, at which he emphatically denied the *L'Express* story and called it a vulgar libel. When questioned about who might have given the story to the French publication, he refused to name names, but resorted to such expressions as 'it's not difficult to guess' and 'certainly not someone concerned about my welfare'.

That night Peres issued a statement denouncing the publication in *L'Express* and denying that any such cheque was in his hands. In response to this announcement, Rabin demanded that Peres sign an affidavit 'to aid him in the libel suit which he intends to pursue against the French paper'. Peres instantly agreed.

Three days later Rabin appeared before the Committee of Newspaper Editors, the forum he chose to prove that he had paid the fine out of his own pocket. He showed the editors a photocopy of a cheque in the amount of 25,000 Israeli pounds made out to the Court Treasury in Tel Aviv and signed by his wife, Leah. 'I'm just embarrassed that I have to spell all this out,' he said, in what was generally an emotional appearance before the committee. But shame did not prevent him from telling half-truths even in this voluntary setting. Had he paid the fine out of his pocket after all? Rabin claimed that he had received two loans. One was from a relative in the amount of IL70,000, which he repaid that same year. Far more curious was the second loan, which he claimed to have received from an American friend named Norman Bernstein. This amounted to $10,000, without interest, and was still outstanding. Then he produced a bank statement from a Ramat Aviv branch showing his account to be overdrawn. The overall impression was of a man in difficult financial straits because of the heavy fine.

A few days later, however, it emerged that the account Rabin had presented before the editors was not the only one he held in that branch. He failed to mention that he also had a foreign-currency account in which the balance was $73,000! Why did he present only part of the picture to the editors? Why hadn't he paid back the $10,000 to Norman Bernstein out of the $73,000 in his account? And why did he borrow $10,000 – without interest and without any due date – in the first place? There were journalists who wanted to air these questions, but they came up against a wall of opposition from their editors. Even the existence of the second bank account was suppressed, for there was a widespread feeling that the L'Express story had been a grave injustice to Rabin and that publishing any additional material would be viewed as collusion. So the questions simply went unanswered. On the other hand, after due consultation between Peres's and Rabin's lawyers, Peres signed the affidavit that Rabin had asked for. The former Prime Minister entered a claim of libel against L'Express, which led to a settlement by which the paper agreed to retract its story.

The entire affair ran back to back with the elections for the branch delegates to the Party convention, in which the rate of participation was among the highest ever known.

Once the results began to come in, it was clear that Peres had scored a victory. But there were differences in opinion about its magnitude, because not all the delegates chosen to attend the convention were clearly identified with one camp or another. Peres, the eternal optimist, started out by speaking of carrying 80 per cent of the vote against 20 per cent for Rabin. His people warned him to lower his sights, because there was no chance of achieving that margin. Instead, they spoke in terms of 70 to 30 per cent. Meanwhile, Rabin's people claimed that the balance of forces was 65:35, perhaps even 60:40. The only way to know for sure was to wait for the vote at the convention itself.

But Rabin did not content himself with an optimistic assessment of the results. Immediately after the count was announced, he shot off a barrage of charges about forgeries and other disorders at the polling-booths. Sticking to his inimitable style, he chose an image which remains etched in the memory and was hardly likely to win him a larger following. 'I will take pills against nausea', he proclaimed, 'and keep going.' Once again Rabin proved how out of touch he was with the thinking of a Party stalwart. No loyalist wants to hear that the Party nauseates a pretender to its top post. And if that's how the candidate feels, the rank and file will probably give him good reason to be ill.

The Third Convention of the Israel Labour Party opened in a festive atmosphere at the *Binyanei Ha'uma* Convention Centre in Jerusalem on the evening of Wednesday, 17 December 1980. The opening session was devoted to speeches by honoured guests and a programmatic address by the Chairman of the Party. The delegates in the hall could see only the flags, the slogans and the smiles, but behind the scenes feelings were running high.

The next morning the convention moved to the Mann Auditorium in Tel Aviv, where the balloting for the Party Chairman and candidate for premiership was held during the morning hours in an indescribably tense atmosphere. Activists of the two camps scurried between the polling-stations to check whether the people pledged to them were voting. Just before 2 p.m., the time when the booths were scheduled to close, Aharon Harel, the head of Peres's campaign, suddenly felt faint. None of the Arabs and Druze who had committed themselves to Peres had voted yet. He began to search for them, but they were nowhere to be found. Harel was sure that they were playing a trick on him, which meant the loss of 100 votes – which constituted 3 per cent of the ballot, when the whole struggle was essentially over 5 per cent of the vote!

After a considerable search, Harel discovered that the Arabs and the Druze had left the building to attend a reception being held by the Egyptian Ambassador. He sent messengers to the Egyptian Embassy, and at 1.55 a long convoy of cars screeched to a halt at the entrance to the building and spewed out their passengers – mostly men in traditional costume – who made a dash for the polling-stations.

Peres and his aides waited for the results in the chamber which Rabin had occupied during the two previous contests – the conductor's dressing-room. Rabin and his supporters sat in the room formerly occupied by Peres. The first results began to come in and augured a clear victory for Peres – even a decisive one. He still refused to believe it. But when the final results were in, the victory was even greater than he had dared imagine: Peres 'broke the 70 per cent barrier' with 71.12 per cent *vs.* 28.8 per cent of the vote. It was the largest majority that any candidate had received in the history of the Labour Party.

Shimon Peres strode onto the stage of the Mann Auditorium to the sound of thunderous applause. After brief opening remarks, he announced his intent to shake hands with Yitzhak Rabin, who was seated nearby, and approached his rival with an outstretched hand. The TV cameras zoomed in on Rabin's face. He looked like a wounded animal who knows that the hunters have closed in on him. His expression was twisted as he glanced from side to side, as if seeking a way out. But there was no way out this time. Finally Rabin stood up, thrust out his hand and quickly resumed his seat, his pale face set in a half-frown. The gesture drove the delegates wild. They applauded and stamped their feet with total abandon. Just then they were in love with themselves, with their Party and with their leader.

That evening a few friends gathered at Peres's apartment. Journalist Mira Avrech walked over to the bar and took out a bottle of Armagnac Napoleon Brandy, for which Peres has a special taste. She had brought it as a gift on one of her trips abroad, and they had decided to open it on the night of victory. Carrying the bottle over to Peres, she said, 'Now you can open it.' But Peres took the brandy from her and put it back on the bar. 'Not yet,' he said. 'This isn't the victory yet.'

Now the struggle with Menachem Begin had begun.

6
Epilogue

It looked to be a pathetically uneven contest long before it began. In one corner stood Shimon Peres, a self-confident winner leading the Party that the polls predicted would score a landslide victory, perhaps even gain an absolute majority in the Tenth Knesset. In the other stood an ailing, depressed, bemused Menachem Begin – his Government in disarray, riddled by leaks and internal bickering; his Party steeped in despair and reconciled to a drubbing at the polls.

Begin looked ghastly during this period. When he bothered to come to the Knesset, he could be seen slightly slouched in his seat, staring blankly into space. It seemed as if he had lost all interest in what was going on around him, a man waiting for his political demise to put him out of his misery. On 11 January 1981, he suffered yet another blow. Finance Minister Yigal Horowitz (the second Finance Minister of the Begin Government) submitted his resignation rather than yield to the country's elementary- and high-school teachers, who were striking for higher pay. All of Begin's pleas fell on deaf ears. 'Why are you doing this?' he moaned to Horowitz at a Cabinet meeting. 'After all, no decision has been made yet.'

The answer to that question was twofold: Horowitz had tried to rehabilitate the country's inflation-ridden economy by resorting to drastic budget cuts. But his programme was repeatedly sabotaged by Ministers who refused to accept the cut-backs in their Ministries' budgets. The frustrated Finance Minister felt that without backing from the Premier, who was increasingly apathetic and out of touch with the events being played out on every side, he had no hope of implementing his policy. But there was another, politically motivated reason for Horowitz's departure. The *Likud* Government was perceived as a sinking ship. Clearly its days were numbered, and

Horowitz feared that if he stayed aboard, he would go down with it. By resigning from the Cabinet, he hoped to topple the Government once and for all and win credit for the *coup de grâce* at the polls.

After a series of desperate attempts to remedy the situation, even Begin came to the conclusion that there was no choice but to bring the elections forward. On 10 February, by a large majority, the Knesset confirmed that the date of the elections would be advanced from November to 30 June 1981. Thus, in effect, Horowitz achieved his goal of bringing the Government down, but his departure also set in train one of the most curious and dramatic political come-backs in the history of Israeli politics. Like the mythical phoenix, the *Likud* – and with it Menachem Begin – rose from the ashes of its self-destruction to embark on a brand-new life.

This remarkable process was initiated by Horowitz's successor in the Finance Ministry, Yoram Aridor, and his formula was excruciatingly simple. As soon as he entered office, Aridor reversed Horowitz's economic approach. Gone were the days of the 'empty-hand policy'; no more did the citizens of Israel hear the bleak refrain, 'I haven't any money'; silenced were the calls for belt-tightening. The era of plenty had arrived, and the Government embarked on a programme of unprecedented reductions in prices. Thanks to Aridor, colour television sets, cars, air-conditioners – everything the public could desire – were suddenly 30, even 40 per cent cheaper. An orgy of buying began. Shops groaned under the weight of new customers. This latest departure was unquestionably a shameless and vulgar squandering of the state's fiscal resources for the sake of electoral gain, but it worked more effectively than even Aridor had dared to dream. The public was delighted; more – it felt beholden to the *Likud*. In no time at all, the three and a half years of galloping inflation and disastrous economic policy were simply forgotten.

Caught completely off guard, the Labour Party was unprepared to deal with this challenge. Practically speaking, it was caught in a trap, and its response was to try to focus attention on the grave consequences Aridor's policy would have after the elections. But the public, exulting in its great sense of relief after years of relentless price rises, did not wish to hear criticism of the new economic policy. Moreover, the electorate understood that if the Labour Party were voted into power the spree would come to an abrupt halt, whereas Aridor continued to promise that if the *Likud* were returned to government the reductions would continue. As to the debate over what was best for the country's economy, few people showed much interest, and those who did had trouble deciding whom to believe.

Peres was scheduled to travel to Geneva in the middle of March to inaugurate the United Jewish Appeal Campaign. As in the past, his itinerary developed far beyond its original format. A few days before leaving, he received a call from his friend Jean Friedman in Paris, who said that a representative of King Hassan of Morocco had called him and asked that Peres 'drop over' to Rabat in the course of his European tour. Peres's initial reaction was negative. He knew how such a meeting would be interpreted in Israel – coming as it did in the midst of an election campaign – so he asked Friedman to fly to Morocco and explain his problem to the King. Friedman was also told to stress that under the circumstances, he could not guarantee that the meeting would remain secret. Friedman accepted the role of intermediary and, after returning from Rabat, reported that King Hassan would be deeply insulted if his invitation were turned down. With a pronounced lack of desire, but for lack of any choice, Peres decided to defer to the royal bidding.

He left for Geneva, as scheduled, on 16 March, and after discharging his duty to the UJA returned to his hotel to find a call awaiting him from London. On the line was Lord Marcus Sieff, one of the owners of the Marks and Spencer chain and a leader of the British Jewish community. Sieff told Peres that King Hussein's brother was in London and had suggested that they lunch together. Peres, who naturally assumed they were talking about Jordan's Crown Prince Hassan, was more than amenable to the idea and immediately made plans to go to London.

The meeting took place in Sieff's home, and included Peres, Sieff, Al Schwimmer and the Jordanian King's brother. From the very first, Peres's eyes were glued on the Prince's face. He looked to be about thirty-five or forty, on the heavy side, with an impeccably trimmed moustache. The more he peered, the stronger grew the doubt in Peres's mind. He had met Hussein a number of times, and the man sitting opposite him did bear a resemblance to the King. But although he had never met Prince Hassan, he had seen several photographs of him – and this man who was introduced as King Hussein's brother did not resemble Hassan in the least! Something very strange was going on, but Peres did not know quite how to broach the subject.

The enigma was solved in the course of the conversation, and, as Peres suspected, the man he had come to London to meet was not the Crown Prince. He was another of Hussein's siblings, Mohammed, who was hardly known outside of Jordan. It was a classic case of serendipity in reverse. The Prince wanted to hear an explanation of the 'Jordanian option', and Peres obliged, stating that the thesis was based on the assumption that Jordan might find herself standing alone facing a Syrian threat, an estranged Egypt and an Iraqi defeat. But Mohammed expressed his doubts about such a forecast coming to pass. The threat from Syria, he said, only intensified Jordanian unity, and Syria was as wary of Jordan as Jordan was of her northern neighbour. For all that, though, Mohammed expressed support for the Jordanian option and said that he would speak of it to his brother, the King.

Peres embarked upon his journey to see King Hassan the next day. At noon he left from a private airfield near London for Paris, where Jean Friedman was awaiting him in King Hassan's private plane. They took off immediately for Marrakesh.

The plane landed at a deserted airfield outside the town, and cars were waiting to take the Israeli contingent through the tourist-filled city. After passing through the walls of Old Marrakesh, the cars came to a halt in front of a villa surrounded by a large garden with a swimming-pool in the centre. 'The King would like you to rest,' his Moroccan escort told Peres. 'If it is not too inconvenient, come to see him at the palace at about seven. There's no need to rush. He wants to talk to you alone.'

The palace Peres entered that evening was six hundred years old and built in the form of a square with a floor of gleaming marble. The guests were greeted by the court chamberlain, a retired general, who led them to a room pleasantly perfumed by incense, tiled in a mosaic and lit by Venetian chandeliers. About half an hour later a side door opened and King Hassan entered the room. He shook Peres's hand and led him to one of the circular tables in the courtyard. Hassan ordered hot Moroccan tea and offered his guest a choice of cigarettes. Speaking alternately in French and English, the King opened the conversation with a series of questions about events in Israel. What were the Labour Party's chances of winning the election? Peres reported the latest public-opinion poll published in *Ha'aretz*, and the King asked why Shulamit Aloni's Citizens' Rights List was given better odds than Moshe Dayan's new Party, showing his familiarity with the minutiae of the local political scene.

Then the King asked his guest for a *tour d'horizon*. Peres began with the United States, explaining how President Reagan's approach to the Middle East was fundamentally different from his predecessor's.

Carter's outlook moved from a local level to a regional and, finally, to a global one. Reagan's thinking worked in exactly the opposite way: from global considerations to regional ones and from there down to the local level. He drew a sharp distinction between friends and enemies and seemed prepared to build an American military presence in the Middle East.

The Iraqi-Iranian war, Peres continued, had shifted attention from the Israeli-Arab dispute to the Persian Gulf. At this point the King expressed the view that Iraq had mellowed and was beginning to glance furtively towards the West. It wasn't out of the question, he ventured, that President Saddam Hussein might throw the Russians out, just as Sadat had done.

What was needed today in the Middle East, said Peres, was a double-barrel policy. On the one hand, there was room for a regional organization which would embrace Egypt, Saudi Arabia, Jordan, Sudan and, if the North African countries were interested, them as well – with the active participation of the United States. Such an organization was needed to stand up to the communist threat, to terrorism and to the threat of nuclear proliferation. At the same time, a solution must be found for the Israeli-Arab conflict, though that could only be achieved gradually and in full partnership with Egypt. Peres stressed that the King of Morocco could play an important role in both of these processes, for he was the only Arab leader who knew the Jews from his own experience, and that of his father, and because he had already played a productive role on the eve of the Camp David talks.

The King wanted to know whether a future Israeli Government headed by Peres would agree to a 'small' change in Security Council Resolution 242, namely, the addition of a clause referring to the rights of the Palestinians and a solution to the refugee problem. 'Definitely not,' Peres replied. Any attempt to amend Resolution 242 would not be the last, he said, and in the end nothing would remain of the original resolution.

What, then, the King asked, could be done about this matter. Peres suggested that the negotiations on autonomy for the Arabs of the West Bank and Gaza be taken through to their conclusion, with the plan being implemented in Gaza first. An agreement must also be reached on the holy places in Jerusalem, without re-dividing the city. Then came the stage of negotiations with Jordan, which could be effected either through residents of Judea and Samaria appointed by Jordan or directly with the Jordan Government. There was also a third possibility: beginning with economic negotiations regarding the area from the Dead Sea to the Red Sea. King Hassan displayed interest in this idea and asked for further details. Peres sketched a map showing the port of Aqaba facing the port of Eilat, airport facing airport, potassium plant facing potassium plant. The King picked it up, studied it silently, then folded it and tucked it away in his pocket.

'Why do you prefer Jordan to the PLO?' Hassan asked. Because, Peres replied, if any one wants to topple Hussein, the best way to do it is to give Arafat a base. Then he launched into a long lecture on the relations between Hussein and Arafat. Finally, he went on to discuss Egypt and explained how the Moroccan monarch could make a great contribution to the peace process by supporting President Sadat and the Camp David accords. But the King complained that Sadat made things difficult for him by refusing to make even the least gesture towards the Arab world. 'Let's say that Sadat would,' Peres hypothesized. 'How would it help?' Instead of bringing the Arab world closer to Sadat, the vanguard on the road to peace, it would create the opposite impression, namely, that Sadat was being swept up in the wake of the Arab world fleeing from peace.

A welcome that was far from royal awaited Peres back in Israel, and it was a painful illustration of the stark change that had occurred in Israeli public opinion. On 6 April he went to Jerusalem to address thousands of North African Jews who were celebrating the holiday known as the Maimouna (following the last day of Passover) in Sacher Park. Prime Minister Begin was also to attend the event. When Begin walked onto the stage, he was received with an enthusiasm that verged on frenzy. When Peres's turn came, he was greeted by a salvo of tomatoes and forced to stand down from the platform without saying a word.

The elections to the *Histadrut* were held next day. A few months earlier no one harboured a doubt that the white- and blue-collar workers would punish the *Likud* for the plague of inflation which had eroded their salaries for four years. Everyone was expecting a smashing victory for Labour and a crushing defeat for the *Likud*. The Labour Party did score a victory of sorts by increasing the absolute majority it had always had in the *Histadrut*. The fact is that the *Likud* received less than half the number of votes culled by Labour. Nevertheless, the election results were considered a victory for the *Likud*, and the reason was simple: before the elections *Likud* people mused that they would be happy to get 20 per cent of the vote. They ended up with 26 per cent and, like Labour, increased their representation in the *Histadrut*.

On the night the election results were announced, Menachem Begin underwent a mystical transformation that he himself defined as a 'resurrection'. Suddenly it dawned on him that all was not lost, and this realization affected him the way that spinach affected Popeye the Sailor. His political muscles began to bulge, his chest puffed out and he assailed his enemies with a vengeance. It was a medical and political miracle rolled into one. His lethargy, depression and apathy vanished, as if his health had never suffered in the least. The more he worked – especially at oratory – the greater his vitality grew.

The first consequence of this extraordinary metamorphosis was the Lebanese missile crisis, which began with Begin giving the air force permission to shoot down two Syrian helicopters on their way to attack Lebanese-Christian civilians in the besieged town of Zahle. The attack on the Syrian aircraft was a glaring departure from the tacit *status quo* which had existed between Israel and Syria for years. Damascus reacted with a departure of her own by stationing surface-to-air missile launchers outside Beirut.

No sooner were the missile launchers in place than Begin demanded their immediate removal. If the Syrians did not comply, he warned, Israel would send her planes in to destroy them. The crisis quickly escalated to a point that looked like the brink of war. With tension at a peak, President Reagan sent Philip Habib to the region as a special ambassador to try and mediate between the sides.

Now the Lebanese crisis hogged the headlines and became the main issue of the election campaign. Begin claimed that it was prompted by Israel's commitment to the security of the Christians in Lebanon, but both Peres and Rabin retorted that throughout the years that commitment had expressed itself in the provision of aid, no more. Extending it to include active military protection meant that Israel would be forced to go into action as a result of moves made by the Lebanese Christian community even when such action was contrary to her own interests – a patently dangerous situation.

During the subsequent Knesset debate on the missile crisis, Peres refuted Begin's claim that there was a national consensus on the affair. He came down particularly hard on Begin's provocative statements, which, he observed, only aggravated the crisis. 'The fate of this country must not be placed in the hands of a man whose moods swing up and down, from incontinent euphoria to paralytic depression.'

But the public lapped up the euphoric declarations, and Begin began to dish them out in bigger doses, using his tongue as a weapon to lash out at whoever crossed his path. The pro-Palestinian statements of West German Chancellor Helmut Schmidt and French President Valéry Giscard d'Estaing prompted a sharp response from Begin: 'Those who speak like Schmidt and Giscard are avaricious men! Only two things hover before their eyes: how to sell weapons for a high price and buy oil cheaply.' Next in line was Dutch Foreign Minister van der Klauuw. At a meeting in Jerusalem, he told Begin that he had met Arafat. 'You shook a hand stained with Jewish blood,' Begin preached to him. From Europe Begin switched his sights to Saudi Arabia. On hearing from Philip Habib that the Saudis might help in finding a solution to the missile crisis in Lebanon, Begin saw fit to express his opinion about them publicly, calling the royal clan 'a wealthy family and a weak regime from the Middle Ages that would not be able to pump oil without the aid of the West'.

And the public stood up and cheered: here was a proud Jew who did not kowtow to the world's leaders and wasn't afraid to talk back to them. Labour's criticism of Begin's irresponsible behaviour and the political damage it caused were interpreted as fawning and defeatism.

Naturally, Begin did not draw the line at insulting people overseas; his choicest pearls were reserved for Peres. Drawing on his impressive rhetorical talents, he ridiculed whatever Peres had to say. But most of all he cast aspersions on his integrity, especially by making a point of reading out selections from Rabin's memoirs.

The battle ranged beyond the bounds of political differences and began to centre on personal attacks. Typical was the exchange between Begin and Peres during a meeting of the Knesset Foreign Affairs and Defence Committee:

Peres: 'You've turned the *Likud* election headquarters into the Government, and you're handling the Lebanese crisis from there.'

Begin: 'We are? What about that ad [in the paper] with my mouth agape about inflation running wild. Who else is running amok?'

Peres: 'In 1977 did you or didn't you blame *me* when a helicopter crashed by accident? . . . And then you go reading from books in the Knesset plenum. That's statesmanlike behaviour?'

Begin: 'That was the reply.'

Peres: 'Read Ezer Weizman, Moshe Dayan and Shumuel Katz – see what they have to say about you!'
Begin: 'You read it.'
Peres: 'You talk about a [civilized] way of speaking? Your Ministers said that Teddy Kollek and I were on the brink of treason. Can't you say something to them?'
Begin: 'Shimon, I'm not your defence attorney. You have a mouth. Defend yourself!'
Peres: 'I need your defence? Israeli society is what has to be defended.'
  And so on and so forth.

The Lebanese crisis supplied Begin with the pretext for another election manoeuvre. What could be more impressive than a summit meeting with President Sadat? He called up 'my friend Anwar' and told him the situation in Lebanon demanded that they have a talk. The Egyptian President agreed and on 4 June came to Ophira (Sharm e-Sheikh, near the tip of the Sinai Peninsula). The summit lasted no more than two hours, and actually accomplished nothing – at least so far as the Lebanese crisis was concerned. But it produced miles of TV film for the *Likud* public-relations people. The results were viewed on the small screen for days afterwards and no doubt added their part to the *Likud* campaign.

And if all this weren't enough, Begin dropped his real bomb four days later. At 4 p.m. on Monday, 8 June 1981, the festival of Shavuot, the newscaster of Israel's state radio, *Kol Yisrael*, informed his astounded listeners that Israeli air force planes had bombed and destroyed the Iraqi atomic reactor outside Baghdad. It was without question a remarkable military feat, but questions naturally arose about its timing. Was it absolutely necessary to execute the operation three weeks before the elections? Begin had his answer all prepared. Israeli Intelligence, he explained, had information to the effect that the reactor would go 'on line' in July or September. Bombing it while it was 'hot' would release nuclear radiation that could devastate the civilian population of Baghdad. Therefore Israel had no choice but to execute the bombing in June.

In reacting to the operation, Peres raised doubts about the validity of this explanation. Iraq had received the atomic reactor from France, and Peres argued that with the election of Israel's friend, François Mitterrand, as the new French President, it would have been possible to ensure through political means that the reactor would not be exploited for military purposes. At any rate, he said, it was unquestionable that in the coming months Mitterrand's France would not supply Iraq with the materials needed to produce an atom bomb. Peres's criticism stopped just short of a complete denunciation of the action, but his statement implied that if diplomatic efforts had failed, he too would have supported the destruction of the reactor.

Then Begin took an unusual step. He sent the Chairman of the Knesset Foreign Affairs and Defence Committee a letter he had received from Peres on 10 May 1981 – the day of the French elections. Peres had written the letter by hand, so that even his secretary would not be privy to its contents, and at the top were the words 'Personal and Highly Confidential'. Begin asked the Chairman to distribute Peres's letter among the members of the committee so that they could see for themselves that his claim to have objected only to the timing of the operation, and not the action *per se*, was a misrepresentation of the facts. As Begin expected and intended, the contents of the letter, plus Begin's covering note to the Chairman, were leaked to the media, and the whole affair became public.

About six months before the bombing of the reactor, Begin brought Peres in on the plan. When the Labour leader asked whether the possible Iraqi response had been taken into consideration, Begin did not reply. Then, on the night of the 9th of May, Peres discovered that the action was scheduled for the next day. Recalling that the elections in France were likewise to take place on the 10th, the following morning he sent Begin a letter cautioning him against executing the action that day so as not to alienate the French. He also added a rider that could be understood as an objection to the operation itself, for he went so far as to note, in code of a kind, that negative consequences might ensue because Israel was equally vulnerable in this area.

Essentially, Peres did not amend his position after the bombing of the reactor, either. At first he refrained from spelling out his views so as not to aggravate the political damage which Israel had suffered. But Begin exploited this reticence to create the impression that there was a considerable gap between the position expressed in his letter and what Peres had said after the fact.

From the viewpoint of electoral gains, Begin accomplished his objective; from the viewpoint of respecting the confidentiality of secret and personal documents, however, it was an appalling move. Begin had crassly violated the trust which Peres had placed in him and, for the sake of campaign points, published a letter despite the fact that it was marked 'Personal and Highly Confidential'.

The dictates of the election campaign also stood behind the official Government communiqué proclaiming Israel's responsibility for the bombing of the reactor. In the past, Israeli Governments had always denied any complicity in operations of this nature. The reason was to make it easier for friendly nations to avoid censuring Israel. So long as there was a shadow of a doubt about who was responsible, such states could limit themselves to a general denunciation of the act. But if Israel made an explicit and official admission of responsibility, they would be forced to adopt a stance designed to appease the Arab states. And that is precisely what happened. The Reagan administration immediately announced that it was suspending shipment of F-16 combat planes despite its contractual commitment – an absolutely unprecedented move and one which sparked off a bitter crisis in relations between the two countries. This clash with the new administration, which until then had been sympathetic to Israel's plight, was caused not by the bombing itself, but by Begin's brazen announcement of Israel's responsibility for it.

If damage were caused to Israel's vital interests, however, once again, from the point of view of the polls, Begin came out ahead. The electorate was intoxicated by the success of the operation and did not wish to hear any criticism of it or see matters as they really stood. Now Peres – and the entire Labour Party – understood that the battle had shifted over to lines of 'catch as catch can'. No ethics, no rules, no deferring to the country's best interests. The ends justified any means. Yet by the time this realization dawned on them, it was already too late. By the middle of June, the *Likud* had made an enormous leap forward, not only catching up with Labour in the polls, but leaving it far behind. The *Likud* had reaped the fruits of the process which had begun with Finance Minister Aridor and continued with the 'resurrection' of Prime Minister Begin, but one cannot ignore the contribution made by Labour itself – which was not inconsiderable.

Peres turned to the task of putting together the Labour Party's election headquarters at a time when the road to power seemed secure. For this reason he was more concerned about ensuring proper representation for the Party's various factions than with creating an effective and functional set-up. The headquarters that consequently came into being was heavily overstaffed, with two or three people in charge of every division. This excess was especially evident in the field of election propaganda, of which no less than three people were in charge, each pulling in a different direction.

What had, therefore, been Peres's strong-point for years now turned into a serious drawback. For four years he had managed to keep the Party unified by appeasing all its factions. But in the crucible of elections, you can't always satisfy everyone. It was imperative to choose the most effective people, without considering their factional identification or ideological leanings, and this was not done.

A good proportion of Peres's declining fortunes could be traced to the fact that Yitzhak Rabin had not vanished from the political scene despite his defeat at the Party convention. Rabin's people were now seeking a settlement that would guarantee their leader the post of Defence Minister in Peres's Government. To put a halt to the speculation about this point, Peres announced that Labour's candidate for Defence Minister was Party Secretary and ex-Chief of Staff Chaim Bar-Lev. Nevertheless, the Rabin people did not lose heart, and items about burying the hatchet appeared in the papers almost daily, further undermining Peres's position.

In the meantime, the *Likud* was making effective use of the Peres-Rabin rift. Its advertisements in the papers and on television generously quoted from Rabin's book, and the tactic proved to be a stroke of near-genius. Peres emerged as a dubious character – an image which dogged him throughout the election campaign. At the same time, the popularity of the man who was responsible for vitiating Peres began to mount. Public-opinion polls showed that Labour's chances of winning the elections would improve if Yitzhak Rabin headed the list.

Rabin did nothing to blunt the edge of the *Likud* attacks on Peres. While he did take part in the election campaign, he would speak about the Labour Party without mentioning the name of its leader. Party activists pleaded with him to demand that the *Likud* cease quoting his book – or at least say something to suggest that despite what he had said and written in the past, he prefered Peres to Begin. But Rabin adamantly refused.

In effect, then, Peres was forced to run a difficult election campaign against the *Likud* while standing up to heavy pressures within his own Party. When the Iraqi reactor was bombed, he temporarily buckled under the weight of it all. One day soon after the Iraqi operation, the members of the Party's Political Committee and its representatives on the Knesset Foreign Affairs and Defence Committee convened to prepare for the Knesset committee session called specially to discuss the issue of the bombing. Peres opened the discussion by declaring that the timing of the Iraqi operation was definitely linked to campaign considerations. He proposed, therefore, that 'we come to the committee and say to the Prime Minister: "You claim that [the bombing] had nothing whatsoever to do with the elections. Please prove that by postponing the elections." If he agrees, that's fine: we won't have to go to the polls with the bombing hovering in the background. If he doesn't, we'll simply say to him: "See, there's your proof that the bombing *was* related to the elections." '

Peres's audience was dumbfounded. Yossi Sarid protested that Begin would depict that proposal as anti-democratic. He would rail that the British went to the polls during a war, and whatever else he might say he certainly would not agree to it. The result would be that while the elections were held on schedule anyway, the notion of postponing them would be read as an admission of defeat long before the polls were opened. The suggestion was dropped then and there.

Six days after the bombing of the Iraqi reactor, Eliezer Zurrabin, head of the public-relations agency working for the Labour Party, and his poll-taker, Dr Mina Tzemach, came to Peres's office in Tel Aviv with bitter news. The poll taken after the Iraqi operation indicated that the *Likud* was leading by an astounding margin of twenty seats. It also indicated that if Rabin were to replace Peres at the head of the list, the Labour Party could close the gap. The conclusion was obvious and Peres could not avoid grasping it. He told the two that he would not stand in the Party's way and expressed his readiness to resign – with one qualification: he wanted the matter thoroughly checked first.

This was one of the grimmest days of Peres's life. The goal towards which he had strived and for which he had struggled throughout his adult life – a goal which just a few months ago had seemed to be secured – now seemed lost forever. The next day he intended to resign as leader of the Labour Party, and for him that could only mean retiring from political life.

That day he continued to act as if nothing had happened. In the evening he made a scheduled appearance before a large rally and returned home late. Sonya was still awake when he came in. Telling her about the talk with Zurrabin and Tzemach, he asked her what she thought. As usual Sonya assured him that she would stand behind him in whatever he decided to do. But he wanted a more definitive answer.

'I think that you should make the decision and go,' she said. But next morning, Zurrabin telephoned Peres to report that the situation had reversed itself again. The latest poll indicated that the *Likud* was leading by only six seats and that Labour would pick up additional seats right up to the last moment. There was no longer any need for Peres to resign. What had happened? A post-mortem on the affair revealed that the poll indicating a large victory for the *Likud* was flawed by a number of serious errors. Peres's political career might have come to an end because of a single unsound poll.

There was also a development on the other side of the fence. The same problem that had worked against Labour at the start of the campaign now began to plague the *Likud*: an excess of self-confidence. Coasting on a wave of popularity whose magnitude surprised even an old pro like himself, Menachem Begin was swept into the outer spheres of rhetorical ebullience with no one able to bridle him. For quite a while the results were dazzling, from his Party's standpoint – until he got too carried away with himself.

That occurred on Sunday, 14 June. Begin arrived at an election rally in the seaside town of Netanya and to a scene that had become familiar to him: a crowd of overwrought voters chanting 'Begin, Begin' and 'Begin, King of Israel'. Every sentence that emerged from his mouth was met with a roar of approval mixed with adulation. Begin's face was flushed with excitement and drenched with sweat. Wagging his finger in the air, he jeered: 'Beware, Assad. Yanoush and Raful* are waiting.' (A rumble of delight.) 'Special Ambassador Philip Habib will arrive here on Wednesday and I shall ask him: "Well, are you going to remove the missiles from Lebanon or not? Because if *you* don't get them out, we *will!*" ' (A deafening roar.)

When a film clip of this part of Begin's speech was broadcast, it sent a pang of astonishment tinged with disgust through a large section of the Israeli public. That same night, moreover, Peres appeared before a rally in the town of Petah Tikvah and he, too, received the welcome to which he had become accustomed: a barrage of tomatoes and chants of 'Begin, Begin' by *Likud* supporters who had come for the express purpose of disrupting the Labour rally. But this time he wasn't the only target. Labour supporters in the crowd were beaten up, cars were set alight and shop windows bearing Labour Party stickers were shattered. 'Violence!' the Labour Party howled in alarm. 'These are the true colours of the *Likud* and of its leader.' In response to the ugly

---

* oc Northern Command Avigdor Ben-Gal and Chief of Staff Rafael Eitan.

spate of arson, vandalism and threats, artists, academicians and other respected public figures rallied to the Labour Party's aid under the banner 'Anything But the *Likud*'.

These were Peres's greatest days. Facing down the violent disruptions that marked all his appearances, he began to earn admiration for his sheer grit and nerves of steel. He exhibited a quality of leadership that breathed new life into the Party's activists. They lifted their heads, squared their shoulders and marched out to fight as if it were the last battle – and soon the polls pointed to a neck-and-neck race. Now the final event of the campaign – the televised debate between Peres and Begin – began to take on decisive importance. Peres had forced the contest on his aides and advisers. Memories of the fiasco in 1977 were still fresh in their minds and, with Begin at the peak of his rhetorical prowess, they feared that he would tear Peres to shreds. But Peres insisted. It was unthinkable that he should back down from a debate, he argued. Far more important, deep inside he was confident that he could whip Menachem Begin.

Once again Yossi Sarid was charged with the preparation of the debate on behalf of Labour. Meanwhile, Peres prepared for it in a thorough-going manner. He even held three 'dry runs' in which Sarid took Begin's part. Sarid played a vindictive, mocking, rancorous Begin and more than once sparked Peres's anger. But the result was that when Peres arrived at the debate, he was equipped with a comeback for every word that Begin was likely to pronounce.

A few days before the debate was taped, Zurrabin and Tzemach were catalysts in another event that would shape the end of the campaign. This time they showed Peres a poll indicating that if Rabin replaced Bar-Lev as the man slated for Defence Minister, the Labour Party could automatically pick up six or seven seats. Peres rebuffed them with the pronouncement that he had no intention of making any change in the lead team, but that didn't stop Zurrabin. He approached Aharon Yariv, a former chief of military Intelligence and a friend of both Rabin and Peres, told him about the poll and asked him to intervene. Yariv went to see Bar-Lev, with the result that two nights before the debate, at 1.30 in the morning, a telephone call woke Peres from a deep sleep. Bar-Lev was on the line, his slow, hypnotic voice saying that he was prepared to pass his mandate on to Rabin. Peres replied curtly that he refused to accept such a sacrifice – and at any rate it wasn't a subject to be discussed over the telephone.

It was against this background that Peres arrived at Kfar Hamacca-biah, where the debate was to be taped. When it was over, the general consensus was that Peres had won. His presentation came across as aggressive, determined, reasoned. Begin, who usually speaks ex-temporaneously, read extensively from notes and appeared to be set off balance by his rival's frontal attack.

As Peres walked out of the studio, he was approached by Mussa Harif, the secretary of the Party's kibbutz movement, who told him that a group of people wanted to talk to him. Together with Harif were Yisrael Galili and Arik Nehemkin, two other representatives of the kibbutz and moshav sector of the Party. They returned to the idea of making Rabin the Party's candidate for Defence Minister, arguing that Bar-Lev did not object and that Rabin had expressed his willingness to announce that he was turning over a new leaf.

That was at two in the afternoon. Peres said first of all that he wanted to talk to Bar-Lev. Because two election rallies awaited him that day, he suggested they meet in his office at 8.30 in the evening and that Rabin and Bar-Lev take part in the meeting as well.

But while Peres was speaking at the rallies, word of the change in Labour's line-up leaked to the media – undoubtedly by the instigators of the move. They also invited the press and electronic media to a news conference with Peres and Rabin at 10.30 that night. When Peres got wind of this, he was livid, but he realized that cancelling the press conference would be very damaging.

At nine that evening Peres returned to Tel Aviv exhausted – after a sleepless night, the taping of the debate and two rallies – and 'I knew it was all over'. The public was waiting for an announcement about the great reconciliation, and by then it was too late to back down. He knew that the leaders of the kibbutz movement had manoeuvred him into a corner from which there was no escape. Nevertheless, he did stipulate one condition: that Bar-Lev accept another post – Deputy Prime Minister. Once Bar-Lev agreed to that, the three men left for the press conference. Peres announced the changes in the Party's list, and Rabin followed with a statement recanting his disqualification of Peres as a candidate for the premiership and adding, as a pledge, that he was drawing a line across the past.

In the end, therefore, all the Party contests and victories had been pointless. Rabin returned to the fold and got the appointment he wanted. The irony was that by all indications, this happened at a time when it would no longer have any meaningful effect on the public's voting pattern. For the poll conducted that night confirmed that a large majority of the voters believed that Peres had won the debate with Begin.

On Election Day, 30 June, Peres toured various neighbourhoods in Tel Aviv. He returned to his office afterwards, and at close to eight o'clock was shown the results of the last poll conducted by Mina Tzemach. It pointed to a *Likud* victory by a seven-seat margin. Exhausted and depressed, he went home to change his clothes and returned to his office. A few minutes after arriving, he received a telephone call from Rabin. 'I've heard about the final poll,' his erstwhile rival said. 'I want to tell you that I consider myself a partner with full responsibility for the defeat.' Peres felt his throat constrict with emotion. 'I appreciate that,' he croaked.

Two hours later, the picture looked quite different. A stone rolled off Peres's heart when he heard the TV anchorman announce that according to the prediction of the television's statistician, Hanoch Smith, the race between the *Likud* and Labour was tied, with perhaps a lead of one seat for Labour. About an hour later, Peres was tingling with excitement when Hanoch Smith announced a difference of four seats in Labour's favour – 51 to 47. He rushed to the Party's election headquarters in the Hotel Deborah, where he was received by hundreds of ecstatic supporters. As he made his way up to the dais, people shook his hand and slapped him on the back. Once he was up on the platform and in full view of the TV cameras, Rabin stood up and approached him. To the echo of wild applause, the two fell into each other's arms.

'Ladies and gentlemen, I am pleased to present the next Prime Minister of Israel,' said the campaign spokesman as soon as Peres was seated. For Shimon Peres a tortuous, years-long struggle, often filled with drama, seemed to have climaxed in a smashing victory. Prime Minister Menachem Begin had been defeated.

Distant and current visions flashed through Peres's mind: his childhood in the youth village of Ben-Shemen, his youth on Kibbutz Alumot, his daring arms-acquisition operations, the aircraft industry, the Mystère and Mirage planes, guided missiles, the atomic reactor, the Entebbe rescue operation. And most of all, the special relations he had cultivated with the great men of the world – especially with the leaders of France and Germany – on which he built the foundations of Israel's security.

And his mind was brimming with plans for the future: developing the Negev into an industrial area comparable to the Ruhr, settling the Galilee, bold political initiatives that would lead to a comprehensive peace with the Arab states.

Above all, looming before him during these moments was the image of the man whom he had had the privilege to serve for so many years and towards whom he felt the admiration of a disciple and the love of a son – David Ben-Gurion. He had already filled one of his revered mentor's posts when he served as Minister of Defence (1974–7). Soon he would take over the other position, the loftiest of all – the premiership.

Peres sat before the cameras and the lights in the crowded headquarters and pledged to form the next Government of the State of Israel. Suddenly one of the newsmen asked him: 'Mr Peres, do you know that the television's prediction has changed again and Labour is no longer in the lead?'

Peres's eyes went out of focus. For a split second he felt totally disoriented, but he soon got a grip of himself. 'Yes, I know,' he said with an odd air of confidence. 'I will form the next Government.'

What was the man talking about? He vaguely recalled that someone had whispered a hurried sentence in his ear on his way up to the dais, but in the tumult he couldn't quite hear. And if he did hear, he couldn't quite assimilate it. His mind refused to take in the statistics he was being fed. It couldn't be that the tide had turned again. It was not possible that victory could be snatched from his hands.

But not only was it possible, it had happened. The revised prediction was wrong. The elation was premature. The correct results were a tie, and everyone understood what that meant. Labour had increased its strength appreciably, from 32 to 47 seats. But this figure would not enable it to form a government, for the religious parties, which would decide the election, had already announced their preference for joining a coalition headed by Menachem Begin.

The songs and cries of victory fell silent at the Hotel Deborah, and the headquarters were soon deserted. Peres returned home, frustrated and weary. Again fate had mocked him. Again he had been deprived of the grand prize within reach – actually with his grasp. He would not be the man to head the Government of Israel – at least not this time. He would return to lead the opposition, and perhaps to another struggle for the leadership of his party.

There was a great temptation to turn his back on it all – the struggles, the party hacks, the ungrateful public; to lay down his arms and quietly disappear; to free himself for his second love, perhaps his first – writing. No. Not his first. That was and always would be Sonya.

But if that was how Peres had lived his life so far, Israel would not have an aircraft industry, a properly equipped army or atomic potential. His inner strength was nourished by hardship, boosted by helpless odds, galvanized by challenges. If he fled the battle now, his life would surely be quieter, more comfortable; but he wouldn't be Shimon Peres.

Index